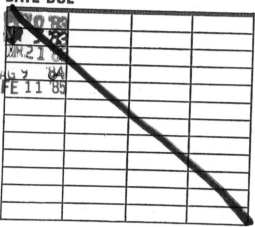

The Gifted Child

The Gifted Child

Cyril Burt

A HALSTED PRESS BOOK

JOHN WILEY & SONS
New York

Published in the U.S.A.
by Halsted Press, a Division of
John Wiley & Sons, Inc.
New York

Library of Congress Cataloging in Publication Data

Burt, Sir Cyril Lodowic, 1883–1971.
  The gifted child.

  "A Halsted Press book."
  Includes bibliographical references and index.
  1. Gifted children—Education. I. Title.
LC3993.B87 1975   371.9'5   75–12892
ISBN 0–470–12532–2

Printed in Great Britain

Editorial note

Professor Sir Cyril Burt finished this book just before he died, when the greater part had already been typed in final form. Outstanding were only two hand-written tables headed 'For book—Chapter 9' and parts of the same chapter for which tables and material needed putting together from articles already published, to replace parts of the original draft. Nothing has been altered from the form which Burt intended; the two hand-written tables have been appended at the end of Chapter 9 and the tables and formulae from other work added to complete the chapter according to his pencilled instructions.

Some readers may notice that the siblings and unrelated children with whom twins are compared throughout the discussion on inheritance vary in number. I am grateful to Professor Jensen for drawing my attention to this. Unfortunately, although Burt kept all his documents and working papers scrupulously, some were mislaid after his death—the data on twins among them. Thus it has been impossible to check the figures. In one case a typing or type-setting error in a previous article had been corrected; but the other differences have been left, most of them probably true ones. If the use of slightly varying samples at different times had no significant effect on the results, it is highly likely that Burt simply used them interchangeably, without comment, as they came to hand. He had many samples of test results, gathered from children of all kinds during his time as psychologist to the London County Council, and he used them in later papers, combining some, adding others, and reworking earlier analyses.

Unlike many psychologists writing on theories of intelligence, Burt had first-hand experience of testing children individually and talking to them, their families and teachers, to elicit intelligence, attainments and the sources of maladjustment. *The Gifted Child* combines his early observations and practical results with later, highly theoretical discoveries, and represents, in a very real sense, the culmination of a long life's work on intelligence—a subject which Burt himself, without doubt, considered of the greatest importance to psychology.

Charlotte Banks

Preface

This book is based on a number of research papers, already published, dealing with the problems of mental inheritance and mental differences between individuals. But almost every paper has been revised and largely rewritten to form a consecutive series of chapters. Children differing from the normal towards the lower end of the scale—the dull, the backward, the neurotic, the delinquent—I have already discussed in considerable detail in my various books. Here, therefore, I shall deal mainly with the gifted. These, in my view, are today unduly neglected.

The book is intended primarily for teachers in training. It is my conviction that the psychological aspects of educational problems should be treated far more scientifically than is usually the practice in most colleges of education. At present, issues of the kind I have mentioned are discussed almost entirely in verbal terms, and the arguments used are based largely on ideological assumptions. Such an approach is bound to be inconclusive and will often be misleading. Quantitative analysis is essential; and every teacher should know something of its basic principles. In the following chapters the algebra and arithmetic should be well within the scope of the ordinary teacher.

I hope, however, that the book may also interest educational and clinical psychologists, particularly those wishing to undertake surveys or research of their own. I have therefore supplemented the simple arguments in the text with a detailed list of references. Apart from the mathematical sections, I fancy the rest of the book may also be of interest and use to other members of the public— education officials, sociologists, social workers, and even perhaps members of parliament interested in education.

Cyril Burt

Contents

A*

CHAPTER ONE

The problem of the gifted

The ideal society

'You, citizens, are all brothers. But the God who created you has put different metals into your composition—gold into those who are fit to be rulers, silver into those who are to act as their executives, and in those whose task will be to cultivate the soil or manufacture goods he has mixed iron or brass. Most children resemble their parents. Yet occasionally a golden parent may beget a silver child or a silver parent a child of gold; indeed, any kind of parent may at times give birth to any kind of child. The rulers therefore have received this paramount charge from the gods—that first and foremost they shall scrutinize each child to see what metal has gone to his making, and then allocate or promote him accordingly: for an oracle has predicted that our state will be doomed to disaster so soon as its guardianship falls into the hands of men of baser metal.'

Here, in picturesque allegory, is how Plato introduces his own blueprint for a Brave New World. The golden age of Pericles had vanished, no one could quite understand why. Plato himself in his early youth had witnessed the collapse of the Athenian empire; he had watched the trial and execution of his friend and teacher, Socrates, who had 'proved himself too good to be allowed to live'; and Athens itself was now distracted by the ceaseless struggles of oligarchs and democrats, the Thirty Tyrants and the rival demagogues, who between them were manifestly helping to complete the final downfall of the city they sought to dominate. A golden age, so he believed, could only be inaugurated afresh by making sure that in future the chosen leaders of the state would be 'men with hearts and intellects of gold'.

His plan was to take the more gifted children, earmarked as it were for the highest functions in the state, and to train and educate them for the responsible parts they were to play as 'rulers' or 'executives'. Nature (φύσις) and nurture (τροφή), we are told, are the two essential factors which make up human character. 'Without proper nurture the best nature is as likely to turn out ill as to turn out well, to seek private wealth and power rather than the public good of the whole body of citizens.' On the other hand, nurture of itself cannot create the requisite nature. Accordingly, to ensure that there shall be an unfailing supply of able individuals, he proposes to institute a kind of human stud-farm.

'I notice', Socrates remarks to Glaucon (Plato's brother), 'you keep dogs for hunting. Do you find that some of them grow up to be much better than the rest?'

'Certainly.'

'Then do you take account of this when you allow them to pair? Do you just breed from all alike or mainly from the best?'

'Oh, only from the best.'

'And if you did not trouble to breed in this way, would your stock degenerate?'

'I am sure they would.'

'And what about horses and other animals? Do you suppose this is also true of them?'

'Only a fool would think otherwise.'

'Fancy then!' exclaims Socrates, 'what first-rate rulers we might have if the same practice were to be adopted for human beings' (*Republic* III, 415 A–C, V, 459 A–B, abridged).

Plato's proposals have been discussed, defended, modified, and violently attacked by a long line of philosophical writers from Aristotle down to the more ardent eugenists of the present day. His arguments, it will be seen, rest on two fundamental assumptions, both of them psychological. First, he assumes that the efficiency, and indeed the ultimate survival, of any civilized society depends on a frank acceptance of the principle which later economists have called the 'division of labour'. The notion that any citizen is capable of carrying out any or all the various types of work required is repudiated as false in theory and disastrous in practice. Social functions require different individual qualities—physical, mental, and moral. Secondly, the differences which everyone recognizes between different individuals are, so he assumes, to a large extent inborn. Education and habit may mould or reinforce them; but a man's natural endowment sets an upper limit to the efficiency with which he can perform the various activities which the everyday business of the state requires.

Both assumptions have been repeatedly challenged, most frequently perhaps by British writers. Our two greatest Chancellors, Thomas More and Francis Bacon, have each followed Plato's method and planned in imagination an ideal commonwealth, and given us a detailed picture of an ideal community as they conceived it. Both, however, have departed widely from the original Platonic scheme. Of this pair of sociological romances Bacon's *New Atlantis* has appealed only to the scholar; More's *Utopia*, on the other hand, has remained the most fascinating and the most influential of the many attempts at this brand of science fiction. Whereas Plato's ideal republic was based on class distinctions, More's was virtually a classless society. More and Bacon, however, each in his own distinctive way, opened up new problems for future discussion, and each displayed remarkable foresight in their anticipations of 'the shape of things to come'.

More's account was written shortly after the young king, Henry VIII, ascended the throne. The medieval world was then rapidly merging into the modern world as we know it today. The Wars of the Roses had ended in a break-up of the old feudal system; a new middle class was gaining power; and signs were already discernible of a steadily increasing commercialism, with the many evils that it seems inevitably to bring in its train. For the appropriate remedies Bacon looked to the development of science and its utilitarian applications; More put his faith in a more equal distribution of wealth and education.

The classless society

More's narrative professes to relate how, while serving on one of Henry's embassies to Holland, he met with a kind of Portuguese 'Captain Gulliver'—'a man now well stricken in age, with a long beard and sunburnt face, and a sailor's cloak about his shoulders'. 'Sitting on a bench in a Dutch garden', this 'ancient mariner' proceeded to tell his story. 'Desiring to see far distant countries', he had joined Amerigo Vespucci, presumably on the famous voyage around the southern coast of the continent that now bears the explorer's name. Eventually, however, the young captain and his companions broke away in a smaller ship of their own, and, after adventures almost as hair-raising as those of Coleridge's less fortunate hero, set foot on an inhabited island, which (so he was told) took its name from a former king called Utopus. In size and in the position of its rivers and cities, one gathers that the island was very much like our own; and the description of the place and its inhabitants turns out to be a witty and satirical commentary on the state of England in More's day, with a set of specific proposals for its reform. Unlike London, the capital of Utopia has broad and handsome streets, clean and well laid out; all the houses are large and roomy with extensive gardens at the back. There are no idle rich. As far as possible each citizen with his family is expected to be self-sufficient; he is required to rule himself and his wife and children, to grow his own food, make his own clothes and tools, but also to follow some definite craft. His leisure hours are devoted to study and reading; and, though he detests warfare, he is at need a soldier. Plato proposed to educate only those who were to hold higher posts in his republic; in More's Utopia every child is to be educated, and educated alike.

There was still a prince with his council to bear rule. There were likewise magistrates and executives, forerunners of our present-day civil servants, to assist in the administration. There were clerks who could read, write and study, ploughmen to till the ground, and manufacturers and merchants to make and sell goods. And, as in Plato's community, each man usually had one specific job and one job only. Thus, a division of labour was still regarded as essential; but the distinctions were reduced to a minimum. And each man's vocation was a matter for his personal choice, not something imposed on him by the alleged limitations of his innate endowment, much less dictated by the authorities of the state.

With minor adaptations to bring them more in line with the changing conditions of contemporary communities or states, the model commonwealths of Plato and More have found many later imitations—from Campanella's *City of the Sun* to Morris's *News from Nowhere* and Wells's *Modern Utopia*; and during recent years egalitarian principles, like those of More, have had a strong attraction for sociological and educational theorists. At the beginning of the present century John Dewey, 'the most influential educationist the United States have produced', argued in several of his earlier writings that the ideal society would be one in which 'all class distinctions are abolished'. Such a society, he believed, could best be developed, not by any abrupt revolution or reform, but by a reorganization of the schools in which the younger generation would be trained. Being itself an embryonic community, the school, he maintained, should reflect and embody, not the actual conditions of the state at the time, but the principles underlying the ideal state towards which society should be moving. And Dewey's suggestions are warmly supported by many British educationists at the present day. 'Our class-ridden society', we are told, 'should be replaced by a genuinely classless society; and the surest way to achieve this overdue reform is by revolutionizing our educational system. Instead of perpetuating class differences by providing a superior type of education for the privileged few in separate schools or institutions, all should be educated alike.'[1]★

The equality of man

Underlying these later schemes there is, implicitly if not explicitly, a rejection of the second of Plato's two basic assumptions, namely, that in virtue of their natural endowment individuals differ, widely and inevitably, in their capacities and character. In the past the most vigorous exponent of this egalitarian view was C. A. Schweizer, more usually known by the Latinized form of his name, Helvétius (*De L'esprit*, 1758; *De L'homme*, 1773). Helvétius accepted the materialist conception of mind expounded by La Mettrie (*L'homme machine*, 1748), and endeavoured to deduce the practical consequences for social and political theory. His chief conclusion is summed up in his oft-quoted maxim 'L'éducation peut tout'. The first of his two books was condemned to be publicly burned by the hangman; but that merely served to enhance its popularity among the younger French intellectuals. It exercised a still greater influence in America: we all remember the celebrated clause in the Declaration of Independence, which proclaimed the belief that 'all men are created equal'.

The arguments of the French *philosophes* and the eloquence of Jean-Jacques Rousseau, with his plea for 'le retour à la nature' and government by 'la volonté generale', fired the enthusiasm of many young romantics in Great Britain. Of these perhaps the keenest in his youthful days was the poet Southey. He coined the word 'pantisocracy' to designate the ideal society as he conceived it—'a society in which all are recognized as equal and all equally

★ Notes and references are given at the end of each chapter.

bear rule'. He and Coleridge resolved to found a 'model pantiso-cratic settlement' on the banks of the Susquehanna. This chimerical project, however, collapsed for lack of funds. Other attempts were made a little later by English, German, and French idealists. None survived more than three or four years; 'all failed', says the historian, 'from the want of a leader, which their principles for-bad'.

Many years afterwards, however, Southey, now a high Tory and Poet Laureate, related how, sitting one evening in his study at Keswick, he was visited by an elderly stranger, 'dignified and handsome except for an ugly red streak around his neck'. The visitor announced himself as the ghost of Sir Thomas More; the scar, he explained, was the mark left by his decapitation. In the discussions that followed, More argued that the humanitarian principles which he had urged on the royal master who had con-demned him could be applied to correct the many evils from which England was suffering in consequence of the industrial revolution. In the new Utopia the envy, greed, and constant class conflicts that were generated by a social system still semi-feudal could, he maintained, be forestalled by training each child to per-form for himself all that was needed for 'the happy life'.[2]

The associationists

The doctrines of Helvétius and his philosophic followers in France exerted a considerable influence on a far more powerful group of British writers—those variously known as 'utilitarians', 'associationists', or 'philosophic radicals'—the forerunners of the twentieth-century 'behaviourists'. Their leader was Jeremy Bentham. James Mill, his most intimate companion and disciple, is commonly regarded as 'the supreme exponent of association-ism'. All men, so he assumes, are born equal in ability; the mind at birth is a *tabula rasa*—a plain wax tablet on which experience can imprint a variety of patterns. As a result of our experiences the objects we perceive, the ideas we retain in our memories, and the various overt reactions we make in response to outer or inner stimuli, become linked together by the 'associations' thus ac-quired; these, according to Hartley, are merely physiological con-nections formed within the brain. Since different children have widely different experiences, the patterns of thought and action thus established are highly diversified. All the observable differences between one individual and another are therefore held to be the product of experience. It followed, as Mill put it (quoting Helvétius), that 'education can do everything, or, if it cannot do everything, there is hardly anything that it cannot do'. And, as a father, Mill put his theories into practice by applying them to the education of his still more famous son, John Stuart Mill.

The eugenists

The environmentalist doctrines of the associationist school received a temporary setback from the biological conclusions drawn by the British evolutionists—Spencer, Darwin, Huxley and Galton. In a series of pamphlets, beginning with an essay 'On the natural inequality of man', Huxley endeavoured to set forth the social and educational implications of Darwin's theory of natural selection. He makes a trenchant attack on Rousseau's 'Discours sur l'origine de l'inégalité parmi les hommes' and on the educational theories advocated by many contemporary teachers. Darwin's detailed demonstration of the evolution of *Homo sapiens* from some primitive type of primate depends essentially on the assumption of inheritable individual variations. Galton carried the argument further by maintaining that the rise and fall of nations, and the progress of human civilization generally, was dependent on the innate qualities of the race and its constituent communities, and in particular on the distinctive innate qualities of their chosen leaders: 'the social stratification which has existed in every progressive society is correlated with a corresponding stratification of inborn moral and intellectual qualities: without such an organization into a hierarchy of classes no industrial civilization could survive'.

To popularize the practical consequences of these 'biosocial' theories the Eugenics Education Society was founded, with Galton as its first president; and we find almost everyone who writes on eugenics starting off with a cry of 'back to Plato'. Psychology entered the lists in the person of McDougall, who published his own view of a utopian commonwealth in a Platonic dialogue reporting a visit to the 'island of Eugenia'. This, as he later admitted, was just a 'youthful philosophical phantasy'; but it was subsequently reprinted in *National Welfare and National Decay* (1921). As in Plato's republic, 'citizens with an intellectual and moral endowment are encouraged to have large families; the dull and the unstable are to refrain from breeding or else be deprived of membership of the state. . . . Schools are re-organized so as to make the most and the best of the human material which nature supplies. The children are brought up in the spirit of world service.' But the training is by no means exclusively intellectual: every pupil is taught a trade, and learns to use his hands as well as his head. Every man devotes his leisure hours to useful practical labour: the professor of astronomy milks cows; the expert in chemistry drives a tractor on the farm; and the lecturer in philosophy finds 'relief from his classes in looking after pigs'.

The behaviourists

As the critics of those days were quick to point out, all such far-reaching proposals were based more on inference and conjecture than on ascertained fact. Apart from data collected by Galton himself, there was little evidence bearing directly on the transmission of innate mental differences; and analogies drawn from the breeding of dogs and horses for physical qualities furnished rather tenuous grounds for conclusions about the inheritance of intellectual or moral qualities in man.

Pavlov's work on the conditioned reflex provided fresh support for the principle of association; and the physiologists and psychologists who adopted his experimental techniques found new arguments for the time-honoured doctrine that the conspicuous differences in the way different individuals behave result, not from any differences in native endowment, but simply from the manner in which each has been 'conditioned' by his early training and experiences.

'Does the behaviourist then', asks Watson, the apostle of this new creed, 'maintain that differences in verbal ability, arithmetical ability, and musical ability, in memory and in manual skill are all the effects of learning? The answer', he continues, 'is an emphatic "Yes". The geneticist and eugenist are fighting under the old banner of a discredited faculty psychology; and we no longer believe in faculties or any stereotyped patterns of behaviour that go under the names of "talents" or "capacities". Give me', he declares, 'a dozen healthy infants, and my own world to bring them up in, and I'll guarantee to take any one at random and train him to become whatever type you like to select—doctor, lawyer, artist, merchant chief, factory hand, ploughboy, beggar man, or thief' (*Behaviourism*, 1931). One has only to glance through the current journals of general or applied psychology, or the correspondence columns of *The Times Educational Supplement*, to see how many psychologists, sociologists, educationists and teachers still adhere, with only minor reservations, to the egalitarian doctrines thus proclaimed by Professor Watson fifty years ago.

No one can properly understand the controversies of the present day unless he knows something of their historical origins; and this brief review, I hope, may have served to fix and clarify the essential issues that are at stake and the widely differing solutions that have been propounded. It will be noted that the champions of the rival theories base their conclusions almost wholly on ideological grounds: unproved postulates, suiting the writer's personal prepossessions, are dogmatically affirmed; and from these his conclusions follow, if they follow at all, by purely deductive inference. Watson himself qualified his challenge by parenthetically observing: 'I am going beyond my facts, and I admit it; but so have the advocates of the contrary opinion, and they have been doing it for thousands of years.' Anyone with a genuine regard for scientific method is therefore bound to ask—why not undertake a few well-planned experiments or a few systematic inquiries to see how far the ascertainable data support one side or the other?

Now, though most educationists and nearly every journalist who seeks to inform public opinion seems unaware of it, a rapidly increasing number of *ad hoc* inquiries have been carried out during the last forty years or so. Unfortunately the reports are dispersed among a wide variety of technical journals, published in half a dozen different countries. What is more, the problems raised have proved to be far more complex than was previously assumed. To reach any sound conclusion by means of verbal arguments is consequently out of the question: quantitative measurements and statistical analyses are essential; and these are usually set out by specialists in numerical tables and algebraic inferences intelligible only to other specialists, working in similar fields. Accordingly, one of my chief objects in the chapters which follow will be to collect the scattered evidence, explain the techniques employed in language as simple and as comprehensible as the nature of the subject permits, and then, after weighing both pros and cons, consider what practical conclusions, if any, can be safely drawn.

Notes and references

1 J. Dewey, *Democracy and Education*, 1916; Julienne Ford, *Social Class and the Comprehensive School*, 1969; D. Rubinstein and C. Stoneman, *Education for Democracy*, 1970; Frances Stevens, *The New Inheritors*, 1970.

2 R. Southey, *Sir Thomas More: or colloquies on the progress and prospects of society*, 1829. I have borrowed some of my comments from Macaulay's review of the book when it first appeared.

CHAPTER TWO

The subnormal and the supernormal

The range of individual differences

Before we start discussing the *causes* of individual differences, we ought first to consider their *nature and range*. Most of us are accustomed to mix chiefly with persons of our own intellectual standing, and we fail to realize how wide are the differences between one individual and another in the general population. Even teachers commonly work each in one particular type of school, which usually recruits its pupils from similar social backgrounds. It is therefore scarcely surprising if many of them are inclined to attribute the minor differences they observe in the classroom to differences in the children's opportunities at home or to the obvious fact that some children are lazier or less ambitious than others. Let us therefore start by looking at a few typical specimens drawn from either end of the scale. Only by keeping in mind concrete case-histories can the statistical data which are to follow be realistically interpreted.

Merely to cite numerical results obtained with the psychologist's tests of intelligence or with tests of the stock school subjects—reading, spelling, arithmetic, and the like—will convey little to readers who are not themselves regularly engaged in applying such tests; so let me take instead a rather different type of test that I found particularly illuminating. The only apparatus required is a set of coloured reproductions, postcard size, of pictures specially selected for the purpose. The cards are dealt out to the children in class, and they are asked to write a 'composition' on the picture before them. One of the pictures I used for children aged ten to eleven was a copy of Watts's well-known painting, *Hope*. The following was written by a girl attending an ordinary elementary school in north London:

Hope

Sublimely, majestically sorrowful she seems. Yet her name is Hope. Cowering low, not in submission to Fate, but longing for happiness, she sits, blindfolded; and fingers, lovingly and musingly, the one vibrating string of her lyre, striving to create sweet melody. The first beam of sunshine is kissing her feet; and in her innermost soul she wonders whether the time will come when it will kiss her drooping head.

She is the good spirit of the world, and the ruler of the minds of those who dwell in it. In the darkest hour of the night she visits us to wait patiently for dawn and the light.

Hope cannot read the future. But the morning star, the eye of Heaven, is a prophet; and though Hope cannot see it, she feels its light shining in her heart. It puts into her soul dreams of happiness, thoughts of the realization of her ideals, and the winning of eternal bliss.

In the most unhappy moments of the life of man, she comes to him, drives away despair, and teaches him patience. She is like a sparkling and refreshing fountain to a thirsty flower, or a light seen in the darkness by some weary footsore traveller.

The writer was a child aged ten years eight months, with an intelligence quotient of 155; in tests of reading, arithmetic and other school subjects her performance was of the same high order. She was the daughter of a headmaster at a neighbouring school, and therefore enjoyed the additional advantage of an educated home background. I printed her essay, soon after it was written, in my book on *Mental and Scholastic Tests*. Some twelve years later I received a letter saying: 'I came across your book in the college library, and would like to thank you for the comments. . . . Father thought you would like to know that I was accepted as a student at this university and gained an honours degree (first class) in science, and am now studying to be a doctor.' Here too she succeeded.

The reader will find it instructive to compare her effort with those of professional writers—Chesterton's analysis of the same picture in his book on Watts, or Pater's celebrated rhapsody on Leonardo's masterpiece, written, so the student of literature will observe, with the same paeonic rhythm. The shortcomings and the occasional banalities in the child's brief essay will then be sufficiently obvious. There is none of Chesterton's ingenuity in the thought; none of the polished elegance of Pater in the style; merely the naive and somewhat sentimental reflections of a child struggling to express

'Some fragment of her dream of human life,
Shaped by herself with newly-learned art.'

Yet how many children, aged barely eleven, taught only in a Council school, could produce so neat a trifle?

A couple of streets away from her school lived a boy, who among all the normal children of the same age, resident in the same London borough, was poorest at scholastic work. Composed under precisely the same conditions, with the same picture in front of him and the same free allowance of time, his attempt reads, or rather runs, as follows:

'Wos a pon a tim a putr of a lrg situdan was out a bot ro stne no.'

('Once upon a time a picture of a girl sitting down without any boots or stockings on', was how he read it over to me: I have not attempted to indicate the cockney pronunciation which his own orthography suggests.)

This is the startling kind of diversity one encounters in making a survey of an entire school population or of a complete age-group numbering many hundreds. But now let us look at a few typical examples for which case-histories are available in fuller detail.

The subnormal

'John Doe' (the name, of course, is fictitious) was the eldest son of a well-to-do Harley Street physician. His mother was an attractive and vivacious woman, a competent housekeeper, but of no more than average intelligence. On the father's side most of the men had been professional people—doctors or lawyers, often eminent in their own particular line. The mother's family were humble country folk; and several remoter relatives, she said, had never learnt to read or write. The child's birth was perfectly normal, and his health excellent. But he did not start to walk until he was nearly two years old, nor to talk until six months later. A medical specialist who saw him about that time suggested trying hormone therapy; but this had no effect.

I first saw him when he was six and a half. He had apparently inherited his mother's good looks. Physically he was quite strong, and appeared happy, lively and eager to please. With the usual tests for general ability his performances were those of a child of four: his I.Q. was therefore $(4/6\cdot5) \times 100 = 62$. He could read neither letters nor numerals; he could count, a little hesitantly, up to ten, but no further. As his two younger brothers, both exceptionally bright, were now rapidly overtaking him, his parents feared that in the near future John might become distressed or jealous. I was therefore asked to recommend a residential institution; this, in fact, was the chief reason for the consultation. We found an excellent but rather expensive school where he remained happily for three years, and made some slight progress.

I saw him again just after his tenth birthday. His intelligence was (as one might have predicted) that of a six-year-old. But his performances in reading, spelling and arithmetic were those of a child of seven. Disparities of this kind often puzzle critics of mental testing: if a boy's innate capacity is that of a six-year-old, how can his attainments reach those of a child of seven? The answer is simple. By the attainments of a child of six or seven, the psychologist means the *average* performances of children at those ages; and some individuals naturally do better than the average and others do worse. This boy had received skilful coaching in the three Rs such as few ordinary children of his type would obtain; and the results were merely a testimony to the efficiency of the school.

I need only add that, when fully grown, John was quite unable to look after himself. He lived with his parents in their country house near the south coast. He could find his way about the village, and enjoyed swimming and simple games. In running a race he could beat both his brothers and some young cousins with whom he used to stay. Except for an attack of scarlet fever, his health remained excellent, until quite unexpectedly at the age of forty-three he collapsed and died, while visiting his aunt. An apoplectic stroke was at first suspected by the local doctor; and for that and other reasons a post-mortem examination was performed. His brain appeared perfectly healthy, and the cause of death was stated as 'heart failure', due, it was suggested, to overexertion. From all these details it seems clear that his subnormality could not be put down to any organic disease, either before or after birth; and it is still more obvious that it could not be attributed to environmental limitations. Apparently, therefore, this was essentially a case of innate but perfectly normal variation; older writers would probably have considered it a throwback to one of those maternal ancestors who, according to the mother, were dull and almost ineducable at school.

During school age, children such as John plainly need an education, or rather a training, very different from that of the average child. If throughout their lives they are never likely to develop beyond the mental level of a child of seven, then that should be kept in mind by those who teach them. To hammer in the formal rudiments of arithmetic, reading and spelling is a waste of time and effort; such things have no meaning to them, and will never be put to use. What they require is a training in those everyday activities which an intelligent child picks up for himself, and a few interesting hobbies and recreations to occupy their leisure hours. And this can be provided only in a special type of school, equipped with materials and apparatus for a more concrete and practical education.

The supernormal

Let us now turn to cases from the opposite end of the scale. Examples from my own studies of Liverpool and London children I shall give later on; none of them, however, could be regarded as instances of the highest genius. Of these the example most frequently cited is that of John Stuart Mill. In Catharine Cox's biographical studies of three hundred geniuses he is the only one whom she assigns to her highest category, that of persons with I.Q.s between 190 and 200. For his early life the chief sources are Mill's own autobiography and a critical study published shortly after his death by Alexander Bain, a Scottish psychologist who was personally acquainted with the family.

Until he was fourteen, John was educated at home by his father. James Mill's 'fundamental doctrine', as John tells us, was 'the formation of human character by circumstances, through the universal Principle of Association, and the consequent possibility of improving the intellectual and moral condition of mankind by education . . . he had scarcely any belief in pleasure'. The boy's education began with the study of Greek at the age of three, and Latin a few years later. Greek he was able to understand for himself, as well as books on English history, by the age of four. At six and a half he wrote *A History of Rome*—'a production', we are assured by those who read it, 'quite extraordinary for so young a lad'. By the age of seven he was reading Plato, Thucydides, Demosthenes, and three Greek dramatists (almost as much as an Oxford undergraduate would have read by the age of twenty); Homer, Pindar, Aeschines, as well as Cicero and Livy he worked at in the following year. He then turned to textbooks on astronomy and mechanics (his 'special delight') and some of the English classics. Physics and chemistry he studied 'in a theoretical not a practical sense' (an omission which he greatly regretted). At the age of twelve he was learning logic; 'nothing', he found, 'tends so much to form clear and exact thinking'. At fourteen he was reading Helvétius, Condillac, and other French philosophical writers; and, young as he was, he received permission to attend lectures on zoology and metaphysics at Montpellier University. Two essays on political economy, written when he was sixteen, were published in a journal called *The Traveller*.

In many subjects, notably in higher mathematics (e.g. the differential calculus, which he took up when he was eleven), Mill was virtually self-taught. Part of his training consisted of daily debates with his father on various new and abstruse subjects, e.g. the foundations of geometry; and Bain, who listened to them both, thought the 'son often evinced his superiority to his father . . . I have never known a similar case of precocity', he says; 'his innate aptitudes must have been very great.' Yet Mill himself believed that 'in natural gifts [he] was below rather than above par'!

Among all the world's famous men there is no one whose pedigree and early development have been so fully documented as those of Francis Galton.[1] According to Terman, Galton's I.Q. was probably even higher than Mill's—approximately 200. His ancestral history is typical of many eminent men belonging to what would nowadays be called the upper professional class. Working backwards, we come first to a well-to-do father and grandfather, often either themselves members of a learned profession or successful men of business (Francis's father, a wealthy banker, was elected High Bailiff of Birmingham and Deputy Lieutenant of the county; his maternal grandfather was Erasmus

Darwin, MD, FRS, famous in his day as the author of philosophical poems on biological subjects). Still working backwards, we then usually come to shrewd and industrious merchants or shopkeepers, born in the country, but migrating early to a nearby town; and so back eventually to the older yeomanry, the small farmer and 'the rude forefathers of the hamlet', sleeping beneath the scarcely decipherable tombstones in the village churchyard (in this case the village of Galton in Dorset). The number of famous relatives in Galton's pedigree is astonishing: they include not only the Darwins, but the Barclays, the Wedgwoods, and many others who were Fellows of the Royal Society or celebrated men of letters. Among them we find eminent scientists like Sir Henry Savile, tutor to Queen Elizabeth I and founder of the Savilian professorships of geometry and astronomy at Oxford, and Sir William Sedley, founder of the Sedleian chair on natural philosophy. Sedley's son married Savile's daughter—the 'gifted child' of whom the poet Waller later wrote:

'Here lies the learned Savile's heir,
So early wise and lasting fair,
That none, except her years they told,
Thought her a child or thought her old.'

Their son was the playwright, Sir Charles Sedley, still remembered as the author of 'Phyllis is my only joy'. It was one of his descendants who married Dr Erasmus Darwin, the 'poetical physician', and so became Francis's 'beloved grandmother'.

Francis was the little Benjamin of his family—the last of nine children, 'the pet of us all', writes Mrs Galton Wheler, who was the oldest. His early education was undertaken by another of his sisters, Adèle. When he was twelve months old he 'knew all the capital letters', and eighteen months later 'could read simple fairy stories'. The following is one of the earliest of his many letters which the family has treasured:

'My dear Adèle, I am 4 years old and can read any English book. I can say all the Latin substantives and adjectives and active verbs, besides fifty-two lines of Latin poetry. I can cast up any sum in addition, and can multiply by 2, 3, 4, 5, 6, 7, 8, (9), 10, (11). I can also say the pence table. I read French a little and I know the clock. Francis Galton, Febuary 15, 1827.' [The figures

'9' and '11' have been erased, and the misspelling of February corrected.]

The next year the maid who was sent to fetch him home found him holding a group of small boys at bay, and shouting:

'Come one, come all! This rock shall fly
From its firm base as soon as I.'

By the age of six he had mastered the *Iliad* and the *Odyssey* in Greek. The next year a friend of his father (the first secretary of University College, London) visited the family, and kept quizzing him about the *Odyssey*. At length little Francis replied: 'Pray, Mr Homer, look at the last line in the twelfth book.' (In my copy of Lang's translation the last line reads: 'All this I have told thee already, and it like me not to repeat a twice-told tale.') Unlike Mill, he dabbled in the practical side of science: a 'Last Will and Testament', which he 'signed, sealed, and delivered' on his eighth birthday, bequeathed to his various brothers and sisters his scientific collections of shells, beetles, minerals, and 'to Lucy my hygrometer'. Later on, chemistry became a favourite hobby; and when he was thirteen, he drew a set of drawings for a flying machine which he thought of constructing, and labelled them 'Francis Galton's Aerostatic Project'.

He was sent early to school—first, when barely eight, to a 'boarding establishment for sons of the professional classes'. Here he was placed in one of the top classes with boys of fourteen and fifteen. A few years later he was admitted at King Edward's School, Birmingham. But always he found the lessons and curriculum far too easy. Again and again he wrote to his parents begging that they should 'arrange for [him] to do work more varied and advanced in character. I am not getting on in the least', he complains; 'only six books of Euclid is not much for two years.' And in his *Memories* he repeats: 'I chafed at the limitations; I craved for an abundance of good reading, solid science, and well-taught mathematics.' To make up for this 'period of stagnation' he embarked on a plan of self-instruction during the weekends and vacations; his comments remind one of Osbert Sitwell's entry in *Who's Who* under 'Education': 'During the holidays from Eton.'

To my mind, however, the most remarkable attainments recorded of any young person are those of William Hamilton; not his Scottish namesake, the philosopher, but, as one of his compatriots describes him, 'the greatest man of science Ireland has ever produced'. Strange to say, he appears neither in Galton's list of geniuses nor in the lists of Havelock Ellis and Cox. Hamilton's early education was supervised by his uncle, a village curate who was apparently a versatile linguist, and hoped to turn the boy into a scholarly divine. By the age of five 'little Willie' could read Latin, Greek and Hebrew, and recite long passages from Homer and Milton. Before he was eight he had added French and Italian, and a couple of years later Sanskrit and 'Chaldee' (i.e. the Aramaic tongue in which parts of *Ezra* and *Daniel* are written). At thirteen he boasted that he had mastered one foreign language for every year of his life. Twelve months later he presented a flowery address of welcome in Persian to the Persian Ambassador who was visiting Dublin.

Just before this, however, he had met the calculating prodigy, Zerah Colburn, and (as he relates) 'resolved to penetrate the secret of the young man's method', which Colburn himself did not fully understand. The consequence, to the uncle's dismay, was that William now became passionately engrossed in all kinds of mathematical problems—at first, so he declared, 'purely by way of recreation'. Here he was almost entirely self-taught. In the course of these early studies he made several novel discoveries and incidentally detected errors in Laplace's proof of the parallelogram of forces. Before he was eighteen he passed, easily first out of a hundred candidates, into Trinity College, Dublin. There he carried off almost all the available prizes and obtained top marks in both classics and mathematics. Meanwhile he was conducting experiments which laid the foundations for his highly original theory of optics. When he presented his first memoir to the Royal Irish Academy, one of the members at once announced that 'this young man—I do not say *will be*, but already *is*—the first mathematician of his age'. Shortly afterwards, when only twenty-two, he was elected professor of astronomy.

In all the cases I have so far described the 'gifted child' was the son of a gifted father, and received from his earliest years an exceptionally erudite tuition from a learned relative at home. Is not this, the critic may say, sufficient proof that 'l'éducation peut tout'? Before we decide, let us turn to instances where the child was reared in an extremely poor and often illiterate home. Of the older scientists known to fame the one of whose family history and early life we have the most detailed records is Johannes Kepler.[2] When he was twenty-six, Kepler drew up horoscopes for himself, his ancestors, and various other relatives; and to each he appended a systematic character sketch. The data these contain can be amplified and checked by existing documents. Kepler tells us to the very minute, not only the time of his birth, but also the time of his conception, from which, it appears, he must have been born prematurely. Owing to the straitened circumstances of his home, he was ill-nourished and often sickly. His father was a drunken innkeeper in a small town in Swabia; who, when times were bad, went off as a mercenary to fight in the Dutch wars, spending all his money on liquor, and on one occasion narrowly escaping the gallows. Kepler's great-aunt was burnt as a witch; and he only just managed to rescue his mother from the same fate. Nevertheless, on both sides of the family some of the boy's ancestors were men of ability, holding responsible posts in the state.

Kepler's schooling was constantly interrupted. He had to serve as pot-boy in his father's tavern, and, to eke out the family income, later became a farm-hand on a neighbour's land. He too, as he tells us, was largely self-taught. 'I spent much time', he says, 'on difficult tasks'—inventing problems, and then trying to solve them, working out far-fetched comparisons, discovering highly ingenious theorems in mathematics, which he subsequently found others had discovered before him. He even wrote lyrical poems, and attempted a comedy in verse. Books for private study he borrowed from the University of Tübingen. His exceptional gifts and remarkable originality soon attracted the notice of his school teachers and even members of the Protestant University. The Dukes of Württemberg, having embraced the Lutheran faith, found they needed able and learned clergy to defend the change to new doctrines amid the fierce religious controversies then raging throughout Germany. They resolved to organize what was a new educational system. New schools were endowed, and scholarships established for 'children of the poor and faithful who are adept and diligent in their learning'.

When twelve years of age, Kepler was selected for a Protestant seminary, and at the age of twenty graduated in Arts at the University of Tübingen, and then spent four years in the Faculty of Theology. In 1595, when their official 'mathematicus' died, the University of Graz (capital of Styria), as was usual, applied to

Tübingen for a new incumbent. Kepler was recommended. In addition to lecturing on mathematics, Virgil, and rhetoric, one of his duties was to publish an annual calendar of astrological forecasts. He apparently interpreted his horoscopes by the aid of a sagacious insight into current trends; his first calendar predicted an exceptional spell of cold weather and an invasion by the Turks. Both prophecies were fulfilled, and this greatly enhanced his reputation. Astrology turned his interest to astronomy; here once again his fondness for posing new problems, and his ingenuity in devising new solutions, led him to ask and answer questions about the orbits and velocities of the planets and their distances from the sun. The answers eventually appeared in the shape of what we now know as 'Kepler's three laws'. But it was the novelty of his scientific approach to fundamental questions in astronomy, dynamics and optics—utterly different from the *a priori* methods which had lasted for a thousand years—that is the hallmark of his genius.

Still more striking is the early history of C. F. Gauss, whom Professor Bell has called 'the Prince of Mathematicians'.[3] There are innumerable anecdotes about his early precocity, several of which were related to Professor Bell by surviving members of the family, and bear out Gauss's own reminiscences. He was born in a miserable hovel in Brunswick. His father, an uncouth and somewhat brutal bricklayer, intended the boy to follow in his steps and provide for his parents' old age; he therefore 'did all in his power to thwart the child's intellectual interests, and prevent him going off to acquire an education suited to his unusual gifts'. Gauss's maternal uncle, however, a weaver of damasks, was evidently a man of some intelligence; he had, we are told, 'an exceptionally inventive mind', but unfortunately died in early manhood: 'in him', says Gauss, 'a born genius was lost.' The boy taught himself to read and count, and in arithmetic achieved local fame as an infant prodigy. One Saturday, when his father was making out the weekly pay-roll, little Carl, not yet three years old, piped up and said: 'Father, you've reckoned it wrong. It ought to be [so and so]'; and he gave the correct figure, which his father quickly verified. He went to the local school; but here the pupils did not start arithmetic until the age of ten. Carl solved many of the problems in mental arithmetic almost as they were announced. 'He is quite beyond me', said the headmaster, who taught the class. 'I can teach him nothing more.'

By a lucky chance there came to the school as a sort of pupil-teacher, another youth named Bartels, with the same passion for knowledge. In the large classroom it was apparently his main task to watch the boys at work, correct their exercises, and cut their quill-pens. Between the two lads there sprang up an intimate friendship; and, when school hours were over, they worked together at algebra, geometry and other subjects, teaching themselves Latin, since most technical books were then printed in that language. It is to Bartels, from whom I have already been quoting, that we owe much of our information about young Gauss's early accomplishments. During the next two or three years Gauss and Bartels between them started to query the implicit assumptions underlying the traditional proofs of Newton's binomial theorem and of the postulates on which Euclidean geometry was based. The highly original work they then began on 'infinite processes' and what is now known as 'non-Euclidean geometry' was to change the whole aspect of mathematics.

Gauss's fame as a 'lightning calculator' reached the ears of the Duke of Brunswick. Accordingly, just after he attained his fourteenth birthday, the boy was summoned to Court to exhibit his powers. His extraordinary speed in mental computation, so he afterwards explained, was largely due to a number of ingenious tricks, dodges and short-cuts, which he had worked out for himself. The Duke was so much impressed that he undertook to pay for the boy's further education, and supported him financially during most of his later life. The lad entered Caroline College in Brunswick at the age of fifteen; and, having now mastered various ancient and modern languages through private study, he became for a while a devotee of the new philological inquiries which then interested German scholars. At the age of eighteen he went to the University of Göttingen, still undecided about his future career. He had, however, already devised the invaluable 'method of least squares' and was pondering on what is today known as the 'Gaussian' curve of errors (the 'normal curve').

Geniuses in their early years are often as versatile as they are precocious; and Gauss's youthful indecision was a perpetual worry to his family. His father continued to abuse the lad as 'Ein ganzer Taugenichts', while his mother still fondly hoped he would at last settle down. One day, when a young stranger from Hungary, Wolfgang Bolyai (the poet and dramatist), had called to see him, she timidly asked whether her son would ever justify her hopes. 'Madam,' replied Bolyai, 'he is already the greatest mathematician in Europe.' Frau Gauss burst into tears.

Gauss kept what he called a *Notizenjournal* (a kind of scientific diary). In it he records that on 20 March 1796 (exactly a month before his nineteenth birthday) he found the solution to a time-honoured problem that had baffled mathematicians since the days of the Greeks, namely, when is it possible to construct with compass and straight edge a polygon with an odd number of sides. The date marks the turning point in his career; for this discovery, so he tells us, finally decided him to choose mathematics for his 'main life work', though he still dabbled in comparative philology as a private hobby.

For one last example let us come nearer home. Michael Faraday's father was a journeyman blacksmith from a Yorkshire village who settled in Newington, which was then just another village south of London. Michael went first to a dame-school, and at ten to a local day school. Here, however, the teaching went no further than the rudiments of reading, writing and arithmetic. When he was thirteen, his father moved north of the Thames; and Michael, to supplement the scanty family income, obtained a job as errand-boy for a bookbinder and bookseller, who subsequently took him on as an apprentice. At home he often read some of the books he helped to bind, particularly works of science and an *Encyclopedia*. He seems also to have carried out simple experiments in chemistry, magnetism and electricity with home-made apparatus. One day a friendly customer, interested in science, gave him tickets for Sir Humphry Davy's lectures at the Royal Institution, which was within walking distance from his home. At length, having conceived the desire (as he put it in his letter) 'to enter the service of science', he ventured to write to the great man himself, enclosing, in lieu of testimonials, notes he had taken of Davy's lectures, with diagrams and incidental comments. Davy was so impressed that he at once appointed him assistant in his laboratory. There is no need to relate how quickly and how remarkably Faraday outdistanced his master, or how, having been unanimously proposed as President of the Royal Society, he modestly refused. 'Michael Faraday', says his biographer, 'was probably the most original experimental philosopher the world has ever known, and almost entirely self taught.'[4]

These few instances will suffice to show how widely individuals at opposite ends of the intellectual scale differ from each other and from the general mass of mankind. But their sporadic occurrence on the pages of history clearly raises far more questions than it answers. A few tentative inferences suggest themselves. It would seem that the highest intellectual attainments are only achieved when an exceptionally bright child is a member of a family in which one or more of his nearest relatives is almost equally gifted, and is at once eager, and able, to superintend his education from the earliest years. Where no such relative exists, the child must take his own initiative and teach himself. It is unlikely that he will get very far, unless by some lucky accident he gains access to books, and later on is fortunate enough to encounter a patron who will recognize him as a child of promise, assist him by putting him in the way of appropriate instruction, and, what is almost always just as essential, give him some financial support. I would add that sheer chance seems frequently to play a crucial part in another way: usually at the critical period there lies close at hand some new and pregnant problem calling for solution, which the youth has the sagacity to perceive and the enterprise and ingenuity to attack by some hitherto untried procedure.

One further point is worth noting—the extraordinary versatility of several of our youthful prodigies. Hamilton, the mathematician, was also a brilliant linguist. Gauss might have made his mark as a pioneer of the new science of philology. Galton was already famous as a meteorologist and an African explorer before he turned his mind to the problem of heredity and the study of mental differences. Is this wide range of interest and ability an intrinsic feature of genius as such or merely an occasional trait—a consequence perhaps of adolescent instability or of the competing claims of the age into which the man was born? Popular as they have been, biological studies are powerless to settle such questions: they can illustrate, but never prove.

Notes and references

1 The chief details are summarized in my centenary paper, 'Francis Galton' (*Br. J. statist. Psychol.*, 15, 1962, 1–50); see also K. Pearson, *Life, Letters and Labours of Francis Galton*, 1924–30 and F. Galton, *Memories of My Life*, 1908. Some of the details given above I owe to my father, who was physician to the Galton family, and to Mrs Galton Wheler, who later inherited the Galton house and estate at Claverdon.

2 See C. Frisch, *Joannis Kepler Opera Omnia*, 8 vols, 1858–71; C. Baumgardt, *Johannes Kepler, Life and Letters*, 1951.

3 E. T. Bell, *Man of Mathematics*, 1937; cf. H. Mack, *C. F. Gauss und die Seinen*, 1927.

4 H. B. Jones, *Life and Letters of Faraday*, 2 vols, 1867.

CHAPTER THREE

Hereditary genius

Need for a scientific approach

We now come to the crucial problem—what are the basic causes
of the mental differences we have observed, and how are those
causes to be ascertained? Are these wide variations the effects of
each individual's innate constitution, or are they simply due to the
way he has been taught, trained and moulded by his home and his
school? If both types of cause are operative, what is the relative
influence of each on the particular characteristics we have in
view? For two thousand years, from the days of Plato onwards,
philosophers and social reformers have discussed these questions,
taking now one side, now the other; and yet, until quite recently,
not one thought of investigating the matter by some kind of
rigorous scientific procedure. The first to make such an attempt
was Sir Francis Galton, Darwin's cousin.

When Galton embarked on his inquiries, the most popular
method of assessing an individual's mental qualities was based on
a system developed by a Viennese anatomist named Gall. He
originally called it 'cranioscopy' (inspecting the skull). His treatise
ran to two volumes with the long and elaborate title (in French)
'Anatomy and Physiology of the Nervous System in General and
the Brain in Particular, with observations on the possibility of
recognizing intellectual and moral dispositions of human beings
by the configuration of their heads' (1810). It was written in col-
laboration with a young and enthusiastic disciple named Spurzheim, who proposed that the 'new science' should be rechristened
'phrenology'. Most people will have come across those bald
white heads of plaster, mapped out into some thirty-five divisions,
duly numbered and named in accordance with a key-list of
'intellectual' and 'affective' faculties—'observation', 'memory',

'language', 'mathematics', 'amativeness', 'benevolence', 'philo-progenitiveness', and the like. This classification Gall took over from the traditional faculty theory of the 'mental philosophers' of his day. The scheme itself goes back to Aristotle and Plato; but the full details, as finally adopted by the two phrenologists, was due to the so-called 'Scottish school'. Each faculty, Gall maintained, must be localized in a specific 'organ' of the brain—the 'intellectual' at the front of the head and the 'affective' at the back. If any specific faculty was strongly developed, the corresponding organ would be enlarged; and this would produce a 'palpable elevation' or 'bump' on the skull.

In Britain the doctrine was widely popularized first by Spurzheim himself, who settled in London, and after his death by George Combe, who wrote several textbooks on the subject and founded a professorship at the University of Edinburgh 'for the study of mental phenomena'. Today the George Combe Chair ranks as the oldest chair of psychology in the United Kingdom. In 1850 Queen Victoria herself summoned Combe to Buckingham Palace to discuss the education and the future of the royal children. Herbert Spencer arranged for his two young friends, George Eliot and Beatrice Potter (later Mrs Sidney Webb) to have their skulls examined. George Eliot regularly described the characters in her novels in the psychological vocabulary adopted by the phrenologists; and today the same vocabulary is sometimes used by teachers, and occasionally by school doctors and psychologists, in reporting on school children. I myself remember how, less than fifty years ago, one local education authority paid a well-known phrenologist to examine the heads of pupils nominated by school teachers for scholarships to a grammar school. Among teachers and parents there is still a widespread impression that children with large and prominent foreheads are likely to be highly intelligent.

Galton, who had received a medical training at Birmingham, realized that there was little evidence to support these physiological speculations; and towards the close of the century the work of experimental neurologists like Ferrier and Sherrington demonstrated that, although certain mental functions appeared to be localized in the brain, the processes involved were all relatively simple, namely the different sensory processes, specific muscular movements, and what were vaguely termed 'associative functions'. The cerebellum or 'little brain' at the back of the head, where Gall located 'philoprogenitiveness', is concerned with general muscular co-ordination and more especially with the maintenance of bodily equilibrium or balance.

Quantitative techniques

It was Galton's firm conviction that the essential feature of all scientific research consisted in the use of quantitative measurement. Accordingly, he set himself to devise methods of measuring first the chief mental characteristics in which individuals appeared to differ, and secondly the correspondence between measurements obtained for members of the same family, and between measurements of mental characteristics and the signs or symptoms used to estimate them (e.g. the actual size of the head). In the earliest of his more important publications in this field, *Hereditary Genius* (1869), he claimed to be 'the first to treat the subject in a statistical manner, and so arrive at precise numerical results'.

He began by accepting the widely held view that all mental activities have three main aspects—knowing, feeling, and willing, or, as later writers termed them, the cognitive, affective, and conative aspects. And from his preliminary biographical studies he concluded that 'those who may be accounted of outstanding achievement' are distinguished, not merely by high intellectual capacity, but also by a keen emotional interest in whatever they may have taken in hand, and by a resolute will to work hard, intently and persistently. His starting point, however, so he decided, should be a systematic study of the first of these three qualities, since intellectual capacity necessarily sets an upper limit to what a man can accomplish. Each of the three qualities, he believed, was largely 'an award of inheritance', but the decisive factor was 'the gift of high ability'.

The elaborate classification of abilities adopted by the traditional faculty psychologists he considered to be of little practical use. Instead he distinguished between two different kinds of ability—a single 'general ability', entering into all we think, do, or say, and a small number of 'special aptitudes'. The former, in his view, was by far the most important. 'Numerous instances', he writes, 'recorded in this book show in how small a degree eminence can be considered due to purely special powers. People lay too much stress on apparent specialities, thinking that, because a man is devoted to some particular pursuit, he cannot possibly succeed in anything else. They might just as well say that, because a youth has fallen in love with a brunette, he could not possibly fall in love with a blonde; it is as probable as not that the affair was mainly or wholly due to a *general* amorousness.' It is just the same, he contended, with intellectual pursuits: 'Without a special aptitude or interest for mathematics a man cannot become a mathematician; but without a high degree of general ability he will never make a great mathematician.' Much the same had been affirmed by Dr Johnson. Robertson, the historian, had argued that it was in virtue of their distinctive gifts that Caesar became a great commander, Shakespeare a great poet, and Newton a great scientist. 'No,' replied Johnson, 'it is only that one man has more mind than another. He may direct it differently or prefer this study to that. Sir, the man who has vigour may walk to the North as well as to the South, to the East as well as to the West.'

Galton, it will be observed, assumes three important distinctions, which lead to a threefold cross-classification. First, he distinguishes between those tendencies which are inborn and those which have developed out of them or been incidentally acquired during the individual's own lifetime; secondly, he distinguishes between cognitive capacities on the one hand, and what we may broadly describe as motivational tendencies on the other; and finally, he distinguishes between a kind of superfaculty covering the whole range of cognitive activity and a number of capacities of more limited range which, as we have seen, he usually calls special aptitudes. This threefold cross-classification, so it seemed to me, suggests a concept defined by three attributes, namely 'an innate, general, cognitive factor'. According to the aspect he is emphasizing at the moment, Galton himself refers to it as 'natural ability', 'general ability', 'intellectual ability', or, in a single word, as 'intelligence'; and it is this last designation that has since been most frequently adopted.

The measurement of intelligence

Most educated people who think about the matter are ready to admit that there may be a few outstanding geniuses, like Newton or Shakespeare, whose exceptional abilities are inborn, and at the other end of the scale a few mentally deficient individuals, whose lack of ability is also due to their innate constitution. Geniuses and defectives alike they regard as nature's freaks. The individuals who make up the general mass of the population they assume to be born with more or less equal abilities, the observable differences being superimposed by differences in opportunity or education. Galton, on the other hand—and this is one of the first points he seeks to demonstrate—holds that between the two extremes every grade and shade of inborn variation may be discerned. 'There is', he says, 'a *continuity* of natural ability, reaching from one knows not what height and descending to one can hardly say what depth.' Men are not divided into three distinct classes—the geniuses, the defectives, and the normal; the differences between them are all a matter of degree.

That being so, the first requirement for any genuinely scientific investigation is to seek some method of measuring the various degrees, just as we should if we were investigating the causes for differences in weight or stature. Now for any scale of measurement two things are needed—a zero point and a unit. In measuring the height of any upright object your zero point is the ground on which the thing or the person stands; and your unit is an inch or a centimetre measured with a tape-measure. For ability it is impossible to indicate any absolute zero, and there is no tape-measure. Accordingly, in measuring ability, Galton proposed to take for the zero point the average or *mean* of the whole population, or in the case of children, of a whole age-group, and to take as the measure for any individual the amount by which he deviates above or below this mean, much as you measure the latitude of a place by its distance north or south of the equator. Since the distribution appears to be symmetrical, there will be just as many individuals above the mean as below it: in other words, the mean divides the whole population into two sections, equal in number. The next step is to imagine each of these halves divided into two again, with equal numbers in each. To make his meaning clear Galton took the case of stature, for which, he believed, the distribution of individual differences is much the same as for intelligence. For Englishmen, he found, the average height was 5 ft 7½ in. (67·5 inches). Half of them fell within the range of 65·8 and 69·2 inches, deviations of ±1·7 inches above or below the mean. This deviation, dividing the whole distribution into four quarters, Galton proposed to adopt as the unit of measurement for his scale of ability.

The normal distribution

How are the different individuals that make up the whole population distributed along this scale? Here Galton was plainly influenced by his own novel theory as to the causal mechanism that underlies human inheritance. Unlike Darwin, but like Mendel, whose work was completely unknown at that time, Galton believed that what parents pass on to their children are not whole traits or characteristics as such, but innumerable minute causal factors or tendencies (nowadays called genes), and that the number of such causal factors which are transmitted to any particular child may be regarded as a matter of chance. In short, he maintained that heredity was, as he put it, 'atomic' or 'particulate'. This was a remarkable anticipation of twentieth-century genetics. Mendel's experiments and statistical theories were not rediscovered until Galton was nearly eighty—as Mendel would have been, had he lived; for, by an odd coincidence, they were born in the same year.

The type of frequency distribution that arises when variations are due to a very large number of very small causes (which is what we mean by 'chance') has long been known to mathematicians. It was first discovered by a French Huguenot, named De Moivre, who fled from France after the revocation of the Edict of Nantes and settled in London. He became a close friend of Newton, and a Fellow of the Royal Society. To supplement his meagre earnings he undertook to solve problems for wealthy gamblers, and so helped to lay the foundations of the theory of probability.

Suppose you toss nine coins over and over again, and count the number of heads obtained with each throw of nine. With 512 tosses the distribution will approximate to the following figures:

Number of heads	0	1	2	3	4	5	6	7	8	9	Total
Frequency	1	9	36	84	126	126	84	36	9	1	512

The mathematician will see at once that this is a binomial distribution, derived from the expansion of $(p + q)n$, where $p = q = \frac{1}{2}$ (the probability of getting a head or tail with a single toss) and $n = 9$. The distribution is symmetrical: the frequencies from 0 to 4 are identical with those from 9 to 5. In general the mean of such a distribution will be pn (here $4\frac{1}{2}$), and the standard deviation

$\sqrt{pqn}$ (here $\sqrt{2\frac{1}{4}}$). Moreover, the mean and a deviation on either side of it equal to approximately $\frac{2}{3}\sqrt{pqn}$ will cut the distribution into four quarters. Here $\frac{2}{3}\sqrt{pqn} = 1$: in this case, therefore, Galton's unit would coincide with the unit of measurement; and it will be seen that the numbers lying between $3\frac{1}{2}$ and $4\frac{1}{2}$ and between $4\frac{1}{2}$ and $5\frac{1}{2}$ are each 126, which is approximately one-quarter of the total (512). Thus, although the whole distribution extends from 0 to 9, about one-half of the total number lies between $3\frac{1}{2}$ and $5\frac{1}{2}$.

De Moivre's formula ('De mensura sortis', *Phil. Trans. Roy. Soc.*, 1711) gives the limiting expression for such a distribution in the more general case in which n is unknown, but assumed to be indefinitely large. Hence its importance for our present problem. All the theoretical frequencies can then be computed from the actual values obtained for the mean and standard deviation. Following Spearman, many writers in Britain attribute its discovery to Gauss. As we have already seen, Gauss rediscovered the formula nearly a century later, and demonstrated its utility in the study of errors of measurement (e.g. in astronomy and other physical sciences) and of errors in gunnery (a favourite illustration with Galton). Hence the curve has become generally known as the 'normal curve of error'; and the value which Galton proposed to take for his unit (the semi-interquartile range) was termed the 'probable error'.

Some years later Quetelet, the Astronomer Royal of Belgium, became interested in vital statistics, and, in the course of his investigations, noted that measurements obtained for the heights and other physical characteristics of French conscripts conformed to the normal curve of distribution (*On Man and the Development of His Faculties*, 1835). Galton owed his knowledge of Quetelet's statistical techniques to Florence Nightingale, who, after her return from the Crimea, devoted herself to the systematic study of the health of soldiers, and had become acquainted with the work of Quetelet on continental conscripts. Galton was firmly convinced that mental characteristics are inherited in the same manner as bodily characteristics, and so conceived the idea of applying the same formulae to express the distribution of mental measurements. In his book and other published articles he takes lists of marks obtained in school and university examinations, and compares the frequencies with the theoretical percentages set out in Quetelet's mathematical tables (reprinted in full in Galton's book).

The method which Galton finally adopted for constructing his scale of mental measurements is as follows. Consider, he says, a population of exactly a million adults, and take the assessments for the abilities of the brightest and the stupidest as indicating the extreme range for the entire population; then divide the interval between these two values into fourteen equal grades, seven above and seven below the mean. The distance separating the border-lines for any one grade will then form the unit for our scale. A simple calculation from the theoretical frequencies given for each grade shows that the unit is once again approximately equal to the probable error.

The definition of genius

Instead of marks or numbers, Galton assigns letters to his various grades, e.g. A to G for those above the average, *a* to *g* for those below; and, to illustrate their nature, he attaches verbal descriptions to each—'mediocre', 'good average', 'those having the ability of the foremen of juries', and so on. He then tries to find an exact numerical definition of 'genius'. For this purpose he begins by counting up the number of acknowledged 'geniuses' actually existing in the contemporary population. This he estimates in various ways—e.g. from obituary notices over a period of ten years, from the number of names in Routledge's list of *Men of the Time*, and from other similar sources. He concluded that, roughly speaking, there appeared to be among every million of the population about 250 persons whom most biographers would class as geniuses. The figure corresponds with the number in his two top grades F and G. F is the fifth grade above the general average, so that the borderline for a genius is approximately $+5$ times the probable error, which in terms of current terminology would mean about 150 I.Q. Grade F, who number about 235 per million, he calls 'eminent', and grade G, who number about 15 per million, he calls 'illustrious'. He notes that there are analogous grades at the lower end of the scale; medical surveys, he says, indicate that the proportion of grossly defective persons is about 1 in 4,000 (i.e. 250 per million), and the two could be split into two grades or groups, namely, grade *f*, the 'imbeciles', and grade *g*, the rarer 'idiots', those terms being used as in the semi-official inquiries then being carried out on the problem.

The inheritance of ability

Galton's chief purpose, however, was to demonstrate that the outstanding achievements of geniuses are due mainly to their exceptional innate endowment. In his early investigation he relies almost exclusively on the study of pedigrees. He formulates his problem in these terms: suppose that a boy is the son of a genius; how far, if at all, does this increase the probability that the boy will turn out to be a genius? Similarly, suppose that he has a grandfather who is a genius, or perhaps, like young Newton, one or two remoter relatives in or near this high category of whom he may never have heard; how could this affect our estimate of his chances? To answer these questions he collected family histories for nearly a thousand 'eminent' or 'illustrious' men in various walks of life, and supplemented them by a brief biographical study of each to justify his classification. A genius, it will be remembered, was defined as the ablest in a random sample of 4,000 male adults. Hence the probability that any boy picked by sheer chance from the school population will be a genius is 1 in 4,000. But, if his father was a genius, then, as Galton's data indicates, the probability is increased to 1 in 4; if only his grandfather was a genius, it would be about 1 in 29; if an uncle, 1 in 40; if a first cousin, 1 in 200—still twenty times the probability of a boy chosen at random.

Now Galton did not (as his critics so often declare) ignore the fact that a gifted father might provide his son with better opportunities—more books, a better school, personal tuition, or the like. This point he meets in two ways. First, he seeks 'two groups of men with equal social advantages in one of which they have high hereditary gifts, while in the other they have not', and then points out how much greater were the achievements of sons in the former class. Secondly, he mentions numerous cases in which the eminent relative could not have exercised any direct influence over the child. D'Alembert, for example, was an infant abandoned on the steps of a Parisian church one winter night, and there picked up by the parish beadle. He was boarded out as a pauper with an impoverished glazier, and christened after the church near which he was found. As a child he was eager to learn. But the glazier and his wife did all they could to thwart his attempts at study, intending him to follow the same humble trade. The boy managed to buy books and read them in secret. He taught himself mathematics; and eventually his youthful discoveries in that subject were so original that he was elected a member of the Académie at the age of only twenty-four. It turned out that he was the illegitimate son of a famous French novelist, who had been the mistress of several still more famous men of genius. Her relatives included a cardinal, a dramatist, and a celebrated critic (Comte d'Argental, who became the intimate companion and literary executor of Voltaire). Galton adds that 'abundant instances of this emergence from obscurity are to be found in the pages of [his] book'; and it is easy to add to his list. We have already noted the cases of Kepler, Gauss and Faraday. Laplace, whose fame as a mathematician is almost as great as Gauss's, was the son of a farm labourer; Wolsey and Defoe were sons of butchers; Watt, Whewell and Lincoln of carpenters; Marlowe, Winckelmann, Hans Andersen and James Mill of cobblers; Luther, Zwingli, Gassendi, Knox and Burns of peasants; Kant's father was a strapmaker, Franklin's a soap-boiler, Bunyan's a tinker, Carlyle's a mason, Sir Humphry Davy's a shiftless wood-carver, Cardinal Richelieu's a soldier of the guard; and so one might go on.

In his later publication Galton devoted considerable attention to revising his rating scale, and sought to supplement it by what was then the novel device of standardized mental tests. Most of those he described in detail are tests of sensory discrimination, generally suggested by the experiments carried out by Fechner and Wundt in Germany. But he also emphasized the need for tests of 'higher mental processes'. His ideas were quickly taken up by many of his followers. As early as 1881, C. H. Lake, a London teacher, started applying tests of discrimination and retentiveness to the children in his school at Chelsea; and a little later Professor Sully devised and applied a test of attention, which he believed gave better indications of intelligence than Galton's tests of discrimination. Another of Galton's disciples, Miss Sophie Bryant, headmistress of the Camden High School, administered a variety of tests to her pupils ('Experiments in testing school children', *J. Anthrop. Inst.*, 15, 1886, 338–49, the earliest publication reporting detailed results from a research of this kind). Later, being a biologist by training, she reverted to the study of shrimps, which, she says, 'formed a welcome change'.

CHAPTER FOUR

The assessment of intelligence

Alternative methods of assessment

Galton, as we have seen, proposed to define 'genius' and other intellectual labels in terms of percentages. Thus 'the talented, in the sense of those who obtained the ordinary prizes of life' (classes D and upwards) are defined as 'the ablest 2 per cent', the 'highly gifted' (E and upwards) as the ablest 0·2 per cent, and the 'geniuses' as the ablest 0·025 per cent; similarly with his definitions of the various grades of mental deficiency. He realized, however, that, as several critics observed, 'definitions in terms of percentages will in practice be difficult to use, and for many people difficult to understand'. So in his book, and in later publications dealing with work among school children, he tentatively suggests alternative methods of measuring intelligence.

In his studies of human stature he noted that from five to fifteen 'a boy increases in height by almost exactly 2 inches every year. . . . Since therefore the rate of growth is fairly uniform, the annual increments are equal, and would therefore provide a convenient unit of measurement. . . . For general purposes it would be far more intelligible to say "This boy of twelve has the height of an average boy of ten" than to say "His height is only 4 ft 4 in.".' And in order to reduce results from his various tests to a comparable scale he suggested that mental and scholastic abilities might also be assessed in terms of annual increments.

This principle had in effect already been adopted by the officials of the Education Department. The Code which they drew up to regulate the payment of grants specified in some detail the attainments to be expected of pupils during each year at public elementary schools from seven years onward. To ascertain whether the majority of pupils in each age-group came up to standard, the inspectors took round with them sets of test-cards, and used them to examine the children's performances in spelling and arithmetic, and at the later stages in more general topics. The normal performance of a child of seven was described as 'standard I', that of a child of eight as 'standard II', and so on, up to 'standard VII' for age thirteen. A little later a 'standard Ex. VII' was added for the brightest thirteen-year-olds and any fourteen-year-olds who had stayed on (for the correlation between ages and standards see my report to the London County Council on *The Distribution and Relation of Educational Abilities*, 1917, table V). In those days it was the custom of teachers to nominate for possible certification as mentally defective any pupil aged nine who could not do the work of standard I, and was thus at least three years behindhand. It was the task of the school doctor or psychologist to determine whether the backwardness was due to innate disability or merely the result of laziness, physical ill-health, or some other adverse circumstance.

Mental age

Much the same principle was adopted, explicitly and more systematically, by Alfred Binet. Binet was one of the most original psychologists of his generation. In 1889 he founded the laboratory of experimental psychology at the Sorbonne—the first to be established in France—and published several books and articles on individual psychology. He was subsequently asked by the Minister of Public Instruction to assist a commission set up to inquire into the problem of subnormal school children. While working in his early years at a biological laboratory, he had conceived a great admiration for the British evolutionists, Darwin, Spencer, and above all Francis Galton, who greatly influenced his ideas. Like Galton, he distinguished between cognitive and motivational characteristics: thus, of the pupils who caused persistent difficulties in school, some, he said, were intellectually subnormal, others temperamentally or morally subnormal; 'their intellectual faculties may be perfectly intact, and their backwardness merely a secondary consequence of their emotional instability'. Secondly, and again like Galton, he distinguished between innate capacities and acquired attainments: to assess the latter he devised a series of 'pedagogical scales', consisting of standardized tests for elementary school attainments, and to assess the former he proposed to construct 'a psychological scale'. Thirdly, he adopted Galton's distinction between 'general ability' and 'special aptitudes'. The French form of the word 'ability' (*habilité*) means something quite different from the English; so Binet fell back on the term used by Spencer and his French admirers, such as Taine—the term 'intelligence'.

'How', he asks, 'are we to understand this term? . . . Intellectual processes form a hierarchy'—the theory of mental structure which, it will be remembered, had been suggested by Spencer. 'There is', he continues, 'one fundamental capacity of the utmost importance in all practical life—the faculty of *adapting* oneself to circumstances' —another notion taken over from Spencer. From this basic capacity the rest develop and evolve. Thus 'all the phenomena with which psychology is concerned are phenomena of intelligence—sensation, perception, memory, etc., as much as reasoning'. How, then, are we to test it? 'Are we to examine all the child's psychological processes?' Plainly that would be impracticable. Except at the earliest stages of development 'sensory tests, after the manner of the psychophysicists', he argues, are of little value, though he retains Galton's test of weight discrimination. Partly on the basis of general insight, partly after trying a variety of mental tasks, he decides that tests of the higher mental levels, relatively complex in nature—tasks involving 'logical processes of comprehension, judgement, and reasoning'—will be the most effective. Accordingly, he proposes to 'discard all the laboratory instruments of the German band, and rely solely on activities which require little else besides a pencil, some paper, and a few objects to be found in any household' (e.g. a knife, a key, the commoner coins).

Binet published several versions of his scale, gradually increasing his compilation of tasks and questions. In its final form the various items were arranged according to the ages at which they could normally be answered. The level of intelligence possessed by any given child was then measured by 'taking the highest age at which he passes all the tests for that age, with an allowance of one failure' ('Le développement de l'intelligence chez les enfants', *L'Année psychologique*, *14*, 1908, 1–94; cf. *ibid.*, *17*, 1911, 145–201, for the final version).

For the diagnosis of mentally subnormal children he suggests as a borderline a backwardness of three years at about the middle of their school career. Thus a boy aged ten by the calendar with a mental age of seven or less would be regarded as subnormal. There is, however, an obvious difficulty about this simple criterion: it is useless for the diagnosis of very young children or of older children and adults. Clearly a child of only two and a half could not be backward by three years, and few could tell whether a man of thirty was backward by three years or less; a backwardness of so many years plainly means very different things at different stages of life. In a later paper Binet himself put forward alternative criteria for use in diagnosing adults. In testing and classifying persons over school age he suggests 'a mental age of eight or nine as the borderline for the feebleminded, six or seven for imbeciles, and two or three for idiots'. These limits, he explained, were based on applications of his scale to adult and adolescent men and women already diagnosed as mentally deficient and accepted as inmates of a mental hospital or institution. However, this still leaves us without any guide when examining young children, e.g. the five-year-olds just entering school or the seven-year-olds entering the junior department—the stage at which teachers started looking for likely scholarship winners or recommended backward pupils for transference to a school for the mentally defective.

Mental ratio (I.Q.)

Galton himself had already indicated a way of meeting this difficulty. In his book on *Hereditary Genius* he notes that, judging by published accounts of the capabilities of adult defectives trained in institutions, it appeared that a feebleminded person was capable of working 'like two-thirds of a normal man', while an imbecile worked with only half of the efficiency of a normal man, and an idiot with only one-third. Similarly a genius, he suggests, might be described as 'a man whose mental efficiency was one and a half, or even twice, that of the average'. And in an address to doctors and teachers on the testing of school children he argued that these proportions, so far as they were due to innate limitations, would remain pretty much the same for the same individual throughout the whole period of growth. The pediatricians, however, raised several objections. Galton's assumptions, they asserted, did not apply to physical measurements, where exact figures were already on record. A few maintained that the rate of growth itself was necessarily 'logarithmic', by which they meant it followed a law of compound interest; thus if at the age of five a slow or fast developer was backward or advanced by 10 per cent (about 4 in.), you would not expect that at the age of fifteen he would be backward or advanced by the same percentage (i.e. by 6 in.); and, since Galton professed to base his views about mental characteristics on analogies drawn from physical characteristics, he could not (they maintained) reasonably assume that in the latter case the proportions or percentages he suggested would remain constant throughout the whole stage of mental growth.

In my early investigations with mental and scholastic tests I endeavoured to check the accuracy of Galton's proposals and of his critics' objections. To reach a definite conclusion it seemed essential to express his hypothesis in a precise mathematical form. The assumption that the proportions mentioned would remain constant from year to year was plainly tantamount to assuming that the actual amount of the children's retardation at any given age would be a linear function of their age. Now the most general expression for a linear function is given by the equation $y = ax + b$, where in the present case x denotes the child's chronological age, y the amount by which his mental age differs from his chronological age (the degree of retardation if he is backward), and a and b are constants to be determined from the data. Plotted on a graph, this means that the child's rate of growth can be represented by a straight line, with a slope or gradient indicated by a. To determine whether this holds good generally, let us consider, not the deviation of a few particular individuals, but the average deviation for the whole age-group, or rather the standard deviation, since that provides a more reliable measure. On plotting the standard deviations of each age-group from five to thirteen, I found that they did in fact fall very nearly on a straight line.[1] In constructing such a graph, the base-line represents the chronological age, and the point of origin from which chronological age is ordinarily measured is the time of birth. When the sloping line that had been fitted to the standard deviation was produced until it cut the base-line, it passed almost exactly through the point of origin. This implies that $b = 0$, and consequently $a = y/x$.

Taking Galton's own unit, the 'probable error', as a measure of the average deviation, I found that it was in fact almost exactly 10 per cent from age six to age fifteen. Thus, on an average, a boy who was backward by six months at age five would be backward by about one year at age ten, and one and a half years at age fifteen. With tests of educational attainments, when expressed in terms of the probable errors or standard deviations for the various subjects, the proportions again proved to be fairly constant (cf. Burt, *Distribution and Relations of Educational Abilities*, 1917, pp. 31 ff., and figure 5). In the case of height, a linear equation still gave a pretty good fit, provided the general form of the equation was used, and an empirical value was found for *b* (which in this case is no longer zero). So far, then, Galton's hypothesis seemed to be confirmed.

Now if, as we have seen, $y/x = a$, it follows at once that $(x + y)/x = 1 + a$, or, translating the symbols into words,

$$\frac{\text{Chronological age plus deviation}}{\text{Chronological age}}$$

and therefore

$$\frac{\text{Mental age (M.A.)}}{\text{Chronological age (C.A.)}} = \text{constant}$$

This result suggests that, for purposes of diagnosis, instead of taking (as Binet had done) the *difference* between a child's mental and chronological age, we should take the *ratio*. I called this fraction the 'mental ratio'. The results thus obtained seemed plainly to justify the method proposed by Stern for allowing for differences in chronological age, namely, that the child's mental age should be divided by his chronological age and the quotient expressed as a percentage: this was termed the child's 'intelligence quotient' (usually abridged to I.Q.). In its original form, as will be noted, this coefficient is a ratio of a mental measurement to a measurement of time: in other words, it expresses a rate, namely, the rate at which a child's intellectual capacity grows. A growth rate of this kind therefore enables us, so far as it is reliable, to predict a child's future performances. That, as we shall see, is one of its most important uses.

As I pointed out at the time, these simple formulae are no more than rather rough approximations, and the conclusions reached are subject to certain reservations. In the first place the standard deviations by no means lie exactly on a straight line; and at the earlier and later school ages the discrepancies are rather large. When we plot values obtained during the pre-school stage and again during puberty and the post-school stage, then both physical and mental development exhibit a marked acceleration during the earlier phase and a still more obvious retardation during the later stage (it was doubtless the initial acceleration during earlier years that made the pediatricians talk of a 'logarithmic' curve).

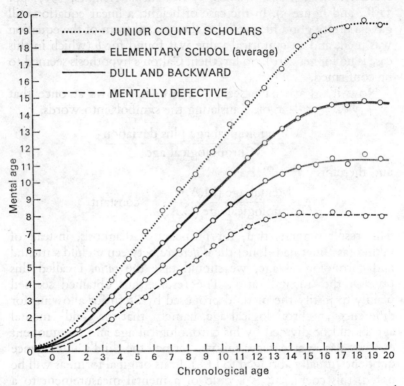

Figure 1. *Curves of mental growth for normal, subnormal, and supernormal children*

Note. The centres of the small circles represent the averages in mental years obtained at each chronological age with tests of intelligence.

Thus a closer fit can be obtained by using the equation for the so-called logistic curve:

$$y = \frac{k}{1 + e^{f(x)}},$$

where k represents the height finally reached when the children are fully grown, e the base of Naperian or natural logarithms, and

$f(x)$ has the form $-c_1x + c_2x^2 - c_3x^3$; the additional powers of x are inserted to allow for the acceleration about the age of six and again just before puberty. Figure 1 shows the curves obtained for representative samples of normal, gifted, dull, and defective children. The curves, it will be noted, meet the horizontal base-line, not at the time of birth, but about nine months earlier, i.e. at the time of conception. Between the ages of five and fifteen (or a little before in the case of the dull and defective) the curves approximate to a straight line. In a graph the incidental fluctuations are too slight to be clearly visible: for a detailed discussion of the various curves that might be used, and their relative merits as compared with the more familiar straight line, see Burt, *The Backward Child*, 1931, appendix II.

Now all these equations and curves, and the generalizations based on them, have been derived from data for large *groups* of children. When we look at the curves published for single in-dividuals, we see that the lines that are plotted waver and undulate far more irregularly. Hence, if we are to use the foregoing generalization for diagnosis and prediction in the case of in-dividuals, it is desirable to have some idea of the amount of in-accuracy likely to be incurred. For this purpose it is necessary to follow up a number of typical individuals to the end of the school period or, if possible, until they are fully developed. The obvious procedure will be to correlate the initial assessments (or the pre-dictions based on them) with the actual assessments subsequently obtained. Since our interest centres on the validity of mental ratios or I.Q.s, all such assessments should be expressed in that form.

The correlations naturally tend to diminish as the interval of time increases. With children tested at the age of 7–8 and retested at 13–14, the correlations I obtained averaged 0·88. With shorter intervals they were higher, declining at an average rate of about 0·01 per annum, more rapidly at first, more slowly later on. Two sets of assessments for the same group of children with the same set of tests made by two independent investigators with an interval of only a few days, still yield a correlation that is far from perfect: in our early studies it averaged approximately 0·94. This can hardly be due to diverse growth rates, and must therefore indicate the margin of error to which these particular tests and assessments are liable—their 'unreliability' (to use the regular but somewhat misleading term). We can correct for this unreli-ability and in doing so we arrive at a corrected correlation of

0·88/0·94 = 0·93, which we can take as the theoretical upper limit for a correlation obtained after an interval of six years.

The meaning of the coefficients becomes more intelligible if we convert them to terms of the average discrepancy between the I.Q.s obtained at the earlier and the later ages. The formula (which, I venture to think, should be far more widely known and used) is quite simple, and follows directly from the ordinary 'difference formula' for calculating correlations. It is $\bar{d} = 1\cdot13\sigma\sqrt{1 - r}$, where $\bar{d}$ denotes the mean of the differences between the two assessments for each individual tested. If we take the standard deviation (σ) of the I.Q.s to be 15 points, then $\bar{d} = 17\sqrt{(1 - r)}$. Thus the observed correlation of 0·88 implies an average change of ± 6 I.Q.s; the theoretical minimum, implied by the 'corrected' correlation of 0·93, would be $\pm 4\cdot5$ I.Q.s. In our own investigations we found that the average amount of change was slightly smaller with the abler children and decidedly larger with those who had achieved relatively low I.Q.s: owing to some temporary and unsuspected handicap at the time of the first testing (undue timidity, slight indisposition, various kinds of emotional disturbance) a child may easily fail to do himself justice.

If, as most other observers have done, one relies merely on results obtained at a single testing, then one occasionally discovers changes of 20 I.Q. points or even more. The interest of other observers, however, has centred on the validity of the particular test they were studying. Here we are interested primarily in the irregularities of mental growth, assessed by the most accurate procedure possible; and that frequently requires the results of a single test to be carefully rechecked, usually because there is some discrepancy between their results and the teachers' ratings. With this more elaborate procedure changes as large as 20 I.Q. points are comparatively rare. Certainly a few children prove to be late developers and make unexpected spurts; others develop precociously and then fail to fulfil their earlier promise: but such cases are far more infrequent than is commonly supposed.

The correlations I have quoted have been criticized on the ground that the coefficients reported by other observers are much lower (e.g. Vernon);[2] the results there cited were seldom based on complete age-groups, and often obtained with written group tests: when due allowance is made for the reduced standard deviations and for low reliability, the adjusted figures agree much more closely with our own.

Perhaps the investigations most nearly comparable with our own are those selected by Cronbach,[3] and based mainly on results obtained with the Stanford–Binet scale (with which each child is tested individually). I reprint the correlations thus obtained with children who were six or more years old when first examined: results from tests given to children below that age are far more unreliable.

Table 1: Correlations between tests applied at different ages

Age at first test	Interval in years between first and second test:			
	1	3	6	12
6	0·86	0·84	0·81	0·77 (W)
7	0·88	0·87	0·73	0·80 (W)
9	0·88	0·82	0·87	—
11	0·93	0·93	0·92	—

Note. The correlations marked '(W)' were obtained when the Wechsler–Bellevue test was used for the last retest.

It will be noted that here too the coefficients decline by about 0·01 per annum as the interval increases; and the predictions obtained at the older ages are in general better than those obtained with younger children. In our own studies, however, we found a rather rapid drop in the correlations during early adolescence, no matter when the first test was applied.

Criticisms

During recent years there have been several vigorous attacks on the use of the intelligence quotient and its alleged constancy (e.g. D. Pidgeon and C. Graham, 'Modern concepts of intelligence', *J. Assoc. educ. Psychol.*, 1970, and A. W. Heim, *The Appraisal of Intelligence Tests*, 2nd edn, 1970). 'Psychometrists', says Dr Heim, 'unhesitatingly express the intelligence of an individual in terms of I.Q., whatever his age, whenever he lived, and however his mental capacity was assessed in the first place'; and she proceeds to criticize what she takes to be the fallacious assumptions on which this practice was originally based. Mr Graham delivers a similar onslaught on what he calls 'the once established position', of which, he says, I was 'the chief protagonist': referring to some of my early publications, he states that I considered the formula 100 (M.A./C.A.) as measuring a child's 'innate and constant ability'. Recent research, we are told, has now demonstrated that 'the absolute constancy once attributed to intelligence quotients and mental ratios by those who originally introduced them is entirely false and devoid of all foundation in fact', and that 'the formula itself is wholly lacking any mathematical or empirical justification'. These and similar utterances are repeatedly quoted by teachers and educationists at their annual conferences and in the correspondence columns of educational journals.

Now, to begin with, no psychologist of repute has ever 'attributed absolute constancy to intelligence quotients or mental ratios'. Indeed, in the first of my LCC reports I expressly deprecated the use of such quotients and ratios for theoretical purposes: 'for scientific work', I contended, 'the standard deviation is the best device' (*op. cit. sup.*, 1917, p. 15). In my next report on the subject I devoted an entire section to discussing and illustrating 'Changes in mental ratio' (*Mental and Scholastic Tests*, 1921, pp. 151 ff.). I argued that the appropriate method of defining special groups (e.g. the subnormal or supernormal) was in terms of percentages (which in practice were based on the accommodation available for them in so-called 'special' or 'secondary', i.e. 'grammar' schools): this was in fact Galton's original procedure. Its advantages are clear: in dealing with individual cases, it indicates the position which any given child holds within his age-group, and, when he is subsequently retested, it enables us to say how far he is maintaining that position from one year to the next. With the mass of normal children, for whom a normal frequency distribution can be assumed, such percentages are equivalent to measurements in terms of the standard deviation of the relevant age-groups. However, in dealing with borderlines for the mentally deficient or for scholarship winners, it is essential to begin with a percentage definition, since later surveys have shown that the tail-ends of the actual distribution no longer correspond with those of the symmetrical normal curve. However, in reports to teachers, magistrates, or members of the education committee on cases they have referred for examination, it would have plainly been absurd to express a child's intelligence in technical terms like percentiles or standard deviations; yet all could readily get a fair impression of the case if one described the child as having (say) only '70 per cent of the ability possessed by a normal or average child'. The assertion that 'I.Q.s are not constant' is perfectly correct; but its implications may be easily misunderstood. As usual, like so many brief verbal statements, it is apt to suggest that there are only two alternatives: either the I.Q. is constant and therefore wholly reliable, or it is not constant and therefore wholly unreliable. But all that 'psychometrists' (as Dr Heim calls them) have ever claimed is that the I.Q. is *approximately* constant, or, as Terman puts it, 'relatively stable'. Hence the real issue is, how close are these approximations?

The answer, as I have indicated, is given by correlations based on 'follow-up studies'. To this, however, Dr Pidgeon replies by saying that 'intelligence tests are self-fulfilling'. Once a child has had an I.Q. hung round his neck, the teacher behaves accordingly: if the child has a low I.Q., he is thereafter treated as dull; if a high I.Q., he is encouraged to live up to it. 'Naturally, therefore, when retested he gets much the same I.Q. as before.' This seems scarcely fair to the teachers; and no factual evidence is produced to support the charge. In any case, the explanation cannot possibly apply to the earlier London studies, since (as was made clear in the detailed report) the teachers knew nothing of the test results. Indeed, part of the purpose of the inquiry was to determine how far the results of such tests agreed with the teachers' ratings; hence it was essential that the teachers remained ignorant of the scores, and that the investigator conducted his tests in ignorance of the teachers' ratings.

Nor is it true to say that 'mathematical and empirical justification is wholly lacking'. Nevertheless, the few mathematical and empirical investigations that have been carried out certainly suggest that still better formulations could be devised; and most of the points urged by our critics are really met by the more elaborate device proposed, namely, by basing both assessments and definitions on a statement of the proportional number in the entire age-groups who exceed, or fall short of, the test score obtained. Since this proposal was originally put forward, many different scales have come into use; these often have widely different standard deviations, and frequently the same scale yields different standard deviations at different ages. This presents still further reasons for adopting the percentage method. With the Terman–Merrill Revision, as we have seen, the standard deviations vary appreciably from age to age; and with other test scales the variations are even greater still. Hence an I.Q. calculated by the stock formula (dividing mental by chronological age) will mean very different things at different ages (the later 1960 Revision, seldom used in Britain, recognizes this obvious flaw, and so prints an alternative conversion, keeping to a constant S.D. of 16). In any case to speak, as critics so often do, of '*the* I.Q.' for a given child is grossly misleading; the test employed should always be specified. Moreover, as mental development slows down at about the age of thirteen and gradually comes to an arrest while chronological age continues inexorably to increase, chronological age can no longer be used as a divisor with adolescents or adults.

Percentages, however, cannot be added. Hence it is desirable to convert them into some kind of standard scale in which the units are equal. For this purpose probably the most convenient is a conventional I.Q., i.e. an I.Q. which is a 'quotient' in name only, and is obtained not by division but by using a conversion table based either on the normal curve or on empirical data. It will be a scale with a mean of 100 and (as a rule) a standard deviation of 15 points at every age. In all our recent work this is the scale that my collaborators and I have used; and it is the scale that will be adopted in the remaining chapters of this book.

Borderlines

So far as intellectual characteristics are concerned, the special categories of school children among whom my work, and indeed that of most educational psychologists, has in the past been carried out are (i) the moderately subnormal, i.e. the so-called 'dull and backward', (ii) the extremely subnormal, i.e. what were formerly described as 'educable mental defectives', (iii) the moderately gifted, and (iv) the exceptionally gifted; the last two together making up what in earlier days would have been classed as 'scholarship winners'. To these should be added (v) those suffering from special educational disabilities, and (vi) those endowed with special talents or aptitudes—both of them categories which fall outside the scope of the present volume.

i. THE DULL AND BACKWARD

Not every child who falls below the theoretical average needs special administrative provision. A pupil who is backward by no more than one year can well be accommodated in the class where the average chronological age is one year below his own: to use the old-fashioned class labels, a boy of ten should normally be working in standard IV; if his abilities are only equal to the work of standard III, practical experience shows that he can quite well be relegated to a class where most of the children are aged about nine without detriment to him or to his fellows. Their mental ages will range from $8\frac{1}{2}$ to $9\frac{1}{2}$. If, however, his own mental age is below $8\frac{1}{2}$, that is, if he were fit only for work equal to that of standard I or II (the average seven- or eight-year-olds), it would be unwise to put him in one of these lower classes, since up into the standards I and II come the brightest entrants of the infants, three or four years younger than himself. Such an association of big and little, side by side in the same classroom, is very apt to lead to disciplinary difficulties and considerable emotional frustration on the part of all concerned. Hence for these so-called 'educationally subnormal' pupils special classes or special schools are desirable. A backwardness of $8\frac{1}{2}$ at the age of ten is equivalent to an I.Q. of 85 points. This therefore was the borderline I proposed for this type of child; and this too was the definition subsequently endorsed and recommended by the Ministry of Education.

ii. THE EDUCABLE DEFECTIVES

Most children of ten with mental ages of 7 to $8\frac{1}{2}$ do best if allowed to mix with others of their own age in the same school during playtime and for non-academic lessons—singing, drawing, handwork, and the like. In general, however, this no longer holds good with those whose mental ages are below seven: all too often they become butts for ridicule, victims of bullies, or are left alone in isolation. Moreover, they need a different type of training and a different educational curriculum—far more concrete and practical work with special materials and workshop facilities, such as cannot usually be provided in the ordinary school. They should therefore be transferred to a school specially designed for cases of this type. Nevertheless, as I have always argued, the question of transfer is a psychological and educational, not a medical matter; still less is it desirable to brand the child with the stigma of medical certification.

At the time of my appointment as psychologist there were in the LCC special schools for the mentally defective sufficient places for just over 1·5 per cent of the children between the ages of seven and fourteen; in the mental hospitals and other institutions there appeared to be a number of ineducable children of the same ages amounting to another 0·6 per cent. In all, therefore, the proportion of so-called 'mental defectives' at the younger ages amounted to 2·1 per cent, or slightly more, if allowance was made for those remaining at home. On the assumption of a normal frequency distribution with a standard deviation of about 15, this was equivalent to an I.Q. of approximately 70. That figure would agree with Binet's borderline—a backwardness of three years at about the age of ten. The class of 'educable defectives' corresponds almost exactly with Galton's grade *d*; the imbeciles and idiots correspond, not quite so closely, with his grades *e* and *f*.

iii. THE GIFTED

For my studies of 'gifted children' I have taken a borderline of 130 I.Q. This is equivalent to defining them as the brightest 2½ per cent of the elementary school population of the same age. I adopted this figure, because in general it appeared to discriminate those children who, when I first began my surveys in the London schools, were obtaining junior county scholarships for entry to secondary ('grammar') schools. I could not use the term 'scholarship winners' for the group I wanted to study, since many bright youngsters whose innate ability qualified them as 'gifted' in my sense, failed to gain scholarships owing to their backwardness in educational attainments. My group would thus include all Galton's classes from D upwards. Terman, in his very extensive study of gifted children, aimed at selecting those who were 'within the highest 1 per cent of the child population'. On a scale with an S.D. of about 15 points this would be equivalent to an I.Q. of 135. Actually, according to his table of test scores, the majority (94 per cent) had I.Q.s of 140 or upwards. His group therefore was rather more highly selected than mine. Were all the gifted children from the *whole* child population included, the number would be considerably increased, since, particularly at the time when I started my surveys, many bright children from the professional and other well-to-do classes were sent as fee-payers to preparatory, public, and other independent schools, which were not under the local authority.

iv. THE POTENTIAL GENIUS

What I have called the 'exceptionally gifted' may be regarded as potential 'geniuses' in the sense in which Galton defines that term, i.e. the grades he labels F and G. Galton's definition, it will be remembered, was 'the brightest in 4,000'. This on a scale with an S.D. of 15 points is roughly equivalent to 150 I.Q. The foregoing assessments, all of them approximate, assume a theoretical frequency distribution for intelligence conforming with the normal curve. But that, as we shall see, tends to underestimate their actual numbers. However, at this stage of our discussion we are merely concerned with broad classifications.

Notes and references

1 This does not hold good of every scale of intelligence. Thus, in the last American revision of the Binet scale the standard deviation (S.D.) with mental age as the unit increases from 0·7 at age six to 1·6 at age ten and 2·7 at age fifteen: the last two are consistent with the average S.D. in terms of the I.Q. (here 16 points); but the marked increase during the earlier years means that the S.D.s of the I.Q.s which, unlike those of the mental ages, should remain approximately constant, increase from only 12 points at six to nearly 16 at ten and 19 at twelve (Q. McNemar, *The Revision of the Stanford–Binet Scale*, 1942, tables 5 and 7). This, I think, is because the Terman–Merrill Revision does not discriminate so well at the early ages as our own revision, but much better at the later ages; it is also appreciably influenced by schooling, so that age-groups which spread over four or five grades show higher S.D.s. Terman's first revision seems more in accord with our own: though detailed figures are not given, he observes that 'the distribution of I.Q.s is practically the same from 5 to 14' (L. Terman, *The Measurement of Intelligence*, 1917, p. 67).

2 P. E. Vernon (ed.), *Secondary School Selection*, 1957.

3 L. J. Cronbach, 1960.

CHAPTER FIVE

The concept of intelligence

Alternative definitions

The new ideas and proposals put forward by Galton and Binet aroused almost at once the interest of a small band of experimental enthusiasts, particularly those concerned with problems of education. In those early days, however, most academic psychologists still regarded their subject as a branch of philosophy; and the notion of actually measuring the mental abilities was dismissed as 'a mere will o' the wisp, deserving no more attention than the fantasies of the palmist, the phrenologist, and the crystal-gazer'. The majority of psychologists therefore scornfully ignored all such proposals; and the rest subjected them to scathing criticism which increased in intensity as time went on. The associationists insisted that all mental differences were due to experience; the faculty psychologists maintained that mental abilities were 'specialized and independent, as distinct as the functions of the liver, lungs, heart, and the other bodily organs'; both rejected the notion of 'a super-faculty called intelligence'.

Among the earlier critics the favourite line of attack was to show that those who talked about intelligence could not agree among themselves about what precisely it was that they were proposing to measure. Accordingly, in 1921 a symposium was organized by the American editor of an American journal of educational psychology ('Intelligence and its measurement,' *J. educ. Psychol.*, 12, 123–47, 195–216). The question asked was 'How should intelligence be defined so as to discover the most satisfactory way of measuring it? How does it function and what is its nature?' The inquiry was addressed to a number of psychologists and educationists; and the result was 'a perfect spate of incongruous replies'. British psychologists apparently thought of it as primarily an 'analytic capacity'. This was in keeping with the theory of cognition introduced by Bain and his followers. 'Intellection', so Sully maintained, 'consists of processes of analysis and synthesis' but 'the discernment of difference is the most fundamental and constant element: it is known as "Discrimination"' (*The Human Mind*, 1, 62). And Spearman, in his earlier articles, emphatically contended that in all manifestations of intelligence sensory discrimination was a universal factor. Aveling treated discrimination as a more general activity, 'not limited solely to the sensory level: any successful attempt to analyse a novel situation into its elements and abstract what is crucial'. American writers laid almost exclusive stress on more complex processes. Terman, who fully accepted Galton's hypothesis, added tests that were more complicated than Binet's, and maintained that 'a person is intelligent in proportion as he is able to carry on abstract thinking'; and later Spearman himself endorsed this view. 'The most effective tests of intelligence', he contended, 'are those depending on the eduction of relations and of correlates', and he cited my test of 'analogies' as a typical example.

Other writers, notably German psychologists like Meumann, Ebbinghaus and Stern, laid almost exclusive stress on the synthetic aspect: 'intelligence', said Meumann, 'is the power of creating new combinations out of old material, new complex thoughts out of simple sensory elements.' Ebbinghaus introduced his well-known 'Kombinationsmethode'—a test depending on the organization of facts or information into an intelligible whole. Educationists adopted a slightly different approach: 'intelligence', they argued, is 'the power to learn' or 'to acquire new habits and new knowledge'; but this seemed tantamount to treating memory as the most important factor. Thorndike contended that 'so-called intelligence as actually measured is simply the sum total of a number of independent constituents'. Perhaps the commonest suggestion was that 'intelligence is the ability to adjust one's thinking to new requirements'—an alternative definition proposed by Stern, and very similar (it will be noted) to the description already given by Spencer and Binet. McDougall sought to reconcile all these discrepant suggestions by saying 'intelligence is that integrative property of the whole brain, or rather of the central nervous system, which enables it, by analysing and recombining sensory experiences and motor reactions, to respond to more or less complex environmental stimuli in a way that is best adjusted to the needs of the moment'. Eventually one final proposal was put forward with a view to circumventing all these conflicting interpretations. Why not, it was asked, adopt an 'operational definition': 'intelligence is simply the capacity or process which intelligence tests measure'? (E. G. Boring, *The New Republic*, 1923, pp. 35 ff.). To this the critics naturally replied that 'mental testers disagree quite as much about which tests are valid as they do about which definition is correct'. 'When', it was asked, 'is an intelligence test not an intelligence test?'

Early criticisms

To many the outcome of all these disputes seemed obvious: 'there is really no such thing'. 'What these theorists have done', said Thomson, 'is to reify an abstract mathematical expression— a dubious formula resulting from a preference for simple linear equations: you take the sum or average of a number of scores obtained in a battery of tests, and call that "intelligence". But a sum or an average is not to be treated as a concrete or objective entity. . . . In any case, a concept so indefinite and elusive as intelligence, capable of such widely varying definitions, is surely not a concept which any genuine scientist can reasonably adopt.' Nevertheless, as some of us ventured to protest, any such adverse verdict was far too hasty. The stereotyped maxim that 'before a scientist can measure a thing he must first determine what precisely is its nature' has long ago been exploded. Who even today can state what is the nature of electricity? Yet electricity is daily produced, measured and retailed to consumers like any other commodity.

Much of the confusion in my opinion appeared to spring from the fact that the word 'definition' was itself open to two distinct interpretations. The older logicians were accustomed to distinguish between what they called 'nominal' definitions (*nomen*, a name) and 'real' definitions (*res*, a thing). The former stated how the term or name was being used; the latter explained what exactly the thing was—how it acted, how it could be recognized, and how it could be assessed or measured. Spencer, Galton, Binet, and their various followers believed that the factual evidence indicated the existence of 'an important human quality or property, which was at once cognitive, general and innate'. They wanted just one single word by means of which they could refer to it without needless circumlocution; as scientists usually do, they went to the classical languages for a suitable technical name, and selected Cicero's word 'intelligence'. Thus 'intelligence' was just a label for the phrase; the phrase was *not* put forward as an ingenious explanation of a concept already recognized and a name already in current use. Questions about how this 'innate, general, cognitive capacity' operates or is to be measured are problems that arise at a later stage, and call for separate experimental investigations; and the answers will probably differ according to the context in which the investigator works.

Verbal controversies such as these are very apt to arise in the early stages of almost every branch of science. Thus, about the middle of the nineteenth century, several physicists commented on the fact that a material body according to its structure, position, velocity, or other conditions was capable of doing useful work: this was a notion of special interest to those who at that date were concerned with the construction of such machines as steam-engines. In a paper 'Über die Erhaltung der Kraft' the youthful Helmholtz put forward on somewhat speculative grounds the notion of a 'general capacity for mechanical work', which manifested itself in many different forms, could be applied to a variety of physical tasks, and in a self-contained system remained constant in amount. To designate this capacity various names were proposed; Joule called it 'living force'; Helmholtz 'innewohnende Kraft'; eventually the single word 'energy', though not wholly appropriate, was accepted and popularized by Kelvin as the most convenient label. A glance at the forgotten publications of those early years will show that much the same objections were urged against the concept of a 'general capacity called energy' as were later hurled against that of 'a general capacity called intelligence'. The doubts and disagreements among the defenders of the principle about the nature of energy and the way it was to be measured were cited as clearly demonstrating the futility of any such notion. Whereabouts in the material body or physical system was it located? And many contended that 'energy' was no more than an illegitimate reification of an abstract mathematical expression—a formula resulting from a preference for differential equations. Nevertheless, despite this flood of criticisms, numerous experiments by engineers as well as by physicists combined to attest both the theoretical plausibility and the practical value of

c

this novel conception. And thus Helmholtz's far-reaching claim, which was at first almost unanimously rejected as 'albern und unsinnig', became a cornerstone of modern physics.

Intelligence as a dispositional property

The modern behaviourist bases his repudiation of innate ability on certain ideological assumptions of his own. Thus Dr Harrison, commenting on the comparison I have just made, maintains that 'All we can observe is behaviour, that is, actions; and actions are described by verbs. Nouns imply things; and to use a noun like "intelligence" suggests that there is an entity carrying that name, which, because of its supposed importance, the faculty psychologist proceeds to reify and deify in a manner highly misleading. As Woodworth has remarked, "We call a child intelligent if he *acts* intelligently." Let us expunge the noun and substitute an adverb. There will then no longer be any temptation to credit the child with an occult substantial or causal something called "intelligence", stored in his brain, much as "energy" is said to be stored in an electric battery, a bent spring, or a charge of gelignite.'

Dr Harrison forgets that there are abstract nouns as well as concrete. Abstract nouns do not designate 'entities' or 'things'; they indicate qualities, tendencies, and properties. The physical sciences make free use of such nouns—'solubility', 'inflammability', 'conductivity', and the like. Some of them, e.g. what the chemist calls 'reaction rate', express, just as the I.Q. does, amount of change per unit of time. For purposes of prediction the most important are what certain logicians have termed 'dispositional properties'. Take solubility as perhaps the most familiar example. If you pour table salt (sodium chloride) into water at a temperature of $18°C$, you will find that about 36 grams will dissolve in a 100 grams of water; as much as 73 grams of calcium chloride will dissolve in the same amount, which accounts for its wide use as a drying agent; on the other hand, chalk (calcium carbonate) is almost insoluble. There are thus degrees of solubility, and they can be measured. By a 'dispositional property' therefore is meant a latent tendency which is expressed by a conditional sentence: '*If* such and such an event occurs to a thing, *then* the thing will behave in such and such a way.'

Modern science usually attempts to relate such properties, at least in theory, with some persistent microstructure of the object in question. Thus, I regard what I call a child's 'actual ability' as a dispositional property, resulting from the microstructure of his brain at the time he is observed or tested; and I regard his 'innate ability' as a dispositional property, resulting from the microstructure of the fertilized cell out of which he has developed (e.g. the number of genes of a particular type, contained in the chromosomes). These hypothetical microstructures are exceedingly difficult to observe, and cannot themselves be precisely specified or measured; but they are presumably related in some approximate fashion to certain actual measurements which we *can* make.

Current criticisms

Many present-day critics, however, take a rather different line. They are prepared to accept the word 'intelligence'; what they object to is the 'definition' that I have proposed. Dr Pidgeon, for example, in criticizing a paper in which I repeated my definition, protests that 'This is not what [he] would understand by intelligence, nor how it is understood by most other writers.' And he agrees with Dr Harrison: when inquiring into the nature of intelligence, the approach we should have adopted was to describe intelligence in terms of behaviour: 'Children are seen to behave in ways to which the adjective "intelligent" is applied, just as for a different kind of behaviour the words "happy" or "industrious" would be used.' And the definition he arrives at is that intelligence denotes 'the set of developed skills which a person has acquired in order to cope with his environment'. Professor Vernon in the same symposium suggests a similar definition: 'Intelligence is not a unitary entity, dependent on particular genes; it is simply the name for the over-all efficiency of an individual's cognitive processes' (*J. Assoc. educ. Psychol.*, 1970). In the United States, Professor McV. Hunt advocated much the same interpretation, namely, 'the conception of intelligence as a set of central processes comprising strategies for processing information that develop in the course of the child's interaction with his environment' (*Intelligence and Experience*, 1961).

All these writers, however, are tacitly or explicitly assuming that 'there is a human quality or type of behaviour which everybody has always recognized and which everybody calls intelligent'. 'We all of us', they say, 'realize that, alike in our dealings with our children and friends, with the shop assistants from whom we buy or the work people we occasionally employ, some are acting more sensibly, more efficiently, more intelligently than others.' Whether 'everybody' recognized this general 'quality or type of behaviour' in Galton's time I venture to doubt; in my own schooldays I can remember neither teachers nor parents describing children and their behaviour as 'intelligent'. They would talk of 'clever' boys or 'efficient' workmen; but the term 'intelligent' had not then filtered into their vocabulary. The critics I have quoted, however, all regard 'intelligence' as 'a word of popular speech, which has been narrowed and misinterpreted by the Galtonian school'. What has happened is that journalists and their readers, and now it would seem a number of educationists, are themselves misusing a technical term—a word chosen because it was seldom used except by scholars and introduced to serve as a name for a newly devised concept. This constantly happens to scientific terms that have drifted into popular usage. There is, of course, no objection to Pidgeon, Vernon and Hunt introducing the notion of 'over-all efficiency', 'developed skills' or 'strategies'. But it merely makes confusion more confounded if they adopt the name 'intelligence' to designate it. And naturally if you redefine 'intelligence' to mean skilled abilities that have been 'developed' or 'acquired', it is easy to show that it is not innate. But in so doing you have manifestly begged the very question at issue.

   The real reason for the change of definition, I suspect, arises from the fact that in their heart of hearts these critics really doubt whether there is indeed anything corresponding to the definition they reject. It may be true, as Professor Vernon argues, that during the last few decades there has been an increasing disinclination both in the United States and more recently in Britain to accept the notion of intelligence as an inherited quality of the individual. But that itself has been due chiefly to the influence of Watson and the behaviourist school; and their oversimplified dogmas are already on the way out. If American psychologists and educationists still continue to reject the notion of mental inheritance, American geneticists have lent it their strong support. But the pendulum of psychological opinion now appears to be rapidly reversing its swing. Professor Jensen's celebrated paper, and the number of writers who have come forward to endorse his conclusions—quite as many as those who have so vehemently criticized them—furnish ample indications of this change of mind. Moreover, it is to be noted that Vernon, Pidgeon, and those who follow them, base their pronouncements more on ideological grounds and on certain obvious prepossessions of their own than on a detailed and impartial scrutiny of the relevant facts.

The evidence

Admittedly there would be little point in assigning a name to the concept I have defined were there no factual support for the assumptions on which it rests. The evidence most frequently cited is chiefly statistical—*a posteriori* deductions from researches deliberately planned to test the hypothesis. But there is also a good deal of antecedent or *a priori* evidence—tentative inferences drawn from general facts already known and acknowledged, which suggest some such hypothetical concept. Let us therefore first glance at these earlier speculations. Then, in later chapters, I shall describe at greater length the numerous *ad hoc* experiments and inquiries carried out to verify the hypothesis, and the newer evidence which has thus been amassed.

Psychological evidence: observational

Psychology began over two thousand years ago with an attempt to distinguish and classify the chief types of mental process. These early efforts were based partly on the observation of other persons in everyday life, partly on self-observation, or, as it is termed, introspection. In the *Republic* Plato, to whom we owe the main lines of our present-day classification, distinguished three 'parts' (i.e. constituents or aspects) of the mind or 'soul' (*Republic*, 435Af, 585B). The later Latin terms—'intellectual', 'emotional' and 'moral', and the more recent terminology 'cognition', 'affection' and 'conation'—suggest convenient but somewhat inexact equivalents for the untranslatable Greek expressions. In a later work he put forward a picturesque analogy which greatly clarifies his view of these basic differences (*Phaedrus*, 253D). The first component he compares to a charioteer who holds the reins, and the other two to a pair of horses which draw the vehicle: the former guides, the latter supply the power; the former is the *cybernetic* element, the latter the *dynamic*. 'The intellect', says Sully, using a slightly different metaphor, 'steers like a rudder; emotion and will supply the steam.'[1]

Aristotle made a further contribution. He contrasts the actual concrete process with the abstract hypothetical potentiality on which it depends. The translators' usual rendering of this term (δύναμις, dynamis), 'power', should not be taken as necessarily implying a causal agency; rather it denotes what I have already called a 'dispositional property'. Plato's threefold classification Aristotle reduces to a twofold. For him the main distinction is what he calls the 'dianoetic' or intellectual capacities of the mind (διανόησις, Descartes' 'cogitatio') and the 'orectic' propensities (ὄρεξις, striving for, desiring. *De Anima*, II, iii, 414a, *Eth. Nic.*, I, xiii, 1102b, *et seq.*). Finally Cicero, in an endeavour to supply a Latin terminology for Greek philosophy, translated Aristotle's term 'dynamis' by *facultas*, 'orexis' by *appetitio* or sometimes *conatus*, while to designate *dianoia* he used and popularized the rather rare word *intelligentia* (i.e. *inter-legentia*, almost a literal rendering of *dia-noia*).

Here, then, we have the origin both of the concept and of the name 'intelligence'. So far from being 'a word of popular speech', whose meaning has been 'narrowed and misinterpreted by the Galtonian school', it is a highly technical expression coined or adopted to designate a highly technical abstraction. From Aristotle and Cicero the term descended to the medieval schoolmen; and the scholastic theories with their Graeco-Latin nomenclature became elaborated into the cut-and-dried schemes of the faculty psychologists and their phrenological followers.

Biological evidence

'The conception of intelligence as a unitary entity', so Professor Guilford justly observes, 'was a gift to psychology from biology through the instrumentality of Herbert Spencer' (*Psychometric Methods*, 1954, p. 471). In Europe, when psychology changed from a department of philosophy to a branch of natural science, it was treated as a section of physiology—indeed, as little more than a new sub-section of the physiology of the brain; in Britain, on the other hand, thanks largely to the influence of Spencer and Darwin, it was regarded as a branch of biology. Biology was defined as 'the science of life in general', and psychology as 'the science of mental life'.

Spencer was the first great evolutionist. It was he who gave the word 'evolution' its modern connotation; and it is to him we owe the phrase 'survival of the fittest'. Evolution he defined in his own portentous style as 'a progress from an indefinite, incoherent homogeneity to a definite, coherent heterogeneity by a process of continual differentiation and integration'. His hypothesis of a 'general law of evolution', covering the history of the inorganic universe as well as the various organic forms of life, was expounded in a dozen thick volumes, entitled *A System of Philosophy*, that appeared between 1862 and 1893, bound in a regal purple which has since turned brown with time. Several of them, strange to say, notably those on *Biology* and *Sociology*, sold to the extent of over 20,000 copies. Today he seems remembered chiefly as an extinct monster of antiquated philosophic speculations. And yet, as Professor Medawar has recently reminded us, 'his ideas have come to life again in the work of men so far apart as Sir Julian Huxley and Father Teilhard de Chardin'. Spencer's two volumes on *The Principles of Psychology* (1870) 'dictated', so he tells us, 'while reclining in a boat on the Serpentine', are still well worth dipping into, though few will have the courage to wade through the whole of his rather chilly exposition. His three instructive chapters on 'the nature of intelligence', 'the laws of intelligence', and 'the growth of intelligence', however, still merit careful study.

Spencer maintained that all progress was the outcome of a twofold process of differentiation and integration (or, as the Greek philosophers would have said, analysis and synthesis). These principles he applied to explain not only the evolution of organic species, but also the development of the individual. On both, he maintained, the fundamental capacity of cognition became increasingly complex and diversified, and at the same time increasingly organized and unified. Like a tree sprouting out into boughs, branches and twigs, it ramified into a hierarchical system of abilities more and more specialized. He recognized four main stages or layers—sensory, perceptual, associative, and relational or rational (I use McDougall's terminology rather than the cumbersome adjectives coined by Spencer).[2] The brain, or rather the central nervous system, he pointed out, appeared to be similarly organized into four corresponding levels of increasing complexity and coherence, with a fifth unconscious level as a basis, consisting of reflex activities. The consequence of this progressive change was that the higher forms and the more mature individuals become more and more successfully adapted to the conditions and events in their immediate environment. Previous writers, extolling the marvels of creation, had noted some of the more conspicuous examples of adaptation—the white fur of the polar bear and the arctic fox, the striped brown fur of creatures living in jungles, the way certain moths and butterflies mimic dead leaves, the elaborate arrangements which allow the human eye to function as a camera. Spencer generalized the notion into an all-pervading principle. It was, he argued, 'the totality of the relations of an organism to its *milieu* which made possible both the survival of the individual and the perpetuation of the species'. A fish out of water will die; and before an amphibian could hope to live wholly on dry land it had to change its structure, its internal functions, and its whole behaviour. Adaptation, therefore, plays a cardinal part in every phase of evolutionary progress.

Spencer's views were taken up even more readily by continental writers than by British. We have already noticed his influence on French writers like Binet and Binet's forerunners (Taine, Ribot, and several others). German physiologists and educationists, such as Vierordt and Meumann, went on to elaborate in still greater detail Spencer's theory of stages in the development of the child. The following indicates the most popular type of scheme, neatly arranged with the chief transitions fixed at the hallowed interval of seven years:

		Age-limits
I	Infancy	
	i Babyhood (pre-school period): mainly sensory processes;	0–4
	ii Infant school period: perceptual processes;	4–7
II	Childhood	
	iii Junior period: associative processes (memory);	7–11
	iv Senior or pre-pubertal period: relational processes (reasoning);	11–14
III	Adolescence	

Piaget (*The Psychology of Intelligence*, 1950, pp. 119, 123) repeatedly acknowledges his indebtedness to Spencer; and his own scheme of developmental stages, with much the same dating and rather more elaborate interpretations, is based on the preceding fourfold plan.

Spencer's conclusions, even in the realms of empirical science, were largely the result of armchair reflection. As grandfather Huxley caustically remarked, 'Spencer's idea of a tragedy would be a beautiful theory killed by a merciless fact.' Certainly many of his speculations—particularly in regard to the child's mental growth and the mental characteristics of primitive races— required to be greatly modified, and sometimes wholly discarded, as a result of first-hand facts later accumulated by actual observation or experiment.

Darwin was strongly influenced by Spencer's evolutionary doctrines, but realized their fragile basis. Unlike Spencer, he hesitated to publish any hypothesis until he had gathered a vast array of supporting data. In the main he endorsed Spencer's conjectures about the course of mental evolution. 'Psychology', he writes, 'will be securely based on the foundation laid by Mr Herbert Spencer—that of the acquirement of each mental power by gradation' (*Origin of Species*, 1859, concluding chapter). In *The Descent of Man* (1871) he again alludes to Spencer's views regarding the evolution of intelligence, and devotes two whole chapters to illustrating 'the influence of natural selection on the development of the intellectual faculties', and (conversely) 'the influence of the intellectual faculties on the processes of natural selection'. *Homo sapiens*, we learn, owes his very existence to the repeated survival of a few ape-like primates who had more brains than their fellows. Empirical evidence, particularly the discovery of 'missing links' in the shape of fossils which were almost unknown when Darwin wrote, have abundantly confirmed these brilliant deductions, and largely helped to fill in the gaps.

Notes and references

1 As all those who are familiar with the recent development of 'cybernetics' will be aware, the Greek noun (from which we get, via the Latin, our own word 'governor') means a 'steersman' or 'director'.

2 H. Spencer, *Essays*, vol. 1, 1868, pp. 420 ff.

CHAPTER SIX

The evolution of man

Man's forerunners

For our purpose it is essential to know something of man's biological development: only in this way can we understand the limitations as well as the capabilities of his various mental processes. Man, by his anatomical structure, manifestly belongs to a peculiar Order of mammalian vertebrates, which Linnaeus grouped together under the name of Primates. Today the chief representatives (in order of increasing physical and mental development) are (1) the tiny squirrel-like tree shrews of southeast Asia—a fairly prolific insectivorous creature, related to our moles and hedgehogs, but possessing brains unexpectedly large for its size; (2) the lemurs of Asia, Madagascar, and the African mainland; (3) the Tarsiers of Borneo and the Philippines; (4) the Old World and New World monkeys; (5) the noisy gregarious gibbons of the Malay peninsula and archipelago; and finally (6) the three great tailless apes, the orang-utan of Borneo, and the gorilla and chimpanzee that inhabit the African forests. These successive types form a roughly graded series, suggesting that man as we know him today has evolved from a small and inconspicuous insect-eating mammal, living among the branches of trees. As the fossil records indicate, this creature first made its appearance about 70 million years ago during what geologists term the Cretaceous era (when the chalk cliffs of Dover were laid down). Owing to a change of climate the dinosaur and other huge reptiles had become extinct, and numerous small mammals of various modern types had already emerged.

In the creatures I have mentioned the sense organs, the bones and musculature, and consequently the brain became adapted to serve an arboreal life. With terrestrial animals that track their prey along the ground a protuberant snout and an acute sense of smell is all-important; but it is useless to creatures living in trees. Sight is far more valuable and becomes the dominant sense; in leaping from bough to bough an accurate judgment of distance is essential; and this is only possible with stereoscopic and therefore binocular vision; so the eyes move round to the front, and the back of the brain, which subserves the sense of vision, is enlarged. The limbs of the mammalian quadruped must be further modified to provide hands that can reach out and grasp, and more or less prehensile feet. This in turn requires more accurate muscular adjustment, and so the areas of the brain which subserve balance and muscular control (at the side of the brain and in the cerebellum) also increase in size. With the gregarious types more especially, hearing is acute; and this entails a development of the temporal lobes.

There is, however, manifestly a wide gap between lower 'prosimian' primates (tree shrews, lemurs and Tarsiers) and the higher man-like apes. And it might be supposed, and has indeed been frequently suggested, that this was bridged by the intervening monkeys. There could scarcely be a more misleading suggestion. It is certainly true that in many of the extant species of monkeys one encounters here and there a peculiarity similar to one or other of those held to be distinctive of man—a shortened arm, a hand which is almost human, an occasional adoption of a two-footed gait, a marked diminution of the large canine teeth, and the complicated folds of the external ear: 'the faces of the more primitive types', so Darwin reminds us, 'are often adorned with whiskers, moustaches, and beards; and the hair on the head of some species grows to an unusual length'—developments which, he believes, originated because of the virile impression which they made on the feminine sex. However, among the monkeys each of these modifications occurred independently in different groups; and all they indicate is that among primates an occasional mutation of certain genes could produce changes characteristic of man. But it is a gross mistake to suppose that the types of primate existing today represent a linear genealogical chain. The New World's flat-nosed monkeys, and the macaques, baboons and gibbons of the Old World are manifestly aberrant side-lines; and the surviving primates are all highly specialized end-products of divergent lines of evolution.

Early primates

To secure a clearer notion of how man evolved we must turn to
the evidence of fossil records. Judged by the all too scanty fossil
remains, man appears to have evolved from the early types of
extinct primate by preserving certain of their more general
characteristics, and avoiding the more specialized modifications
developed by the various side-lines. Possibly because of their
lack of specialization, most of these transitional forms quickly died
out. But the chief stages are now seen fairly clearly; and a brief
chronological outline will indicate their nature.

Precise dating in terms of years, even if we keep to round
figures, is highly conjectural. But the sequence of climatic and
geographical changes is pretty well established. The 'Tertiary
Era', which succeeded the Cretaceous period, is subdivided by
geologists into four periods—Eocene, Oligocene, Miocene, and
Pliocene. These in turn were followed by a period called Quater-
nary or Pleistocene, which gradually merged into recent and
historic times.

During the Eocene period there were, widely dispersed over
the whole world, including Europe and Asia, at least twenty-five
different genera of Tarsiers, some very like the sole modern
survivor. For obvious reasons creatures dwelling in forest trees
are not likely to leave fossil remains; fossils of animals are most
frequently found in sedimentary deposits or in caves, where water
impregnated with lime or other mineral petrifies and so preserves
them. Hence our knowledge of all early arboreal creatures is
extremely meagre. The oldest and most primitive type of ape so
far discovered dates back to the Oligocene period, that is, about
40 million years ago. The earliest fossilized fragments were
found on the banks of a stream in the Fayum. These creatures
seem to have been a small and very general type of anthropoid
ape, still showing marked resemblance to a tarsioid ancestor. The
monkeys—first the New World type and then the Old World
type—had by this time probably diverged from the earlier
tarsioid stem. *Parapithicus*, or some similar transient group,
would seem to have been the precursor of all the Hominoidea
(i.e. the whole group of man-like creatures, including the larger
apes and ourselves, and various intermediate types).

Darwin was convinced that man had evolved, not in Meso-
potamia or anywhere on the Asian continent, but in tropical

Africa. At the turn of the present century, when various Egyptian irrigation schemes were under consideration, the government of the day undertook a survey of Lake Victoria, and (with unusual foresight) suggested the inclusion of an archaeologist to test this speculative notion. He managed to collect a remarkable variety of fossils, but unfortunately was himself collected by a crocodile. Some years later Dr Louis Leakey, born in Kenya, took up the quest, beginning with the hilly tree-covered islands. He found numerous relics of extinct ape-like creatures belonging to the early Miocene period (about 35 million years ago). Tropical Africa at that date, it would seem, provided a kind of experimental breeding ground for the development of a profusion of varying sizes and types. In 1948 Mrs Leakey discovered a complete skull.

Proconsul Africanus, as this famous group of creatures was called, shows comparatively few of the specializations that characterize contemporary apes. It had large protruding jaws, ape-like canine teeth, and a braincase decidedly smaller than that of a modern ape; but its forehead was smooth, without the ape's heavy brow ridges. Like man, it had squarish eye holes instead of the nearly circular openings of the apes and monkeys: like man, too, it had relatively slender thigh bones, and arms shorter than the legs. Evidently it was far more agile, and able to run about more easily than the modern gorilla or chimpanzee. It is therefore quite conceivable that these extinct creatures were the fore-runners alike of modern apes and of man.

The benign Miocene climate, which had turned this part of Africa into a veritable Garden of Eden, lasted about 20 million years. During the Pliocene period that followed, a series of droughts devastated the forests and fertile shrubland, which Darwin believed had formed our ancestral home. Vast savannahs and dusty deserts took their place. The four-handed tree-dwelling fruit-eater had therefore to be transformed into a two-footed flesh-eating hunter; or possibly, when their Kenyan paradise was lost, the tree dwellers found themselves driven out into the forests of the Congo or were able to survive in the Asiatic jungles. Unfortunately, since the lake beds had dried up, the fossil record remains blank for the next 12 million years or so.

It seems pretty clear, however, that quite early in this period the lines of development that led to the arboreal apes and to terre-strial man began very markedly to diverge. Huge carnivores had by now evolved, and were roaming over the more open country. The only means by which our weaker ancestors were able to meet this formidable competition was by developing swift and agile legs, skilful hands, capable of wielding improvised weapons, and above all a quick and cunning brain.

At length the rains returned; and a large number of instructive fossils have recently been found, belonging to the opening stages of the next geological period. The earliest of these finds was discovered in a limestone cave on the edge of the Kalahari desert. It was a hitherto unknown ape-like creature, and was accordingly christened *Australopithecus* ('southern ape'). Numerous specimens have since been found further north. In general the pattern of their brains was very similar to ours, but in size were no larger than those of the modern apes (about 500 cc). The shape of the pelvis suggests an erect posture. Two main types have been distinguished, chiefly as a result of differences in the teeth: one group was apparently vegetarian; the other, which exhibits remarkable anatomical resemblances to ourselves, was partly, if not mainly, carnivorous. It seems evident that during the gradual evolution of man the new conditions of life determined first of all the mode of progression, and therefore the changes of the skeleton and leg bones needed for the erect posture, and then much later an expansion and elaboration of the brain.

The transition from the Pliocene epoch to the Pleistocene is rather arbitrarily fixed at about a million years ago. It was marked by extraordinary fluctuations of temperature affecting the whole planet. These began with a general cooling of the earth's surface, leading to the Great Ice Age. There were four glacial periods, during which the northern half of Europe was covered with one huge sheet of ice; and between them there were shorter inter-glacial periods, when much of Europe seems to have experienced a subtropical climate. During the last of them, when what are now the British Isles still formed part of an extended continental shelf, the hippopotamus, rhinoceros, hyena, monkey, the straight-tusked elephant, and the sabre-toothed tiger, all left their bones in the area that is now the county of Yorkshire as well as further south. In tropical Africa rainy spells coincided with the colder spells further north, resulting in marked fluctuations in vegetation and animal life. Fossil records pointing to man's ancestry now become more numerous, not only in south-east Africa, but in widely separated parts of the world. They reveal one remarkable change—a surprisingly rapid increase in the size of the average brain, from about 500 cc to nearly three times that size in less than a million years.

Modern genetic principles go far to explain how this may have occurred. As we have seen, the various early ape-like groups show an exceptionally wide variability—so wide that the discoverers of a new specimen tend to assign it to some new species. But species are by definition incapable of interbreeding. The nomenclature is therefore misleading. What seems to have happened was this. The drastic climatic changes led to constant migrations. Groups isolated in different areas always tend to form new inheritable characteristics. With another change of climate they move on and eventually meet other members of a slightly different strain. The cross-breeding leads to further variability, and increased adaptability as a result of further selection. Thus evolution is progressively speeded up.

Homo sapiens

At what stage, then, are we prepared to term one of these novel variants 'Man'? And how are we to distinguish *Homo sapiens* from other varieties or subspecies? Since the chief relics left by early prehistoric man in addition to his fossilized bones are the various implements of stone or bone that he shaped and made, anthropologists have found it convenient to confine the term 'Man' or *Homo* to 'those primates that have acquired a level of intelligence which enables them to fabricate tools'. However, quite recently Miss Lawick-Goodall, watching chimpanzees in the wild, has noticed that occasionally they too use and even make temporary tools; and there is now reason to believe that some of the *Australopithecines* used crude pebble-tools. Were it possible to secure clear evidence in doubtful cases, I should myself prefer to fall back on the old definition, that 'man is an animal that can talk', where 'talking' implies not the mere chattering of monkeys or parrots, but the systematic use of articulate speech. The change in the position of the head, in the structure and shape of the jaws and in the size of the teeth, all appear to have led to changes in the finer muscles of the tongue, the lips, and the cheeks, which facilitated the production of vowel and consonantal sounds, and so rendered articulate utterance possible.

Somewhat similar refinements occurred in the musculature of

the hands and fingers. The hands, even of the simpler primates, are able to perform more effectively many acts for which a dog, for example, would use teeth and claws—e.g. carrying and dismembering its prey. But in all the primates these actions still mainly involve the use of the larger muscles only; and in the apes the hands as well as the long arms have been adapted chiefly for climbing and swinging from bough to bough, i.e. for a strong grasp rather than delicate manipulation. The making and shaping of tools, however, demands much finer muscular movements, and a thumb that can be neatly apposed to the finger-tips. Moreover, skilled hand-work entails a division of labour between the two hands; and man therefore at an early stage of his evolution became right-handed.

The use of the hands, and particularly the control of hand and finger movement by the eye, necessitated a further development of the brain. Right-handedness is associated with a dominance (and according to some anatomists a slight enlargement) of the left cerebral hemisphere. In right-handed persons this is also the hemisphere in which we find the so-called 'centres' for speech. Incidentally, it may be noted that theories based on these facts, commonly illustrated by a note on the composite symptoms produced by tumours in this part of the brain, have of late led to many rather dubious suggestions, emanating from certain brain specialists interested in so-called dyslexia, about the frequent association of disturbances of speech, manual dexterity and 'right–left disorientation' in children; and a few anthropologists have even claimed that, by inspecting prehistoric human skulls, it is often possible to deduce whether or not the individual in question was endowed with the gift of speech. But this would scarcely be feasible, even with well-preserved skulls belonging to a relatively late period; and the inferences, I suspect, owe more to fancy than to fact. In any case I would suggest modifying the conventional definition of man and saying that he is 'a primate that *regularly* makes tools and *largely relies* on their use'. Wherever we find a traditional culture which involves the making of particular types or patterns of tool, such as the straight-edged hand-axes found originally at Abbeville and Chelles, or the curved hand-axes found originally at St Acheul, there, I think, we may safely infer a verbal tradition and a verbal co-operation, and therefore speech.

The earliest creatures in order of relative dating to which most anthropologists appear willing to accord the title of 'Man' consist of a group whose first-known representatives were discovered in Java and in China. They had the heavy brows and projecting, chinless, muzzle-like jaws of the ape; but they walked upright, and had brains of about 900 cc, larger than those of any ape. They made implements of quartz; were active hunters; and, judging by the hearths and charred bones found near their fossilized remains, had learnt the use of fire. The animal food which some of the groups appear to have shared in the caves, and the fact that these groups seem to have hunted in small bands, implies that they were able to communicate by speech. Thus culturally they were almost as advanced as the less civilized tribes of today.

The Dutch surgeon who discovered the Javanese skull-cap and thigh bone suggested the name *Pithecanthropus erectus* (i.e. 'upright ape-man'). Numerous specimens have since been found in India and in Africa, not only in Kenya, but as far north as Algeria and Morocco. Crossing the land bridge which linked Africa to Gibraltar, they or a very similar type migrated into Europe. The Heidelberg jaw, discovered in a sandpit at Mauer, probably belonged to this group. Judging from the fossiliferous strata in which such specimens are commonly found, it would appear that they flourished during the first interglacial period, say about half a million years ago.

What more is needed before we can bestow the full title of *Homo sapiens*? The definition commonly suggested is, in addition to the features we have already noted, a cranial capacity approaching at least 1,350 cc, roughly the lower limit for a normal human brain at the present day. This means a skull with a nearly vertical forehead, which seems to be usually accompanied by an eminence on the lower jaw, producing the characteristic human chin. I myself would prefer to make *sapientia* itself the defining characteristic, and then argue that this will seldom be attained without a brain of between 1,300 and 1,500 cc.

By *sapientia* (wisdom) I understand the appreciation of order and value. Under the name of 'reason' the ability to appreciate logical order has often been considered the essential characteristic distinguishing man from animals; but I would also include the ability to appreciate aesthetic order (i.e. what is popularly called a 'sense of beauty') and the ability to appreciate moral order (i.e. a sense of social obligation). Of this threefold endowment there seem to be clear indications in the relics left by *Homo sapiens*

during the Palaeolithic period—the various bone carvings and
cave paintings, the evidence of family organization and quasi-
religious practices, and of an increasingly rational behaviour.

Most of the skulls that I have described as typical of *Homo
sapiens* have been found in conditions pointing to the last glacial
period or a little later. However, in 1936 large pieces of a skull
were found in a gravel pit at Swanscombe in Kent, a little south
of the Thames. With it were discovered bones of the Pleistocene
elephant, the rhinoceros and the red deer, as well as flint hand-
axes and implements of the flake type (so-called Clactonian, since
many of this kind had already been found at Clacton-on-Sea)
which suggest a marked advance in craftsmanship. Fitted together, the fragments of the skull indicate a cranial capacity well
over 1,300 cc. The geological evidence and the nature of the
animal remains point to the second interglacial period, a dating
which has since been confirmed by a recent examination of the
fluorine content of the bones and their radio-activity. Their
antiquity, therefore, can hardly be less than 100,000 years, which
pushes the date for *Homo sapiens* much further back than had
previously been assumed.

From Palaeolithic times onwards there has been a good deal of
diversification, leading to the different races scattered over the
globe at the present day. But there has been no discernible advance
either in general bodily structure or in the size of the brain.
Indeed, one of the divergent types, the Neanderthal, which
eventually died out, had an average skull capacity (1,450 cc) that
was actually larger than that of contemporary Englishmen. Both
during the prehistoric and the historic periods man's further
progress has been due, not to changes in his hereditary nature,
but to the cumulative effects of his innate *sapientia*, and more
especially to the originality, enterprise and leadership of the most
gifted individuals. Cultural evolution has taken the place of biological evolution; and cultural evolution works, not by the slow
process of natural selection operating on genetic innovations, but
by the much swifter process of human and social selection operating on practical and conceptual inventions. Through language,
tradition and education in all its conscious and unconscious forms,
technical, artistic and moral advances, acquired by personal effort
and experience, can be passed on to later generations without the
need to wait for genetic variations and the blind elimination of
the relatively unfit.

Generalization and adaptability

The object of this excursus on the course of human evolution has been partly to provide a biological background for the problems of genetics which will be discussed at a later stage, and partly to emphasize the implication of human biology for practical education. New evidence from fossils and other sources is constantly being laid bare. Hence in details my account may become rapidly out of date. But the main outline is, I think, correct. Accordingly, before we go further let me summarize the salient points.

In the evolution of man, as of all other species, environmental conditions have played an essential part. Unless an organism is by nature fit to survive in its special habitat, whatever changes are likely to occur, it will evidently fail to survive: the maladapted die. Hence the supreme importance not only of adaptation but of adaptability.

As we have seen, adaptability has been secured by avoiding premature specialization. Apparently there are genes, or combinations of genes, which block the development of certain potentialities and thus slow down the rate of maturation and growth. The effects of this principle are so far-reaching that it has received a special name—'paedomorphosis'. It consists in the retention of juvenile ancestral traits by adult descendants. The head and face of an infant ape resemble those of an adult human being even more closely than they do those of its adult parents, and only with maturity does the ape take on the specialized characteristics of an orang, gorilla or chimpanzee. The comparatively unspecialized character of the adult human frame results from a change in growth rates. In most mammals the growth of the braincase is relatively fast during early embryonic life; it then slows down while the jaws, snout and remainder of the body increase their rate of growth. With man the reverse occurs. The braincase continues to grow quite rapidly until well after birth, so that the infant has a bulging forehead and a large skull, out of all proportion to its trunk and limbs. Otherwise, both before and after birth there is a general retardation in the rate of development. Puberty does not arrive until about the age of thirteen, and full maturity is not reached until some years later.

The human infant is thus quite helpless at birth. During the first twelve months it cannot even walk, and consequently needs prolonged maternal care. This is only possible if at each birth the mother produces not a litter of infants, but (with comparatively rare exception) only one; adequate protection necessitates the establishment of the family as a fairly stable unit. To be born only half made, and to remain immature for many years, confers a special advantage. The parents can train and instruct the growing infant, and pass on the cultural tradition of the group. And during the years of play the child is able to acquire a detailed knowledge of his own particular environment. Instead of being wholly committed to a few limited patterns of built-in behaviour, he forms his own individual modes of conduct, fitted to the special circumstances of time and place. Fixed adaptations give way to a freer adaptability.

The principle of generalization is discernible in another peculiarity of the genus *Homo*. Paradoxical as it may sound, greater generalization allows greater variety. When other genera spread over world-wide areas, they tend to split up into distinct species; but there is only one surviving species of mankind, *Homo sapiens*. There are numerous varieties; but they are all capable of interbreeding; and the term 'species' is conventionally used to denote a group whose members are either absolutely infertile with those of other species or yield only infertile hybrids.[1]

During the early stages of the race-making period men scattered far and wide; and so for a while formed geographically isolated groups. These, as a result of natural selection, became differently adapted to their different conditions. When their migrations started once again, owing perhaps to climatic change, different groups would meet and mate. The ensuing recombination of different sets of genes produced still greater variation, and therefore still greater adaptability. Thus the evolution of man from the more primitive types proceeded, not by the selection of favourable mutations, but by the much more rapid process of selecting favourable recombinations.[2]

This in turn provided a gene pool which produced wide individual differences even within the same local group. Those who like to calculate 'coefficients of variation' (a method not without its pitfalls) have little difficulty in showing that the degree of individual variability manifested by *Homo sapiens* is far greater than that of any other species for which such figures have been calculated, and that human variability is greatest for the size of the skull, the volume of the brain, and such mental characteristics as are measurable. The wide variability among the members of a human community who live together and (with certain minor restrictions) breed together permits, and indeed encourages, a 'division of labour', or, to speak more accurately, both a division and a co-operation between those performing different social or economic functions. As history demonstrates, any civilized community which fails to produce, and make full use of, gifted individuals with exceptional capacities quickly begins its decline and fall.

Specialized changes

The cardinal facts of man's evolution throw considerable light on much in contemporary human behaviour that puzzles not only parents and teachers, but also educational and psychological theorists. There are, as we have seen, two important specializations which distinguish man from other anthropoids, and mark successive stages in his evolution. Yet to the untrained eye they seem so slight that they are easily missed: I have known medical students, encountering the skeleton of a chimpanzee for the first time in an anatomical department, mistaking it for a young human being. As T. H. Huxley was so fond of remarking, 'There is less difference in structure between man and the apes than between the apes and any other primate.'

The first of these specialized changes was the alteration in the shape of the hip bone (*ilium*). With *Australopithecus* it becomes shorter, broader and flatter; and there are clear indications on the fossil bones of a marked increase in the size and strength of the gluteal muscles. These modifications were indispensable for the maintenance of an upright stance and an easy striding gait. The change is still more marked in *Pithecanthropus erectus*. Thus man at his first emergence was distinguished more by his buttocks than his brains.

The erect posture freed the hands for skilled manipulation, and the teeth and mouth for articulate utterance. Thus *Homo*, though not yet *sapiens*, developed two 'special abilities' of profound importance for his future development—manual ability and verbal ability. This fact alone, I think, throws doubt on the simplified theories of those who, like Spearman and his earlier followers, sought to ascribe all intellectual differences to a single general factor called intelligence.

The second important change revealed by the fossilized remains was the remarkable increase in the size of the skull, and consequently of the brain which is lodged within it. When we measure the area of the cerebral cortex devoted to the muscles and the muscle sense of the hands, fingers and thumb, we find it much larger than that devoted to both trunk and legs; and the same is true of the area concerned with the muscles and muscle sense of the lips, tongue and larynx. There is also a marked enlargement of the parts devoted to eye and hand co-ordination, and to the co-ordination of hearing with the so-called speech centres. Still more striking is the enlargement of the association areas in the fore-brain. This general expansion of the brain, and the increasing differentiation, integration and systematic organization of the conduction paths within the brain, seems clearly to confirm Spencer's theory of a progressive increase in mental ability proceeding by an increase both in analytic capacities and in synthetic capacities. The lavish supply of association paths allows the formation of innumerable associations between movements and still more between ideas. These form the basis of the skilled habits and the memories that each individual acquires as a result of personal experience. In this way each individual realizes his own adjustments and adaptations. Thus, as we have seen, from palaeolithic times onwards social and cultural evolution has replaced biological evolution. Hence the paramount importance of education.

So far as we can tell, there has been no appreciable change in man's innate constitution or in the general quality of his brain throughout the last 20,000 years. We are each of us born into the Old Stone Age. The instinctive impulses which the young child inherits, even from the most highly civilized parents, are identical with those which actuated our Palaeolithic ancestors before they emerged from barbarism: indeed, many of them are but little changed from those of the earlier mammals. The opposite sex, the young of our kind, our natural food and our natural foes, still arouse the emotions even of the enlightened adult, much as they aroused activities of the primeval savage. All too often the innate motives of fear, anger, sex, curiosity, acquisitiveness, self-assertion, self-submission lead to irrational and anachronistic actions which may prove disastrous to the individual and to the community. These inherited impulses, blind and automatic, had obviously a rough-and-ready value on the savannah or in the cave; but, unless controlled and guided by reason, they are grossly out of place among civilized people.

If, as I have argued, the evolution of the brain virtually ceased with the end of the Palaeolithic period, then it would seem to follow that, so far as innate endowment is concerned, modern man is on much the same level as prehistoric man at the peak of the Old Stone Age. And this I believe to be true. When we consider the limitations in regard to materials, apparatus, traditional techniques and general cultural background, the amazing achievements of man during the closing phases of the Palaeolithic period equal anything that modern man, brought up in similar ignorance and with similar limitations, could possibly accomplish. Examine the thin stone blades of the 'laurel leaf' pattern and try yourself to make one out of a piece of flint with no metal tools to help you; look at the delicate engravings on ivory and bone and exquisite statuettes found with fossils belonging to the same period, or the wall decorations in the caves like those at Altamira and Levira—the vivid pictures of the animals they hunted, drawn not merely in black or white outline, but with appropriate colour shadings, and the quaint representations of female dancers, attired in bell-shaped skirts, tight waists and high coiffures. It would, I think, be difficult to deny that the innate abilities of those primitives were at least as great as those of craftsmen of the present day. The enormous differences in intellectual and technological achievements of stone-age man and space-age man must therefore be due entirely to the stores of knowledge, skill, customs accumulated during the intervening millennia, and handed on by oral tradition, written and printed books, and the various educational, economic and political organizations that instruct, guide and govern us.

Notes and references

1 The second clause is added to allow for such cases as that of the vigorous but infertile mule. In practice the traditional criterion has proved awkward for museum specimens and often inapplicable to plants. But to abandon it in the case of human beings, as a few taxonomists have done, leads only to confusion. Anyhow these verbal questions do not affect the argument from the facts. As to these, Darwin's early discussion is still worth reading (*Descent of Man*, I, vii, pp. 257–80; cf. also A. E. Emerson, 'Taxonomic categories and population genetics', *Ent. News*, 56, 1945).

2 The various genes for blood groups throw far more light on the early movements of human populations than do the more obvious differences of skin colour, hair colour, shape of the face, or minor differences in physique. Today every human community, down to the level of the family, is a mixture

of over a dozen such gene differences. And the impossibility of grafting skin from one individual to another, unless they happen to be identical twins, demonstrates that each of us is innately different from everybody else. (For the physiological and biological evidences for these statements see C. D. Darlington, *The Evolution of Man in Society*, 1969 and refs.)

CHAPTER SEVEN

The neurological evidence

Early speculations

The psychological conclusions that we have so far drawn from biological and anthropological data are both indirect and highly speculative. For direct first-hand evidence it is natural to turn first to detailed studies of the brain itself. If man's abilities are the results of the way his brain has progressively evolved, should it not be possible to discover identifiable mechanisms within the brain which subserve those abilities? To demonstrate their existence and mode of functioning it will clearly be essential, not merely to inspect the visible structures of the brain, but also to carry out *ad hoc* experiments to elicit their activity. This seems so obvious that it is surprising to find that hardly any systematic experiments were attempted until the nineteenth century, and until then many writers on human psychology still held with Aristotle that the brain had nothing to do with mind. With a few notable exceptions, however, this view was not held by medical writers.

A Greek historian tells us that Alcmaeon, a Pythagorean who lived about 500 B.C., carried out actual dissections of the brain and optic nerves; and concluded that it was the organ of sensation. He has consequently been hailed by modern Greek scholars as 'the founder of empirical psychology' (J. Burnet, *Early Greek Philosophy*, 1930, p. 194). Aristotle, who refers to Alcmaeon's theory, dismissed it in favour of the older view that the heart was the seat of consciousness. Wandering over the battlefield of Chaeronea, he observed soldiers whose skulls had been hewn open, still alive and capable of speaking. On touching and pressing their brains, he found that they felt nothing whatever. Galen, physician to the Emperor Marcus Aurelius and a keen experimentalist, reverted to Alcmaeòn's theory, and incidentally noted the occurrence of what we now call reflex actions, e.g. the pupillary reaction to light. On all these matters, as on most questions of physiology, his authority among medical writers remained unimpeachable for well over a thousand years. But since the brain did not respond to physical stimulation, experiments were considered futile. In Christian universities the orthodox version of this view was similar to that formulated by Descartes: conscious processes are essentially a property of the immortal soul; the brain receives sensory impulses and organizes muscular activities; and the soul interacts with the brain at some central point. Descartes suggested the pineal gland.

Gall's 'phrenological' theory that mental faculties are located in various parts or centres of the brain was held to be grossly materialistic and to tend towards atheism. He was consequently compelled to leave Vienna. But in Paris, where he lectured and published, his views became the subject of heated controversy among physiologists and pathologists. Post-mortem examinations of patients who had exhibited various mental symptoms were quoted both as supporting and as disproving Gall's own theories. Pierre Flourens (1794–1861), Sécrétaire Perpétual of the Académie des Sciences, undertook a systematic investigation of the whole problem.

There are two main ways of determining how a particular organ or any particular part of it functions: we can stimulate it, and observe what kind of activity is produced; or we can cut it out, and observe what kind of activity is lost. In her own crude fashion Nature carries out both these two types of experiment in most of the bodily organs. In the case of the brain, however, Flourens believed that both the actual site and the actual consequence of natural disease often eluded precise determination. Stimulating the brain he too regarded as useless, since the brain did not respond to direct artificial stimulation. The only effective procedure, therefore, was to attempt a systematic exploration by extirpating small parts of it in living animals and then noting the effects. His results were published in a critical *Examen de la phrénologie* (1842) and in a series of '*Recherches expérimentales sur les fonctions du système nerveux*'. His main conclusion was summed up as follows: 'all the essentially diverse parts of the nervous system have specific functions, and yet they constitute a unitary and integral system. Removing one part tends to diminish the energy of every other. . . . The brain may rightly be regarded as the seat of sense perception, intelligence, and will; nevertheless, all these processes constitute only one faculty and form only one unit. . . . Thus each part of the central nervous system has both an *action propre* and an *action commune*.' Of the two, so Flourens maintained, the *action commune* was the more important. And this was about as far as the knowledge of the brain had reached when Galton wrote *Hereditary Genius*; Galton's medical training no doubt included a knowledge of contemporary neurology.

It was, however, by no means clear that the results of Flourens' experiments on animals also held true of man. Inspection of the brain, it was argued, showed it to be an almost completely homogeneous mass of tissue; there were no visible signs of separate 'organs'. And so, during the years that followed, a heated controversy continued to be waged between those who upheld a strict localization of mental functions and those who believed that the brain operated as a unitary whole.

Later experimental work

In 1788 Volta, during his endeavours to check Galvani's theory of 'animal electricity', had observed that electrical activity could elicit sensations from the organs of touch, taste and sight. A year or two later his nephew Aldini tried the effects of electrical stimulation on the brain; he began with the brains of animals in the slaughter house, just after they had been killed, and noticed muscular twitches on the opposite side of the body; he then stimulated the brain of a decapitated man, and observed movements on the opposite side of the face. Aldini's experiments, however, passed unnoticed; and for the next ninety years or more it was still almost universally believed that the brain could not be excited by any direct artificial stimulation.

However, in 1870—just a year after Galton had published his book—two German army doctors, walking over the stricken battlefield of Sedan, improved upon Aristotle's gruesome experiment. Using a portable battery, they applied electrical stimuli to various points on the surface of the exposed brains of wounded soldiers. Apparently no pain or sensation was felt as a result; but along a certain convolution it was observed that the stimulation produced involuntary movements of a limb, the action varying consistently with the point excited. Repeating the experiments with rabbits, dogs and apes, they were able to map out what appeared to be definite 'centres' for specific movements. A little later 'centres' were discovered for sensory responses—vision, hearing and touch. Thus, so far as there appeared to be any localization in the brain, the functions located were not complex 'faculties', but relatively simple movements or sensations. It may be added that during the last few decades surgeons, undertaking operations for the removal of cerebral tumours and the like, have been able to lay bare the surface of the patient's brain under a local anaesthetic, and explore it while the patient is still conscious. The early results have been broadly confirmed and considerably amplified.

The hierarchical organization of the nervous system

It has long been known that the peripheral nerves convey messages to or from the spinal cord and brain. If a sword-cut slashes through the nerves of the arm at any point, the parts below the cut will remain both insensitive and paralysed. The peripheral nerves, and the so-called white matter of the spinal cord and brain, consist of minute nerve fibres. And with the improved microscopes that became available during the latter part of the nineteenth century it proved possible to trace, stage by stage, the minute pathways presumably followed by nerve currents in their passage from sense organs to identifiable areas near the surface of the brain, and from other areas down to the muscles. Evidently the brain, like an electronic computer, possesses both input and output channels; and, like a computer, it can therefore be regarded as a complex wiring system for processing information received, and issuing messages or instructions accordingly.

During the present century further improvements in the microscopical techniques, particularly the invention of better methods of staining nerve tissue, have thrown a remarkable light on the minute structure of the brain. The whole nervous system, it can now be seen, is made up of cells of various shapes and sizes, termed 'neurons'. Each consists of a cell body prolonged in one direction to form a nerve fibre which may be many feet long, and in the other direction sprouts into a number of shorter branches and twigs. There are in the human brain something like 10,000,000,000 of these 'neurons'. Formerly the cell bodies were supposed to be independent 'nerve cells', in which, according to some writers, 'ideas' could be stored: it is now known that these cell bodies are concerned chiefly with the neuron's growth and nutrition.

Roughly speaking, these neurons are arranged end to end in serial chains, with the twig-like branches of the longer fibres intertwined with the shorter branches of the next cell or group of cells. Some chains, however, may branch out like railway tracks, into side-lines; others may converge on a single common path, and there are innumerable cross-connections. The function of these chains of nerve cells is to transmit an electrochemical impulse or current from the sense organs to the brain, and thence down to the muscles or glands. Conduction along the nerve fibre may be regarded as essentially electrical; but the transmission of a nerve impulse from one cell to the next is chemical: certain substances are squirted out from the minute terminations of one nerve cell, and thus excite an electrical current in the next. At the junction between one neuron and the next the conditions are constantly changing: the passage of an impulse usually leaves the junction temporarily fatigued; but the frequent passages of impulses, more or less spaced out in time, tends to make subsequent passage easier. This latter change presumably lies at the basis of memory, habit formation, and what used to be called the 'association of ideas', and is now more often described as 'conditioning'. The constant modification of the resistance at different cell junctions serves to guide the currents this way or that, rather like the movable 'points' on a railway line. In the brain, it should be noted, most of the cell bodies and cell junctions are found in what earlier anatomists called the 'grey matter'; the 'white matter' consists chiefly of fibres, which branch out from the cells. The portion of the 'grey matter' which has been studied in greatest detail, is the outer layer that covers the wrinkled surface of the brain, and is called the 'cerebral cortex' (i.e. the 'rind' or 'bark' of the brain).

The entire nervous system, including the brain, is organized (in Sherrington's phrase) as a 'neural hierarchy' (C. S. Sherrington, *The Integrative Action of the Nervous System*, 1906). It consists of subsystems within subsystems, the more complex being, as it were, superimposed on the simpler, and thus controlling and integrating their activities, so that the animal's actions form a more or less coherent set of adaptive reactions. Both the term and the concept of a neural 'hierarchy' are taken over from Spencer; and, as a glance at the textbooks of the earlier systemizers will show, there has been a general tendency to group the processes involved into five main levels very like those originally proposed by Spencer. They are characterized by an increased complexity of the processes which they mediate, and roughly correspond with the main stages of psychophysiological evolution and development already distinguished by these earlier theorists.

1. The simplest conceivable type of neural system would consist of a chain or 'arc' made up of three neurons only—a sensory neuron running from a sense organ on the surface of the body (or in some cases within the body) up to the spinal cord, a motor neuron running down to certain muscles (or in some cases to glands), and a connecting neuron within the spinal cord linking the sensory neuron with the motor. If, for example, you pinch the toe of a decapitated frog in which only the peripheral nerves and the spinal cord are left to function, a nerve current will rush up to the spinal cord, and is apparently there 'reflected' back to the muscles of the leg. The frog pulls the toe away. A process of this type is termed a 'reflex'—a term first used by Thomas Willis, Sedlerian Professor at Oxford (1664).

Actually, even in the simplest of these processes, the neural pathways consist, not of a chain of single neurons or nerve fibres, but of bundles. The more important activate the physiological reflexes governing respiration, circulation, and digestion; and, when all goes well, they are wholly unconscious. The sense organs function as trigger organs: a very slight stimulus from the outer world may pull the trigger, and the ultimate effect is to release a store of energy in the muscles which immediately explode, as it were, into vigorous action. These simple reactions are the same in all individuals belonging to the same species. They are both automatic and innate. The various receptor cells which compose the different sense organs are highly selective. They respond only to particular kinds of stimuli occurring at particular places, and the muscular reactions are usually locally and clearly adaptive: they seem, as it were, designed to the particular situations which the sensory stimulation signalizes. Those reflexes, which are wholly unconscious, may be regarded as constituting the lowest level in the neural hierarchy.

2. Each sensory nerve fibre, on entering the spinal cord, also makes contact with a further bundle of nerve fibres, which thus

provide an alternative route leading up to the sensory centres in a large ganglion at the head of the spinal cord. There the incoming or 'afferent' fibres make numerous cross-connections which lead eventually to certain motor centres. From the motor centres various outgoing or 'efferent' fibres run back, via the spinal cord, to the muscles or glands. These loop-lines form a second level, consisting of sensori-motor circuits, whose action seems usually to be accompanied by a sensation. Your hand unexpectedly touches a hot stove, and you immediately withdraw it; at the same time you feel a sensation of pain. Reflexes of this higher level are rather more complex, and exhibit less regularity and fixity than the simpler reflexes of the unconscious level. Whether they operate and how they operate depends on the general state of the nervous system at the time: some of the alternative nerve paths may even have the effect of inhibiting muscular action. Of these more complex reflexes perhaps the most typical example is the activity of walking: this involves both simultaneous and successive co-ordinations of what may be regarded as simple reflexes. Both in animals and in man all the most important reflexes have been intensively studied; and for most of them, compound as well as simple, the essential stimuli, the neural pathways, the nerve connections and the muscles concerned are fairly well known. The majority of them depend primarily on sensory stimuli of a single kind—eye movements on visual stimuli, ear movements on auditory, limb movements on stimulation of the skin, though most of the more complex also include kinaesthetic control.

The sense organs of vertebrates consist of very much more than the five traditional senses. They may be regarded as covering three main perceptive fields. (*a*) There are, first of all, the 'interoceptors', as they have been called—minute sense organs situated in the internal viscera, and concerned partly with the primary physiological functions of those viscera, and partly with various emotional reactions (which are almost always accompanied by changes in visceral and glandular activities). (*b*) Secondly, there are what are called 'proprio-ceptors', sense organs situated in the muscles, tendons, joints and inner ear, and concerned chiefly with the balance and orientation of the whole body and with the control of muscular actions generally, operating largely by a kind of feedback. (*c*) Thirdly, there are the 'extero-ceptors', situated on the external surface of the body: these include contact sense organs (for touch, warmth, cold, pain and taste) and the three main distance senses (smell, hearing and sight).

In the course of evolution the head ganglia at the top or forward end of the spinal cord became progressively enlarged to form what we loosely term 'the brain'. It is, however, important to note that the evolution of the brain has proceeded, not by substitution or radical remodelling, but rather by successive additions. Some physiologists have sought to express this by talking of 'three brains'—the 'old brain', 'the later brain', and the 'new brain', with a 'between-brain' to bridge them (Greek designations, specially coined, are commonly preferred). Others call them the 'reptilian', the 'mammalian', and the 'human brain'.[1] These terms serve to remind us that we inherit the cerebral mechanisms characteristic of more primitive animals as well as a distinctive set of mechanisms peculiar to ourselves and our ape-like ancestors; and there are frequent conflicts between them. But the terminology is somewhat fanciful, and is apt to suggest that the distinctions are more clear cut than is actually the case and that the characteristic functions have remained unchanged.

The study of the development of the central nervous system in the human embryo shows that the brain and its various parts begin with an enlargement of the upper or front end of the spinal cord. This bends backwards, forwards, backwards and then forwards again: at and between the curves the cord bulges into four distinguishable swellings. These are most conveniently labelled the 'hind-brain', the 'mid-brain', the 'inter-' or 'between-brain', and the 'end-brain'. The last two are sometimes grouped together under the name of 'fore-brain' (as usual, Greek translations are invented and more frequently adopted in technical textbooks). In the individual the embryological development of the brain appears to recapitulate the stages in the evolution of the brain in vertebrate animals, from fish and reptile up to the anthropoid apes and man. The additions take the form, not so much of entirely new brains, but of increasing enlargements of the successive swellings.

The prolongation of the spinal cord which carries these enlargements, usually known as the 'brain stem', consists mainly of nerve fibres, passing to or from the nerve cells in the enlargements. But in the midst of its substance it also contains an elongated network of cells and fibres, called the 'reticular formation'. This extends upwards from the medulla to the inter-brain, and forms the core of the hind-brain and mid-brain. It consists of a vast number of highly branched neurons and a mass of synapses. Nerve fibres, as they pass upwards and downwards, send branches to its neurons. To a large extent it appears to be concerned with the interoceptive system (nerves going to or from the viscera and glands).

The reticular formation, however, is not a single entity. Different parts have different functions. Some parts seem to have mainly inhibitory functions. Apparently they filter and select the miscellaneous variety of neural inputs arriving from the sense organs: some are suppressed, others reinforced. One part makes for general relaxation and repose, and appears to be a centre for sleep. Other parts have the opposite effect. They arouse the animal and keep it alert and attentive: thus one of its functions is often described as 'vigilance'. Several writers have therefore regarded this part as a centre for 'attention'; and those who, following Ward, treat attention as the essential characteristic of 'intelligence', have claimed that 'here, if anywhere, the faculty of intelligence has its seat'—a view which has found little or no support from neurologists themselves.

The hind-brain or cerebellum is the ganglion for the proprioceptive system: it is largely concerned with the reflexes of posture and movement. In creatures which move in three dimensions—fishes and birds—it is, as we might expect, relatively large. In human beings, suffering from disease of the cerebellum, sensation and sense perception remain unaffected; but there is gross muscular inco-ordination: posture and gait are seriously disturbed. Movements of the hands and arms become extremely clumsy. If, for instance, the patient is asked to touch his left forefinger with his right forefinger while his eyes are closed, he almost always overshoots the mark.

The rest of the brain consists primarily of enlargements resulting from the development of the distance senses; in different animal species it increases greatly in size as smell, hearing or sight increase in general importance. In the humbler mammals the mid-brain executes in more primitive fashion many of those functions which in human beings are performed by the end-brain; in human beings the mid-brain functions chiefly as a set of relay stations. It receives afferent impulses, not only from the spinal cord and hind-brain, but also from the retina through what are miscalled the optic nerves (developmentally the retina is an outgrowth of the brain, and the optic nerves are really brain tracts);

D

from the mid-brain emerge efferent nerve fibres, going to various motor centres and to the external muscles of the eye. Provided its mid-brain is left intact, a dog can still stand erect and right itself when laid on its side, even after its entire fore-brain has been removed: this, of course, would be impossible in a human sufferer.

In all the processes I have so far described there is nothing like 'perception' as the psychologist uses that term, i.e. the recognition of concrete things, situations, or other animals. But with the last group of processes—the more complex—there appears to be, at any rate in the lower animals, vague recognitions of this sort; but with human beings it seems to be motivated by higher levels of the brain.

3. The 'inter-brain' (in Greek the 'diencephalon') may be regarded as an extension of the brain stem, a bridge between the parts of the brain already considered and the so-called 'end-brain'. It consists of two main portions, the 'thalamus' (Greek for 'inner room or chamber') and the 'hypothalamus' (a chamber 'beneath' the other). In all vertebrate animals the thalamus, with its many nerve cells and nerve junctions, serves to correlate messages received from various sense organs with each other, and particularly with those from the organs of vision; and it also allows interconnections to be made between these and the efferent centres in the hind- and mid-brain. A frog, whose fore-brain has been removed while the thalamus is left intact, will take its usual posture, jump when touched, and even snap a fly, and a casual observer might note little difference in its behaviour. However, it exhibits little or no spontaneous movement. In higher vertebrates, with a larger fore-brain, the thalamus functions as an elaborate relay station for all incoming impulses.

Close to the thalamus are clusters of nerve cells and nerve junctions—'nuclei', as they are rather confusingly termed—which have an important influence on movements. They are sometimes referred to as the 'basal ganglia'. The most important is the 'corpus striatum' ('striped body'). It is one of the oldest portions of the cerebrum. In the lower vertebrates, where there is little or no cerebral cortex and therefore no motor tract leading from its motor centres to the spinal cord (the 'pyramidal system'), the corpus striatum is the highest motor centre. In birds, after their rudimentary cortex has been removed, visual and auditory sense perception seems but slightly impaired; they can carry out instinctive reactions—feeding, courting, hatching and rearing their young, fighting, avoiding obstacles when flying or walking—in much the same way as before. In human infants the earliest movements are almost wholly effected by this 'extra-pyramidal' motor system. In adults it serves mainly to supply a firm postural background for the voluntary movements performed through the pyramidal system. This seems evident from the disturbances observed when the older system is affected with disease. In the various forms of chorea, both the commoner type seen in children ('St Vitus' dance') and in the rare hereditary type ('Huntingdon's'), in so-called 'paralysis agitans', and in the syndrome called 'Parkinsonism' which often follows encephalitis, signs of degenerative changes in the corpus striatum are frequently found post mortem. The symptoms are fairly familiar: everyone has seen an elderly person whose head and hands become afflicted with a coarse tremor; the fingers often make involuntary movements suggestive of pill rolling; there is usually an apparent stiffness of the limbs and neck: when the person looks round the whole body may turn, not merely the neck; in walking the steps are shortened, the patient bends forward and hurries as though trying to catch up with his centre of gravity.

In the higher vertebrates the hypothalamus is connected with the intero-ceptive system more closely than other parts of the brain seem to be. In warm-blooded animals it keeps the internal temperature steady in the face of wide environmental variations. It receives incoming messages from the various viscera; and, partly through the sympathetic and parasympathetic nervous systems, it sends back instructions to them as well as to the blood vessels and glands of internal secretion. These supplementary nervous systems have their highest subcortical centres in the hypothalamus. To a large extent their functions are antagonistic; the sympathetic increases the heart rate, dilates the bronchi, increases the secretion of sweat, inhibits gastric secretion; the parasympathetic has the opposite effect. Thus the sympathetic is largely active in situations requiring outbursts of muscular energy to meet external emergencies, as in the instinctive reactions of flight or of attack and defence. The parasympathetic is active in instinctive reactions of a milder self-restorative type—feeding, digestion, sex and sleep. Visceral and vascular changes provide a kind of internal sensory resonance for the various emotions. The rapid beating of the heart, the gasping of the lungs, the flushing or blanching of the face, the secretion of the tear glands, the sweat glands, the salivary glands, the sinking feeling due to muscular changes in the stomach and intestines, occasional incontinence, and above all the hormones injected into the blood by the endo-crine glands (pituitary, thyroid, adrenals and sex glands)—all these, often quite visibly, tend to reinforce in various ways the emotional reverberations that accompany the instinctive activities we share in common with other animals—fear and flight, anger and aggres-sion, sorrow, sex, and so on.

Fibres descending to the hypothalamus from the fore-brain are partly able to control these semi-reflex responses. If the brain of a dog is divided *above* the inter-brain, the creature on recovering is much more liable to exhibitions of rage or fear; if it is divided *below* the inter-brain while the mid-brain is left intact, these emotional reactions disappear. By inserting electrodes deep into the brains of rats, cats and monkeys recent investigators have discovered that, on stimulating certain specific sites within the inter-brain, they could evoke symptoms of various quasi-emotional states—hunger, sex, fear, rage, even pleasure and sleep. Somewhat similar experiments have been carried out on human beings. In many patients, diagnosed as schizophrenic, the crucial symptom is the apparent lack of all emotional response: one method of treating such cases has been to implant electrodes which reach certain emotional centres in the diencephalon and thus artificially arouse emotions of fear, anger, sex and the like. Dr Delgado attached a small radio receiver to the head of such patients, and by sending out wireless signals was able to evoke these manifestations of emotion from a distance and almost at will. Electrodes reaching to a pleasure centre, which are operated by the patient pressing a button, have been used as a means of obliter-ating intractable pain felt by those suffering from cancer (J. M. R. Delgado, *Physical Control of the Mind*, 1969; R. G. Heath, 'Electrical self-stimulation of the brain', *Am. J. Psychiat.*, 120, 1963, 571 ff.).

In lower mammals the instinctive actions to which these emotional states lead are largely inborn and fairly stereotyped: complex as they are, they yet need little or no individual experi-ence for their appropriate execution. In man these instinctive and emotional propensities are still discernible; but the localization seems much more widely spread. On the very first occasion that a child sees a huge dog running towards him, he will at once scream in fear and run away; when an older youth sees an attractive girl coming towards him, he too automatically recognizes the possibilities and reacts accordingly.

Disease or damage to the brain is very apt to produce emotional symptoms. When cortical control has been grossly impaired, or when lesions in the hypothalamic centres (e.g. as a result of encephalitis) increase their sensitivity, emotional reactions are greatly enhanced, and the whole personality may be altered. After prefrontal leucotomy has been performed, by which the nerve fibres connecting the frontal part of the brain with the hypothalamus are severed, character changes, sometimes for the better, can be frequently produced.

The various motor activities I have described imply the co-ordination of impulses from several different receptors giving rise to the perception and recognition of fairly definite situations or objects; and the ensuing activities are far too complex and adaptable to be regarded merely as compound reflexes. As a result the whole sensory complex acquires a meaning. James's account of a broody hen's view of the egg she has just laid as 'a never-too-much-to-be-sat-upon object' expresses what is meant by 'meaning' in its simplest form. All such activities therefore may be regarded as involving a third level in the neural hierarchy—the 'perceptual level', as it has been called.

4. In those mammals that possess a well-developed end-brain with a 'mantle' or 'roof-brain' formed by the cerebral cortex, most of the important distinctions which we have noticed seem, as it were, to be mapped out afresh. All the five senses—sight, hearing, touch and kinaesthesis, taste and smell—have separate localization; and there is a separate set of motor centres with the additional cortico-spinal (or 'pyramidal') tract subserving voluntary movements. In this tract the fibres run down, not to separate muscles, but to reflex co-ordination centres in the spinal cord. These cortical localizations, as we have seen, were among the earliest to be discovered experimentally. Around each sensory area there is a further region subserving the more complex experiences that constitute perception. Between these sensory and motor areas there are masses of nerve tissue which, when stimulated during experiments on dogs and apes, failed to yield either movement or any sign of sensation. These are what are commonly recognized as 'association areas'.

Microscopically the different regions can be distinguished by the course taken by the fibres in various minute layers of the cortex and still more readily by the shape of the predominating types of cell—round, pyramidal, star-shaped, spindle-shaped, and so on. Thus the motor areas have numerous large pyramidal cells, the sensory areas numerous small round cells: yet, in spite of the marked difference in the subjective sensations, there is little difference between the visual, auditory, and other sensory types of cortex. The association areas are characterized by a preponderance of long transverse fibres.

These association areas, as we have seen, presumably provide potential connections between the more specialized centres, enabling the individual to acquire new associations and new co-ordinations, adapted to his own peculiar circumstances by dint of personal experience. They are thus the basis of perception and of learning. On the cognitive side they mediate the acquisition of an ever-increasing fund of knowledge; on the motor side they mediate the acquisition of various skilled habits. They form a fourth level in the neural hierarchy—a level subserving what may be termed 'memory' in the broadest sense of the word.

These inferences are confirmed, not only by the effects of actual damage or disease restricted to certain identifiable parts of the brain, but also by direct stimulation of it during operations carried out while the patient is still conscious. If a point in the visual cortex is then electrically stimulated, the patient reports simple visual hallucinations: he sees flashes of light or colour. If the area surrounding the visual cortex is stimulated, he reports definite objects: 'I could see a lot of desks.' If an association area is stimulated, he may report a whole string of memories: 'I was back in the schoolroom, listening to the children singing "Land of Hope and Glory" on the last day of the term just before Christmas': no original thoughts are provoked; all that happens is that, so long as the stimulation lasts, a kind of cinematograph-tape with a sound-track unfolds in his mind, reproducing what the patient saw, heard, and possibly felt and thought on a given occasion in the past. Directly the stimulus ceases, the reproductions cease; if the stimulus is reapplied, the memory may continue from where it broke off, or start from the beginning again, or even fail to re-appear. When for remedial reasons such a spot is surgically removed, the same memory can often be recalled quite voluntarily, though not with the same realistic vividness. Evidently the spots so stimulated do not contain 'storage cells'; they are merely points in the neural network underlying the memories; and as a rule the memories are of quite trivial, often long-forgotten incidents.

Perception involves the synthesis of several sensations or sensory images. I see a globular object of a certain colour and texture; this seems to call up a memory of a soft and semi-solid shape I have handled with a distinctive smell and taste. I may then say to myself the name—'orange'. Except perhaps for the name these sensations and sensory images fuse together into a distinctive whole—an object or thing which is located in outer space. Thus all perception involves integration.

In what is loosely called 'memory' the associated mental images and ideas (often themselves quite complex) remain distinct. To account for what is termed 'learning' various hypotheses have been put forward. On the whole it seems agreed that the essential basis consists, not in any change of pattern *within* the nerve cell but in the formation of new connections between different groups of nerve cells.

i. First, it is supposed that, if a particular nerve cell, A, repeatedly helps to fire a second nerve cell, B, then the resistance offered at the junction of the two cells (the 'synapse') is left permanently lowered, so that the readiness of A to fire B is thereby increased: we may, for example, imagine that some chemical change has taken place at the cell junction which increases conductivity, or that the end branches of A have grown in size or number, so that closer cell contact ensues.

ii. But this merely explains how a path already formed becomes more and more permeable; it may account for the recall, but not for the recording. How was the connection originally made? Here, as elsewhere, 'c'est le premier pas qui coute'. A plausible physiological machinery was first proposed by McDougall. He illustrates it from observations on his small son Angus, showing 'how the burnt child dreads the fire'. The child sees a 'pretty candle flame', leans forward by an innate reflex tendency to touch and grasp whatever attracts his attention: the current flows along a sensori-motor path from eye (A) to visual centre (B) and thence to extensor muscles of arm and finger (C); the painful touch at once excites a still more powerful tendency, and a fresh current flows from the skin (D) to the flexor muscles

(E), which withdraw the hand. All chains of neurons, however, possess possible crosslinks. Since the second channel, C to D, is more powerfully excited, it drains off the current from A to B, by opening up a connecting path from B to D. On the second occasion, therefore, the current from A to B passes through this new path direct to D. And, what Pavlov later called a 'conditioned reflex', was thus formed (W. McDougall, *Physiological Psychology*, 1905, pp. 141 ff. and fig. 8; a somewhat similar scheme had been proposed by James, but in terms of an association of ideas or sensations).

iii. The learning of entirely novel reactions commonly proceeds by 'trial and error'. A rat confined in a maze makes a number of false starts ending in blind alleys, and only after unsuccessful trials at last discovers the correct route. When the situation recurs, the rat tends to omit some of the false reactions, and the last and successful trial reappears more and more quickly on successive occasions. Presumably the physiological processes underlying the unpleasant feeling of failure tend to stamp out the unsuccessful reactions, while those underlying the pleasurable feeling of success tend to 'reinforce' and ultimately hammer home the more satisfying response that ended the whole series of attempts. This two-fold principle, it will be noted, supplies a basis for the familiar method of animal training by punishment and reward. Much the same emotional accompaniments probably play a part in the experiments on 'conditioned reflexes' reported by Pavlov, though he never refers to them: the food which 'conditions' the salivary response to the dog's 'dinner bell' must have had the satisfying effect of a reward; the subsequent refusal of food, which eventually produced 'extinction' of the response, must have aroused disappointment. More recent experiments have shown that learning based on punishment differs appreciably from learning based on reward: it is more resistant to extinction; it extends rather to the situation as a whole than to the specific response; it decays more rapidly when the animal is removed to a different situation.

Partly no doubt for purposes of intelligible exposition, the earlier exponents of these physiological hypotheses usually stated their theories in terms of single chains of neurons. This and the accompanying diagrams, however, are apt to be misleading. It suggests that for each process involved there are fixed, precise, and isolated neuronal connections, like those of a telephone exchange. A clear disproof of this common assumption was given by a series of experiments carried out by Lashley and his followers. Rats were taught to seek their food by choosing one of two alternative routes; one route (not always the same) was brightly lit, the other left dark. When the rat chose the illuminated route, it received a shock; when it chose the dark, it was rewarded with food. Sections across the brain were then made at different places with different rats. It was assumed that, if a definite and unique neural connection had been formed in the brain, one or other of the cuts would have interrupted it. But, provided the rat was neither blinded by destruction of the visual cortex nor paralysed by destruction of the motor cortex, it still made its choice more or less correctly. In later experiments the rats were taught to find their way through mazes of varying degrees of difficulty. They then had various parts of the cortex removed. Once again 'no definite region could be found in the brain where the memory of the maze was stored'. In the experiments the extent to which the rat forgot the appropriate route varied simply with the amount of tissue that had been removed, not with the place from which it had been taken. Similar experiments were later carried out on monkeys and apes, with similar results. Lashley inferred that learning depended not on structural changes, but on dynamic changes: patterns of electrical potential were formed in a continually active field; McDougall suggested that the patterns were formed not in an electric field, but in a psychical field within a mind, interacting with the brain (K. Lashley, *Brain Mechanisms and Intelligence*, 1929; also *id.*, 'The problem of cerebral organization', *Biol. Symp.*, 7, 1942, 301 ff.).

However, an alternative hypothesis seems conceivable. Consider McDougall's illustrations—little Angus learns that a candle flame burns, a nettle leaf stings, and the words 'Mrs William McDougall', whether typed or written, mean Angus's mother. The retinal pattern formed by the stimuli when the child is looking at the flame, leaf or name constantly changes even during a single glance, for the eyes are never perfectly still and his head may move. The child's response therefore is not to a specific set of sensory stimuli but to generalized patterns. Presumably a generalized pattern of nerve impulses proceeds towards the visual area by a variety of different routes. Every single nerve cell in the cortex, with its fibres and branches, is connected with numerous other nerve cells, often with several thousands, running all over the cortex: with so many millions of brain cells there is room for a diversity of patterned routes to be formed all over the brain, converging eventually on the appropriate muscles. If a surgeon or experimentalist destroys some of the patterned routes thus formed, he will leave others nearly, if not wholly, intact. As with the rat, the human brain displays a remarkable resistance to damage; a bullet which would put an electronic computer completely out of action may leave a man's memories wholly unimpaired. What used to be thought of as an 'association path', conceived as an isolated chain or a strictly localized bundle of neurons, must really consist of an organized aggregate of nerve cells, dispersed over almost the whole brain, providing mutiple representations of even the simplest memory or skilled habit, and allowing a variety of alternative paths for retrieval. This is by no means a wholly novel concept. Herbart talked of an 'apperceptive mass'; Stout revived the scholastic term 'disposition' (the Latin sense of 'arrangement'), to which McDougall prefixed the adjective 'physiological'; Nunn proposed the word 'complex' (now monopolized by psychoanalysts); I suggested 'neuronal plexus' (or 'web'); at the moment the fashionable phrase is Hebb's 'cell assembly'.

How far the inferences suggested by the foregoing experiments on rats are in fact applicable to human beings remains a little doubtful. Several recent investigators have claimed that in man the associations formed by learning often appear to be more narrowly localized or limited than Lashley's experiments would suggest. And the processes of memory appear to be more complex than is usually supposed. In certain patients, suffering from epilepsy, it has been necessary to remove large portions of the temporal lobe or of a particular convolution underlying the eaves of the lobe, called the hippocampus. It then frequently appears that memory of recent events may be gravely impaired or even abolished. Some of the patients, it is reported, failed to recognize nurses and doctors whose names and faces had become quite familiar before the operation, and could no longer find their way to the bathroom. On the other hand, their memory for earlier events remained intact (B. Milner and W. Penfield, 'The effect of hippocampal lesion on recent memory', *Trans. Am. Neurol. Ass.*, 53, 1955, 42 ff.; *id.*, and W. B. Seville, *J. Neurol. Psychiat.*, 20, 1957, 11 ff.). In monkeys and apes, it is said, removal of both temporal lobes does not have any specific effect on memory (B. Milner, *Psychol. Bull.*, 51, 1954, 42 ff.).

The interpretation of these results is by no means clear. Psychologists and educationists have long been accustomed to distinguish between 'immediate' or 'recent memory' and 'long-distant memory'. Every student is familiar with the effect of cramming up topics for an impending examination, and the complete oblivion which may ensue as soon as the ordeal is over. Memory, too, is profoundly affected by motivation and feeling; and it is to be noted that the hippocampal region and the adjacent parts of the temporal lobe are among the oldest portions of the cortex, closely connected with the hypothalamus. It is therefore conceivable that what is disturbed by these operations are the emotional components of learning and of recalling. Unfortunately the results obtained by different neuro-surgeons are far from consistent; and those who report or discuss them seldom consider the possible influence of individual differences. Some persons, for example, remember both their past experiences and their surroundings in terms of concrete visual pictures; others apparently carry in their heads a kind of map in purely kinaesthetic imagery; others again are able to recall only those episodes and those items of their local geography which they have previously formulated in words. Since part of the temporal lobe is concerned with verbal activities, it may be chiefly this last group whose memories are impaired by the excision of parts of that lobe. And there is a further difficulty: with human subjects, surgical operations of this kind are only carried out on patients whose brains have already been damaged or disturbed by disease.[2]

Conclusion

But, whatever theory we adopt, it is clear that memory as a neurological process is not just a matter of threading beads on a single string or linking items end to end in a single chain; it consists in the organization of innumerable paths into a systematic network. Thus, at almost every one of the levels we have studied, we find that the efficiency of the processes involved depends on what Sherrington called 'integration'. And efficiency of integration in its turn must depend on the quantity of neurons available and on the number and variety of their branches. These qualities must characterize, not merely certain 'centres' or areas of the brain, but every part of it. (For more technical details the student may refer to D. A. Sholl, *The Organization of the Cerebral Cortex*,

1956, and the references there appended.) Accordingly we may, I think, safely conclude that human biology and neurology amply confirm the views expressed by Spencer and Sherrington about the general nature of intelligence and the hierarchical organization of brain and mind. An obvious corollary would seem to follow. If general and special types of mental ability depend on the physiological structure of the brain, then differences in these abilities are likely to be affected by the individual's genetic constitution, just like other physiological differences. To this further problem we must now turn in the next two chapters.

Notes and references

1 The latest version of the doctrine of three brains is that expounded by Paul Maclean, 'The paranoid streak in man', in Arthur Koestler and J. R. Smythies (eds.), *Beyond Reductionism* (1970): for a fuller account see P. Maclean, 'Man and his animal brains', *Mod. Med.*, *32*, 1964, 94–106.

2 Associationist theories of learning assume that the appropriate explanations must be expressed in terms of the transmission of energy (usually regarded as a current flowing along a channel with variable resistances at certain crucial points); by themselves, such hypotheses involve a gross oversimplification when applied to the cortex. In view of our ignorance of the structure channels involved, hypotheses expressed in terms of the transmission of information are likely to be more effective. The analogy of the servo-mechanism is far more appropriate than that of the telephone exchange. A servo-mechanism is a device which tends to change a material system in such a way that it progressively approaches a specified condition in accordance with instructions given, regarding a condition to be achieved and the condition actually obtained from moment to moment, i.e. from information continuously supplied by special 'feedback' mechanisms. The usual illustration is the 'automatic pilot'. In this, signals indicating the actual height and direction of the aeroplane are compared with a signal indicating the desired height and direction of the target to be reached: the differences between the signals then actuates the ailerons and the rudder so as to keep the aeroplane on its right course; similar methods are adopted for space-craft. In the nervous system the most obvious example is the mechanism which regulates the body temperature in warm-blooded animals: if the body temperature begins to fall, the superficial blood vessels contract, metabolism is increased, and movements (e.g. shivering) initiated, which warm up the body; if the temperature rises, the superficial blood vessels dilate, sweating increases, and so on. Since we are concerned with patterns, not with single variables (e.g. currents and resistances), the natural method of formulating the problems in symbolic terms will be by using matrices: in this way assumptions and hypotheses can be precisely stated, changes formulated by means of algebraic

'operators', consequences formally deduced, and then submitted to experimental testing (cf. C. Burt and E. Foley, 'The statistical analysis of the learning process', *Br. J. statist. Psychol.*, 9, 1956, 49 ff. and refs; W. R. Ashby, *Introduction to Cybernetics*, 1956).

CHAPTER EIGHT

Unifactorial inheritance

The origin of variations

Much of the doubt and criticism that has surrounded the theory of mental inheritance springs from the naive and inaccurate notions commonly held about what inheritance really implies. It is widely supposed that heredity, in the words of the *Oxford Dictionary*, means 'the tendency of like to beget like'. One Greek writer (wrongly supposed to be Aristotle) argued that leopards always beget leopards and camels always beget camels, and that if a leopard mates with a camel the offspring will be a blend which resembles both, namely, a camelopard, or, as we call it, a giraffe. Similarly, he contends, tall parents have tall offspring and short parents have short offspring; but if a tall husband marries a short wife, the height of the children will be the average of the two. Much the same holds good of skin colour, as is shown by the marriages of blacks and whites.

These various types of resemblance, partial or complete, observed or alleged, were commonly explained by ascribing them to the transmission of the parental blood. The older biologists supposed the blood of the father and mother passed into their germ cells, and mingled during sexual reproduction, and was thus transmitted to their offspring. This ancient hypothesis survives in many popular phrases: we talk of 'blood relations', of 'people of a different blood', and of traits and tendencies that 'run in the blood'. Many people, even school teachers, still take such phrases almost literally.

Darwin himself partly accepted this traditional interpretation of the resemblances produced by heredity. However, the evolution of species from earlier forms, which he was principally concerned to establish, implies changes in hereditary characteristics in addition to resemblances. Little or nothing was then known about the actual mechanism of heredity; and one of his greatest problems was to explain how these variations in hereditary characteristics could possibly occur. He suggested two types of causation. To a large extent he relied on a hypothesis put forward by an earlier advocate of evolution, the French naturalist, Antoine Lamarck. Darwin's own version of this conception he called 'pangenesis'. Every organ and tissue in the individual's body is supposed to excrete certain invisible substances or 'germules' (little germs) which enter the blood-stream and collect in the germ cells. If owing to incidents in the individual's life an organ or tissue is changed, the substance excreted would be altered; and this produces a corresponding alteration in the offspring. According to this theory one would expect the bodies of the offspring when fully developed to be, as if were, photographic copies of the parents at the time of reproduction, or at all events to tend in that direction. If a group of animals migrated to a different environment and there acquired new habits, then after several generations these habits would not only be inherited by their progeny, but become permanently fixed. The habits would thus be transformed into instincts. Similarly changes in climate, food, predators, and the like would result in adaptive variations during the individual's lifetime; and, if repeated generation after generation these too would, so Darwin supposed, be transmitted and fixed by inheritance. On the other hand, he also recognized an alternative possibility, and this has proved to be his own most important contribution to the problem. Among every species numerous minor changes may be observed in all directions, good, bad and indifferent, for which no assignable cause can be offered. These he describes as 'due to chance', a phrase (as he points out) which is merely a synonym for ignorance. He cites many interesting examples to illustrate the different types of variability. But, as time went on, he himself seems to have been more and more inclined to emphasize the importance of what for convenience he called 'spontaneous variations'.

Are acquired characteristics transmitted?

The attractive idea that adaptive changes in bodily structure which have been acquired by a parent may often be transmitted to his offspring formed the subject of a prolonged and vehement controversy. Numerous experiments were carried out. One enthusiast, for example, cut off the tails of successive generations of rats. The offspring never turned into tailless Manx rats; nevertheless he was convinced that their tails tended to become slightly shorter. Another experimentalist maintained that salamanders bred for several generations in yellow environments became yellower, and those bred in black environments became blacker. None of these findings have been confirmed by other investigators. In Russia, Pavlov, in one of his early research papers, announced that a certain conditioned reflex he had established in mice was genetically transmitted, increasingly so if repeated during successive generations. Later, however, he withdrew his conclusion, as based on an undetected error. McDougall trained rats to escape from a tank of water by choosing one of two alternative exits—namely that which was dimly illuminated; when they chose the route that was brightly lit they received an electric shock. The time taken to learn the right passage decreased appreciably, so he maintained, in successive generations. His conclusions have not been verified by later experimentalists; it seems possible that, quite unwittingly, McDougall had really been selecting certain families with a better capacity for learning mazes.

Both Marx and Engels were staunch adherents of the view that acquired characteristics become hereditary; and about twenty years ago, at a well-publicized meeting of the Lenin Agricultural Academy, this doctrine became officially recognized in Soviet Russia. Lysenko claimed that by appropriately changing environmental conditions it was possible to change the hereditary characteristics of wheat and other plants far more rapidly than by the slow procedures adopted on theoretical grounds by Western horticulturists. Today, however, these claims seem to have been tacitly discarded even by Russian agriculturists.

The environmentalists' criticisms

So long as these heated controversies and contradictory pronouncements continued, psychologists not unnaturally began to doubt all attempts to apply biological concepts to the problems of individual psychology. Professor Ward, for instance, in a long section on 'The concrete individual and heredity' (*Psychological Principles*, 1918) argued that 'pedigrees alone will not bring us to the concrete individual'. The late Sir Francis Galton's famous book he subjected to a sustained and vigorous criticism. He is still more scathing in his attack on Stern's proposal to make a science out of 'Individuelle Psychologie' by 'constructing psychograms of the concrete individual', and concludes that 'a better *reductio ad absurdum* [of such principles] is scarcely possible'.

The use of psychological tests in the diagnosis of mental deficiency and their subsequent introduction into the 11-plus examination has elicited similar protests expressed in language still more emphatic. 'The so-called science of psychogenetics', declared Dr Davidson in an 'Address to parents', 'is nothing but a pseudo-science. The notion that a psychologist can make a case study of you and your ancestry, and thereby inform you what mental and moral abilities or disabilities your infant child will exhibit—still more the idea that by applying a scale of intelligence tests he can foretell, soon after the youngster has entered school, what progress he will make at his lessons, whether he is fit for a grammar school and possibly a university, or whether he must pass all his days in an institution as a certified defective—all such would-be scientific diagnoses are as worthless as the gypsy's claim to prophesy the date of the boy's death. Individual variations are so wildly erratic and unpredictable that they defy every effort to turn such investigations to practical use. Doubtless, like all other unpredictable events, they are rigidly determined by a string of hidden causal processes. But, mindful of our utter ignorance of their nature, the intrinsic nature, the wise man will treat them as the effects of mere chance, and refrain from gambling. Professor Vernon puts the argument in a nutshell. Like Ward, he admits that the potentialities, mental as well as physical, *which are distinctive of the individual* may conceivably be due in part to his innate endowment; but this, as he rightly warns, "is not of the slightest use to the psychologist, since he has no means of observing, diagnosing, or measuring it".'

In all these allegations there is a grain of truth; but, even allowing for the rhetoric, the way they are expressed is grossly misleading, for most psychologists investigating mental inheritance are interested not in the individual as such, but in individuals as members of a population. Their primary aim is to estimate probabilities. Indeed, the textbook which investigators like myself used in the early days of our biometrical studies (Sir Palin Elderton's useful volume on *Frequency Curves and Correlations*,

1906) was written by an actuary for the Institute of Actuaries. Sir Ronald Fisher begins his book on *The Genetical Theory of Natural Selection* (1930) by stating that he proposes to 'make use of the ideas developed in the actuarial study of human mortality'. The actuary will tell you that, of 100,000 healthy English boys aged 11 in 1970, approximately 50,000 will survive till the age of 69 (a century ago he would have put the age at 46). Thus, had she adopted a frequency theory of probability, Dr Davidson's gypsy could have based her 'date of death' on her guess about the boy's age, and the betting would have been half and half in favour of the view that he would live to very nearly the age announced by the palmist. Of course, in point of fact a few of the 100,000 would die in the following year and one or two live to be centenarians. If trained in statistics, the gypsy could also have indicated the accuracy of her prediction by quoting the 'probable error'— about seven years either way.

It is perhaps not always realized that the psychologist's predictions are of this type. I could, of course, use Dr Davidson's objections to criticize the insurance company and their doctor when I first decided to insure my life. I could argue that I was still alive and that my length of life was a 'potentiality' which the doctor could neither observe, diagnose, nor measure. The actuaries would remain unperturbed; and the doctor would remind me that every branch of science dealt with potentialities which could not be directly measured, but could certainly be estimated with varying degrees of accuracy measurable by a 'probable' or 'standard' error. The psychogeneticist's approach is much the same. In the case of health and illness the predictions and the prognosis are subject to a rather larger margin of error. Hence statistical calculations play a somewhat greater part. Dr Davidson is speaking with more truth than he realizes when he suggests that the effects of heredity are the results of mere chance. But, as the owner of any roulette table could tell him, things that are indeed the results of mere chance can be predicted with considerable accuracy, provided we are content with averages based on large numbers together with a statement of probabilities. There will be no need in what follows to trouble the reader with all the mathematical details of the techniques which the psychologist uses. I shall merely give a few simple deductions and tables which I hope will suffice to demonstrate the general principles and illustrate their practical value.

Statistical genetics

However, before we can hope to give a plausible answer to the problems of mental inheritance it is necessary to know something of the principles of inheritance generally. Inheritance itself is a physical not a mental process. And the remarkable advances made in our knowledge of the physical mechanisms involved is the joint result of two converging lines of approach. The first is essentially an adaptation of the pedigree method: it consists in the collection of data from related individuals, particularly those derived from different types of mating or breeding, and then subjecting the data so obtained to a mathematical analysis. The second is cytological. The microscopic structure, the chemical nature, and the subsequent development of sex cells and their contents have been investigated in the laboratory with the aid of a variety of ingenious techniques. The first line of attack began in the days of Darwin and Galton, though they themselves were ignorant of it; the second is mainly the outcome of researches carried out during the present century, some only during the last ten years or so.

In a monastery garden, a year or two before Darwin published his work on *The Origin of Species*, a young Austrian monk, the son of a gardener, started a systematic study of the effects of hybridizing certain common plants. Unlike Darwin, he had received a training (amongst other subjects) in mathematics; and the novel feature of his research was the application of simple statistical techniques to the results he obtained. He spent eight years developing his methods and collecting his data, and finally announced his conclusions in a paper read to a local natural science society (Gregor Mendel, 'Versuch über Pflanzen Hybriden', *Verhandlungen des Naturforschenden Vereines in Brünn*, 4, 1866, 3–43). His work remained practically unknown until 1900, many years after his death, when both his results and his paper were rediscovered almost simultaneously by three continental botanists.

Mendel begins his account by noting that most horticulturalists who had previously practised cross-breeding had studied the hybrids in their entirety, whereas his method had been to record the results for 'single characters' separately—a procedure which had in fact been adopted by a forgotten experimentalist almost a century before. Moreover, as Mendel observes, 'in spite of the numerous experiments on hybridization no one', he says, 'hitherto attempted to determine the *numbers* of the different types produced or to ascertain their numerical *proportions*'. His own investigations were carried out mainly on different varieties of the kitchen pea. He gives figures for seven different characteristics derived from crossing many hundreds of pure-bred plants. His final generalizations are based chiefly on a comparison of average frequencies. But to show how results from individual plants may fluctuate about the general mean he also prints detailed figures for the first ten plants in each series.

On crossing specimens of a tall variety of pea which had been pure bred with pure-bred dwarfs he found that the first generation of hybrids were all tall. On breeding from these hybrids he noted that the grandchildren (so to speak) sorted out into tall and dwarf in fairly definite proportions (roughly 3 to 1). Shortness thus reappeared as a kind of 'throwback': but there were no plants of an intermediate height. Thus in the first generation tallness apparently dominated over shortness; and shortness, as he put it, was 'recessive', though by no means permanently suppressed. Again, when pure-bred peas bearing white flowers were crossed with pure-breds bearing red flowers, the hybrids of the first generation were all coloured: redness was dominant. Plants of the next generation, however, included both red and white in the same proportions as before: there were no pink blends. These results are sometimes said to indicate 'a law of segregation'.

In later experiments Mendel tried crossing parent plants which differed in two sets of alternative characters, e.g. a tall plant with white flowers and a short plant with red flowers. In these cases he found the various characteristics sorting out quite independently of each other, so that in the second generation every possible combination was obtained—tall plants with red flowers, tall flowers with white, short plants with red flowers, and short plants with white. The proportions were what one would infer from the proportions for the separate characters—approximately $9:3:3:1$. The important point to note is that as a consequence of the recombinations entirely new varieties were produced. These results are commonly taken to indicate a second law—the law of independent assortment.

During the earlier years of the present century, after his results had been resurrected, the experiments of Bateson and others in Britain quickly demonstrated that Mendel's generalizations held good not only of a wide variety of plants, but also of birds and animals. Let us therefore take a couple of examples from the latter, since they come nearer home. In poultry the Andalusian breed has several varieties of colour. If we cross a pure-bred white bird with a pure-bred black, all the offspring are an intermediate grey, or, as poultry fanciers prefer to call them, 'blue'. If we mate these grey birds with one another, the next generation—the grandchildren of the original cross—sort out into three distinct types: in addition to the grey, the white and black types re-emerge. When we cross-breed the 'blue' Andalusians in sufficiently large numbers, and calculate averages, we find that, in the second filial generation, the three types appear in constant proportions. The white and black appear in equal numbers, but the grey are twice as numerous: here therefore the proportions are 1 : 2 : 1. If, following Mendel's procedure with his plants, we continue breeding for further generations, we find that the white and black each breed true, but the offspring of the grey always sort out in the same proportions as before.

The conclusions are obvious. Although with the fowl the observable characteristics appear to blend—the white and black producing grey—the hereditary 'factors', as Mendel called them—the 'genes', as it is now more usual to say—do not blend. Throughout the successive generations they retain their identity. We may suppose that each reproductive cell—egg or sperm (the egg, of course, coming from the hen and the sperm from the cock)—contains a single gene which may appear in one or other of two forms: let us call them B and b. The fertilized cell is a combination of both, and therefore contains two genes, which may either be both B, both b, or one of each. The chicks which develop from the first of these three combinations, BB, will be black, and must obviously breed true; those which develop from the second, bb, will be white and will also breed true; those which develop from bB or Bb will be grey; and when two fowls of this hybrid type breed together, some eggs and sperms will contain a gene for black (B), and some a gene for white (b), in approximately equal numbers. It makes no difference which gene comes from the male parent and which from the female. Evidently, therefore, on fertilization there will be four possible recombinations, namely BB, Bb, bB, and bb; and the several combinations will tend to appear in equal numbers. Since the effects of Bb and bB are identical, the ratio for the observable characters, that is, black, grey and white, will be 1 : 2 : 1. These are the ratios we eventually obtain if we keep tossing two pennies and count the numbers of heads and tails in successive throws. Thus, as Mendel observes, the re-assortment of genes in fertilization obeys the laws of chance; and his theory clearly explains why in later generations the off-spring of hybrids which look the same, will (as the older breeders used to say) often 'revert to type'. Popular lecturers on the subject are fond of quoting Miss Dorothy Sayers' limerick as a mnemonic for Mendel's laws:

> There was a young woman named Starkie
> Who had an affair with a darkie;
> The children she bore
> Amounted to four—
> One white, one black and two khaki.

This bit of poetic science-fiction is inaccurate: for, if Mendel's laws for monohybrids applied (which as a matter of fact they do not in this particular instance), the first generation should all be 'khaki', and the parental types reappear only in the grand-children.

When, as was so frequently the case with Mendel's peas, one type of gene, B, say, dominates over the other, the individuals with two different genes (Bb or bB) will appear to be of the same types as those with two of the dominant genes: there will be no inter-mediate blend and the ratios will therefore be $3 : 1$. For an illus-trative example let us take a case occurring in animals—one which will be familiar to many schoolboys who keep pets. When a pure-bred rabbit of the common or so-called wild type which has brownish fur is mated to the popular albino type which has white fur and pink eyes, then, to the disappointment of the young owners, all the offspring will have brown fur. However, if these in turn are mated, the next generation will produce a few white, but the majority will be brown. With sufficiently large numbers, it will be found that the proportions gradually approximate to the ratio mentioned so often by Mendel, namely, 3 to 1. If mated amongst themselves the albinos will breed true as will some of the brown; but the progeny of the rest will again include both brown and white in much the same proportions as before. The pedigrees for albinism in man (a condition, be it remembered, which carries with it certain mental peculiarities as well—defective vision and a tendency to slight intellectual subnormality) exhibit precisely the same peculiarities. (i) the parents of an albino usually appear normal; nevertheless (ii) *both* will carry the recessive characteristic in latent form; hence (iii) the parents are far more frequently 'relatives by blood', e.g. first cousins. (iv) With large families there will often be more than one albino sib. (v) If, when an albino marries an apparently normal person, he or she produces any albino children at all, there will be in any large family about as many albinos as normals. Finally (vi) the children of two albinos are all albinos.

The chromosome theory

Mendel's 'unit factors' were purely hypothetical entities. It is therefore natural to inquire whether in the sperm and egg the cytologist can discover any visible structures which behave in the way Mendel postulated. In the 1870s, with the improved types of microscope that then became available, several biologists reported the existence of minute threadlike bodies in the nuclei of almost every cell, which at certain stages in the cell division could readily be stained with a carmine dye, and thus could be seen and counted. They were later called 'chromosomes', i.e. 'coloured bodies'. With one notable exception their number is the same in every cell of the same body and in every individual of the same species. They are present in pairs; and (again with the same exception—the chromosomes for sex) the members of a given pair are similar in size and shape. The banana fly, which geneticists have relied on for much intensive study, contains only four pairs; in human beings there are twenty-three. While organisms are growing, the body cells multiply by simple division. The chromosomes in the original cell then split longitudinally into two similar halves, one of which goes to one of the two new cells and the other to the other cell; hence each new cell contains the same number as the original cell. When the sex cells are formed, however, one of the duplicates disappears; consequently a sperm or an egg contains only one member of each pair; but when sperm and egg unite to produce a single fertilized cell, which develops into a new individual, corresponding duplicates come together, so the total number of pairs is restored.

Thus the chromosomes behave in much the same way as Mendel's postulated factors. However, the Mendelian factors, which are necessarily far more numerous than the chromosomes, correspond not with a whole chromosome, but with a certain short region, called a 'locus'—the 'locus' (i.e. 'position') being the same on corresponding chromosomes. Such a region is termed a 'gene'; and this is assumed to have two alternative biochemical forms (sometimes more, as in the genes determining certain blood-groups).

All organisms except the lowest appear in two alternative forms, distinguished by a striking set of differences in certain characteristics which regularly segregate in generation after generation and never blend, namely, those that define the two sexes. The characteristics are determined by a specific pair of chromosomes—the pair already mentioned as usually differing in size and shape—the so-called sex chromosomes. In one sex (the female in mammals, including human beings) the sex chromosomes form an identical pair called X-chromosomes; in the other sex only one X-chromosome is present: its partner, the Y-chromosome, is much smaller and carries very few genes. Thus in human beings the egg cell produced by the mother will contain twenty-two autosomes (as the matching chromosomes are termed) and one X-chromosome, whereas the sperm cell produced by the father will contain twenty-two autosomes and either an X-chromosome or a Y-chromosome. Hence the fertilized cells will contain forty-four autosomes and either two X-chromosomes or one X-chromosome and one Y-chromosome—the two types being produced in approximately equal numbers. The former develop into females, the latter into males.

Now it might be supposed that since each chromosome carries a large number of genes, all the genes that are located on the same chromosome would invariably be transmitted together; consequently they would, as the geneticist puts it, all be 'linked'. This would imply numerous exceptions to Mendel's law of independent segregation. However, during the formation of eggs and sperms homologous chromosomes temporarily lie side by side, and segments of material are exchanged. This exchange produces a 'crossing over' of genes. Genes which lie close together on the chromosome are much more likely to remain linked, while those which lie at a distance from each other will show only a slight linkage.

The most interesting examples of linkage occur in connection with sex. Every reader, I imagine, is familiar with the fact that all tortoiseshell cats are females. Suppose, for example, we mate pure-bred black cats with pure-bred yellow. It will quickly appear that the gene for yellow is sex-linked. Let us call the gene for black *B*, and the rarer alternative gene which produces yellow *b*. Then females may be either *BB*, *Bb*, or *bb*: dominance is incomplete, so that the hybrid *Bb* has the mottled black and yellow markings which we call tortoiseshell. In the males the Y-chromosome can carry no such genes; hence all males are either *B* (black) or *b* (yellow). Six types of matings are therefore possible; and it then appears that the sons must be either black or yellow, while the daughters may be black, yellow or tortoiseshell. In many animals, cattle for example, a knowledge of this type of inheritance has often proved to be of considerable economic importance. In cows the yield and the quality of milk depends largely on genes that are sex-linked. Hence, though the production of milk is limited to females, the character of the milk is even more strongly influenced by selecting bulls than by selecting cows. In Denmark the superior quality of the milk and its butter content (it has been stated) is due to the fact that a large proportion of the dairy cows are descended from two bulls only, which have been used (partly by artificial insemination) to sire cows used for breeding. There is reason to believe that the same principles hold of the inheritance of certain special abilities and disabilities in man. This is one of the many neglected problems in the field of psychogenetics which, it is to be hoped, will attract the attention of research workers in the near future.

The nature of the gene

It has recently been demonstrated that the material responsible for the transmission of genetic tendencies is a complex substance known as deoxyribo-nucleic acid (DNA). This is a large chain molecule consisting of two linked strands spirally coiled. It has certain peculiar properties. First, it is able to reproduce itself. The order in which certain constituents, four 'bases' as the biochemist calls them, are arranged along one of the two backbone strands determines the order in which these bases are arranged on the other strand. The two strands are complementary to one another. Hence, each can serve as a template for the reproduction of the other. Secondly, the order in which the four bases are arranged in any section of the chain acts as a code conveying instructions for synthesizing certain specific proteins; and many of these proteins are known to act as enzymes catalysing definite biochemical and chemical composition of the individual organism and its various parts.

The various types of DNA molecule are extremely stable. Nevertheless, occasionally they undergo minor changes, especially when exposed to certain exceptional conditions, e.g. radiation. We may suppose that the code for some specific protein is altered, so that it fails to function as an enzyme. In his researches, therefore, the geneticist likes to work with fairly specific mutations of this kind which result in the failure or blockage of some identifiable enzymatic reaction. A section of the DNA molecule presumed to be responsible for this failure may be regarded as a specific 'gene'. Indeed, the geneticist's ideal is often expressed by the formula 'one gene, one enzyme'.

The principles underlying this particular process have been discovered by work on micro-organisms, such as bacteria, where the immediate effects of a mutation, experimentally produced, can often be precisely determined. In higher organisms the structure of the chromosomes is more complex. Often all that can be observed in the case of a mutation is some simple change in the visible character of the fully developed organism, e.g. a change in flower colour, such as those studied by Mendel. In some cases, however, the chemical nature of the pigments that produce the colours are well known; and if these chemical substances are taken as the criteria instead of the mere colour, then the modes of transmission are found to agree still more closely with the Mendelian 'laws'. This emphasizes the wide distance which separates the initial genotype from the final phenotype in more complex organisms. Nevertheless, all the available evidence tends to show that in these too the mechanism of inheritance is essentially the same.

So far almost all my illustrations have been drawn from studies of physical characteristics, chiefly in animals or plants. We have now to inquire whether the conclusions thus reached apply to the transmission of mental characteristics in man.

Unifactorial inheritance in human beings

In 1934 a Norwegian biochemist who came to work at an institution for mental defectives observed that many of the inmates exuded a peculiar smell. On studying these particular children more closely he noticed that an unusual number were blue-eyed and with hair and complexion so fair that they reminded him of albinos. The case files indicated that in regard to intelligence the majority were idiots, the rest chiefly imbeciles, a few merely feebleminded or only slightly subnormal, but a remarkable number were related by birth: in several cases the parents were first cousins. On making a chemical study of them he discovered that all regularly excreted in their urine about 1 gram daily of an aromatic substance called phenylpyruvic acid. This can be readily detected by using a strip of paper impregnated with an iron salt (ferric chloride), which is turned blue by this particular acid.

There is in our ordinary diet an essential amino-acid known as phenylalanine. Normally an enzyme in the liver converts this into another amino-acid—tyrosine, which has a dynamic action on the metabolism of tissue cells, and augments the production of certain hormones, such as adrenalin. The defectives in question proved to be lacking in this enzyme. Phenylalanine consequently accumulates in their blood, and is changed into phenylpyruvic acid and other toxic substances. These damage the brain tissue and produce not only mental deficiency but in some cases epileptic manifestations. Growth is often impeded. Since the pigment (melanin) responsible for dark hair and eyes happens to be an end-product of the metabolism of tyrosine, lack of this substance leaves the sufferer with fair hair and blue eyes.

The enzyme in question is manufactured by a specific gene. Most persons inherit two such genes, one from each parent. The mutation of such a gene results in a partial failure to manufacture the enzyme. But if the other gene is normal, a sufficient amount will still be produced. If, however, the child inherits two such modified genes (as, of course, is far more likely to happen if the parents are related), the result will be total failure. The condition thus behaves as a Mendelian recessive. A simple calculation based on the principles outlined above will indicate that if two carriers —two first cousins, it may be—marry and have children, the probability is that one in four of their offspring will be mentally defective; the others will apparently be normal, but two will probably be carriers. The test I have described renders the diagnosis quite easy at an early age; and from infancy onwards the child should then be fed on a diet which is practically free from phenylalanine—with this treatment intellectual development is usually normal or nearly so.

I have described this example in some detail because I wished to emphasize the rather complicated and indirect fashion in which different genes influence the various observable conditions with which psychologists and teachers are concerned. At the same time they indicate how important it is for the clinical psychologist to keep his eyes and other senses alert to note suggestive signs and symptoms besides the lowered I.Q.s recorded by his tests. There are a number of other recessive conditions associated with mental deficiency; but just because they are recessive, such hereditary tendencies are difficult to establish unless a number of rather elaborate pedigrees are available. In the family history the most characteristic feature is the presence of inbreeding: the parents are often closely related and nearly always apparently normal, and there is a marked difference between the affected and the unaffected children. Those tribes or racial groups that are subject to a good deal of inbreeding, the Jews for example, evince a greater liability to recessive disorders.

The types of dominant conditions associated with mental deficiency are fewer in number, because being dominant they are far more liable to be eliminated by natural selection. In fact, were it not for the occurrence of fresh mutations, most dominant defects would rapidly die out. The clearest observable cases are those in which the disorder does not appear until fairly late in life, so that the sufferer may have already produced a fairly large family.

Early in the nineteenth century a boy named George Huntingdon, the son of an American doctor, was driving with his father through a lane in Long Island, when a couple of women stood in their way 'bowing, twisting, grimacing and chattering unintelligibly'. His father explained that they were mother and daughter belonging to a family which had produced many such cases treated by his own father and grandfather. The boy was so impressed that, as he related in an autobiographical note published many years later, he resolved to make the study of this disease his first contribution to medical history. It is now called after him, and known as Huntingdon's chorea.

Many of the American cases have been traced back to two brothers who emigrated to New England in 1630 from the village of Bures in Suffolk. One line, indeed, has been followed up through twelve generations. The pedigrees leave no doubt that the condition is due to a single gene with dominant effects. Since the gene is rare, an affected patient almost invariably carries it on only one of the relevant pair of chromosomes; and, if he or she marries, he will in all probability marry a normal person. It follows that on an average about half the children will receive the gene, and therefore, since it is dominant, suffer from the disorder if they survive long enough. The peculiarity of the disease is that the physical manifestations seldom appear until after the age of about thirty-five or later, that is, after the patient has produced children. The most conspicuous symptoms are a gradual increase in jerky involuntary movements of the hands, face, and ultimately of the whole body. With this goes an increasing intellectual impairment. These manifestations are commonly ushered in by temperamental changes. Alcoholism, violent temper, criminality and sexual misbehaviour are often noted before the patient comes under medical observation; as the pedigrees show, even their legitimate offspring are more numerous than usual. A curious feature is the way the patient during the slow onset of the disease tries to conceal the involuntary character of his movements by making them serve some needless voluntary purpose: if his hand jerks up, he proceeds to smooth his hair; if his body suddenly bends down, he brushes imaginary dust from his trousers. Eliot Slater records a patient who, as a young man, had become the popular clown of an amateur dramatic club, his comical movements and grimaces—the first signs of his chronic chorea—drawing rounds of applause and laughter. Huntingdon records that several of the affected women in the families that his father attended had been burnt as witches. Post-mortem examination reveals that the brain is noticeably atrophied, the frontal lobes and the areas around the so-called motor centres being most conspicuously involved. How the gene comes to produce these changes or why its effects are so long delayed is at present unknown.

Several other clinical types of mental deficiency are due to a single dominant gene, and usually manifest themselves at a comparatively early age. They are all rare, and generally result in defects severe enough to be classed as idiocy or imbecility. In a few cases the disorder may be the result of a mutation of some gene; but in the majority its origin is traceable to a parent who either suffered in much the same way or else was evidently the carrier of a genetic tendency manifested by remoter relatives. It is evident, therefore, that eugenic measures—segregation, sterilization or the use of contraceptives—could appreciably reduce the number suffering from the severer types of mental deficiency.

A few forms of mental deficiency are due to abnormalities in the number of certain chromosomes. The most remarkable example of this is to be seen in so-called 'mongolism'. About 10 per cent of the defectives transferred to mental hospitals belong to this type; and they are not infrequently seen in schools or classes for the mentally deficient. Their appearance is quite distinctive. They are usually short, have small round heads, flat faces with oblique eyes, all suggestive of the stereotyped popular picture of a mongol from east Asia. In character they tend to be cheerful and friendly; they are usually imitative and often musical. During childhood their I.Q.s range from 20 to 75. Some can just learn to read and write. When grown up, however, the mental age even of the brightest is seldom above eight or nine.

About ten years ago a group of French investigators noted in a number of cases which they had studied the presence of an extra chromosome of the type usually numbered 21; occasionally there is a translocation of the pair numbered 22. Since chromosome pairs are numbered in order of decreasing size, this means aberrations in the two smallest pairs. It has long been known that mothers of mongols are rather elderly, and there can be little doubt that their advanced age when these children are conceived may disturb the production of a normal fertilized cell. In a few cases the mothers (never the fathers) are also mongols.

Sex-linked abnormalities

A number of peculiarities other than mental subnormality are caused by a recessive gene carried on the X-chromosome. Of these the disorder that has attracted greatest attention is the condition known as haemophilia. Its essential characteristic is the exceptionally long time taken for the patient's blood to clot. The most celebrated pedigree is that of the descendants of Queen Victoria. Her youngest son Prince Leopold suffered from it, and two of her daughters Princess Alice and Princess Beatrice proved to be carriers. Of Princess Alice's children, Prince Frederick William was a haemophiliac and died when he was three; Princess Irene, who married Prince Henry of Prussia, had two haemophiliac sons; Princess Alexandra married the Tsar Nicholas II, and everyone knows the study of the ill-fated Tsarevitch, who suffered from the disease until he died with the rest of his family, when he was fourteen. Prince Leopold's daughter was the Duchess of Athlone, and one of her sons died of it before he was twelve months old. Princess Beatrice had two sons who died in the same way, and a daughter who married Alfonso XIII of Spain; two of their sons were haemophiliacs. Edward VII was free of the disease, and, as would be expected, none of his descendants has shown it.

Since males have only one X-chromosome, a male will be normal if his X-chromosome is normal, and for the same reason he cannot transmit the disease; if his X-chromosome carries the gene, he will necessarily suffer; and, if he has children, will transmit the gene to half his children: thus one would expect about half his sons to suffer and half his daughters to be carriers. The gene is extremely rare, and a female with both X-chromosomes abnormal has never, I believe, been encountered, and since the condition is recessive, the disease is confined to males.

The commonest abnormality to be transmitted in this way is red–green colour-blindness. It is present in 3 to 5 per cent of west-European males. The percentages vary, because there are not only different degrees, but different forms of this abnormality; and the tests and criteria used differ from one investigator to another. Probably more than one gene is involved. However, all the ordinary forms are definitely sex-linked. The mode of inheritance is similar to that of haemophilia. Colour-blindness is transmitted by female carriers, but decidedly rare in females. However, the first woman who came to me as a postgraduate research student during my appointment at Liverpool was, as her hat and clothes plainly revealed, definitely red–green blind. So, she said, was her father, and her grandfather on the mother's side. Father and mother were first cousins. Colour-blindness is much commoner than haemophilia; such cases are therefore reported and discussed far more frequently in the psychological literature.

Since the genes for both haemophilia and colour-blindness are carried on the X-chromosomes, it is not surprising to find pedigrees in which the two defects regularly occur in the same individuals. However, the female has two X-chromosomes; and in a few pedigrees it appears that the gene for haemophilia may be carried on one and the gene for colour-blindness on the other. In that case, although both defects appear and reappear in successive generations, they may often appear in different individuals.

Several other psychological abnormalities are thought to be sex-linked. Left-handedness often runs in families, and is much commoner in males than in females. In my own school surveys approximately 6 per cent of the boys, but only 4 per cent of the girls were left-handed (*The Backward Child*, 1937, ch. 7). In the family histories it was found that, when both father and mother were left-handed, just over 50 per cent of the children were left-handed. When both were right-handed, less than 5 per cent were left-handed. When only one parent was left-handed, the proportion was just over 25 per cent. This suggests that, when the child receives only one gene for left-handedness, his condition is intermediate, and may readily be modified by training. The problem, however, is extremely complex. There are different varieties of left-handedness; and parents and teachers adopt widely different views about the wisdom of training a left-handed child to use the right hand. Consequently, without prolonged study and testing of each individual concerned the diagnosis is by no means easy. There is clear evidence of sex linkage in many pedigrees; and some investigators have held that congenital left-handedness is in fact a sex-linked recessive, with a varying degree of manifestation. Probably different genes are involved with different modes of transmission.

Speech defects exhibit much the same tendencies and present much the same problems. They are commoner in boys than in girls, and exist in various forms. Many persons with impediments in their speech are also left-handed: Lewis Carroll was one well-known example. The fact that the motor centre for the right hand is in the left hemisphere of the brain, and that in right-handed persons the chief centre for speech lies in the third left frontal convolution, has suggested that variations in both verbal ability and left-handedness are associated with the alleged dominance of one of the two cerebral hemispheres. Among this group of associated symptoms several medical psychologists would include a condition which they describe as 'congenital dyslexia', that is, an 'innate disability in reading'. However, the neurological and the statistical evidence which they adduce is to my mind far from convincing.

I hope I have now said enough to demonstrate that human characteristics are inherited in much the same way as those of animals and plants. And so many of the characteristics mentioned include mental manifestations that I infer that mental tendencies generally are inherited in much the same way as physical, i.e. that their transmission follows the same principles and results from the same mechanism as those described by Mendel and his present-day followers. The critic, however, will be tempted to retort that all the mental characteristics which I have so far enumerated are pathological or at least abnormal, and in many cases decidedly rare. We are therefore still free (so he will contend) to assume that in all normal characteristics of the mind human beings are born equal, and that the observable variations in intellectual ability and in emotional or moral character among normal individuals are the results of postnatal experiences. This is the standpoint adopted by many British sociologists and several writers on educational theory at the present day. 'We may well admit', they say, 'that certain forms of so-called mental and moral deficiency are inborn and ineradicable, and therefore that the mentally subnormal should be segregated and [in their opinion] transferred to a special school or institution. But to apply this to the normal or allegedly supernormal is to fly in the face of all democratic principles. Those who appear to be intellectually superior—those, for example, who score high I.Q.s in, say, the 11-plus examination —generally owe their apparent superiority, not to some innate gift, but to the economic and cultural privileges they enjoy in middle-class homes. To transfer these to a special type of school— a grammar school or one of our venerable public schools—is to perpetuate social divisiveness and to persist in a gross social injustice.' Let us therefore now examine the apparent causation of normal individual differences.

CHAPTER NINE

Multifactorial inheritance

Quantitative variation

The characteristics which we have so far examined are those which differ essentially in quality rather than quantity. They are usually such as will enable us to classify the individuals studied into two distinct and well-defined categories. Mendel's kitchen peas were either dwarf or tall, the pods were either yellow or green, the seeds either round or wrinkled, and so on. Similarly human beings can be classified, though perhaps not quite so sharply, into colour-blind and colour-sensitive, the night-blind, the normal, the right-handed and the left-handed. The reasons for selecting characteristics of this kind are obvious. First of all, the observable manifestations can be readily identified; secondly, they can often be explained in terms of the presence or absence of a single gene, and always suggest such a possibility. Indeed, the earlier Mendelian investigators commonly spoke of a gene *for* this or that colour or *for* this or that specific abnormality, as though the causation was invariable and direct.

Now most normal characteristics, particularly those of interest to the practical psychologist, differ in degree rather than in kind. Unlike Mendel's peas, the height of human beings exhibits continuously graded variations: some may be only 57 inches high, others as much as 77 inches; and, when sufficiently large samples are measured, instances of every intermediate height are found. Similarly in surveys of large numbers of school children the I.Q.s vary from 50 to 150, and between these extremes every shade and grade may be found. If we include mental institutions and public schools the range will be wider still; and, indeed, in theory it is virtually unlimited.

Now this was a phenomenon to which Mendel himself drew

attention towards the end of his paper in a section which has all too often been overlooked. When he turned from his studies with kitchen peas to similar experiments on the common bean (*Phaseolus vulgaris*), he found that the offspring of hybrids sorted out as regards height, colour of pods, type of seeds, in exactly the same way as those of the kitchen pea. He then proceeded to hybridize other varieties of beans, e.g. *Ph. multiflorus* (which has purple flowers) with *Ph. nanus* (which has white). To his astonishment he found that in this case the hybrid plants no longer exhibited one or other of the two colours characteristic of the plants which he crossed; what he obtained was 'a whole series of colours from purple, and paler shades of violet, to white'. But, he immediately adds, 'even these enigmatical results could be explained by the same laws as those governing varieties of peas if we imagine that in this instance the colours observed are, so to speak, compounded of several independent colours, due to factors which individually act like those governing independent and constant colours, as in peas'. And he goes on to suggest an algebraic formula which would explain not only the apparent mixture of colours, but also the relative frequency of the different grades.

The measurement of correlations

To deal with quantitative variation in any systematic fashion new methods of statistical analysis are plainly required. So long as the differences with which we are concerned are differences of class or kind, the amount of resemblance or difference can be expressed in terms of percentages. When the differences are differences of degree, some other measure of resemblance or lack of resemblance is essential. Viewing heredity as essentially a matter of resemblance, earlier psychologists followed Galton and used a coefficient of correlation, which, as we have seen, measured the amount of agreement between two series of figures on a scale ranging from $-1 \cdot 00$ through $0 \cdot 00$ to $+1 \cdot 00$. For instance, in studying the inheritance of height Galton selected two brothers only from each family and took the coefficient of correlation as a measure of heredity. Since the persons measured had all been brought up in much the same environmental conditions, he assumed that the influence of environment could be ignored. And he then went on to calculate coefficients for various degrees of kinship.

In the case of school children drawn from very different types of home, and particularly in dealing with mental characteristics, this simple procedure is plainly inadequate; we need some method of assessing environmental influences.

The psychological factorist naturally thinks of trying factor analysis. Suppose, for example, that we can get pedigrees for relatives belonging to typical families, and included a wide variety of kinships—parents and children, identical and non-identical twins, ordinary sibs, half-sibs, first and second cousins, uncles and nephews, and so forth. If possible, we ought also to include related pairs brought up from infancy in separate homes. (A table of this sort will be found printed in the *Irish J. Educ.*, *3*, 94.) On factorizing such a table four types of factors appear to emerge. (i) There is a 'general factor' entering in various degrees into the assessment for all the individuals belonging to the same families, whether brought up together or apart. This could be interpreted as a *common genetic factor*. (ii) There are distinct group factors affecting in various degrees those brought up in the same homes, whether related by birth or unrelated. These could be regarded as *common environmental factors*. Factors of both the fore-going types would tend to produce resemblances between the individuals concerned, and thus to increase the correlations. (iii) The correlations of identical twins with their elder or younger sibs usually average about 0·40 to 0·50; the correlations between identical twins themselves often rise to 0·70 or over, even when they had been reared apart. The increment therefore seems to indicate a *specific genetic factor*. This result is readily intelligible in terms of current genetic theory. Every child inherits half his genes from his father and half from his mother; which genes he inherits is purely a matter of chance. It follows that two children born of the same parents will have about half their genes in common, the rest being specific to each. But monozygotic twins result from the splitting of one and the same fertilized ovum. Consequently they have all their genes in common. (iv) Nevertheless, the correlations between monozygotic twins never reach unity. In this case, of course, the deficit cannot possibly be due to genetic factors; it must therefore be due to non-genetic factors, such as differences in past or present environmental conditions and in the minor irrelevant influences which together are responsible for the errors and 'unreliability' of the initial assessments. The same doubtless holds good of all other correlations. Evidently, therefore, we must also postulate the influence of *specific environmental factors* (as a rule, no separate estimates were available for 'unreliability'; hence its effects were usually included under the general term 'environmental'). The two types of specific factor, genetic and non-genetic, produce differences between the correlated pairs, and so reduce the size of the correlations between them. If Pearson's method of principal components were used with a strictly orthogonal rotation, the factors thus obtained would be independent and uncorrelated, and the factor variances would indicate their relative importance.

If we accept this conclusion at its face value, it would mean that we may assume our observed measurement for any individual can be partitioned into four independent components: i.e. that we can write

$$x_i = g_{ci} + g_{si} + e_{ci} + e_{si} \qquad \ldots \ (1)$$

where x_i is the measurement for the ith individual (twin, sib, etc., according to the type of kinship we are studying), g denotes genetic factors, e environmental factors, c common factors, and s specific factors. But it is by no means necessary to adopt the cumbersome procedure of collecting members from the same family; nor, indeed, is it possible with the limited data usually available to compile a complete correlation matrix: various substitutions have to be made. If, however, we are content to calculate approximate factor values, we can make do with four observed values only.

Analysis of variance

But what we really need is, not merely a means of demonstrating the existence of these various factors, but some method of comparing their relative influence and importance. A great improvement was achieved when Sir Ronald Fisher introduced what he termed the 'analysis of variance'. This starts from the idea of comparing not so much the amount of resemblance as the amount of difference. The difference between two or more members of the same family can best be measured by taking, not the different pairs, or the various members of the family taken pair by pair, but their differences (or 'deviations') from the common mean. Partly to avoid difficulties arising from the fact that some deviations will be positive, others negative, it is best to square them. The squares are all positive, and so we can add them. The average of all the squared deviations in the group we are studying is called its variance, and the square root of the variance is the standard deviation.

Now if the intra-group (or 'intra-class') correlation be calculated, then it is easy to show that the coefficient so obtained will be equal to the ratio of the variance for the common factors to the total variance. Thus the correlation for ordinary sibs brought up together (r_{st} say), we can write

$$r_{st} = \frac{V_{GC} + V_{EC}}{V_{GC} + V_{GS} + V_{EC} + V_{ES}} \quad \ldots \quad (2)$$

where the suffixes have the same meanings as before. In the case of identical twins we must add V_{GS} to the numerator, and in the case of sibs or twins brought up apart we must omit V_{EC} from the numerator. If we assume that the total variance for all our different groups is virtually the same (an assumption which, of course, should be checked by testing the statistical significance of any differences in the data as observed), we can set the denominators in all these equations equal to unity. We then have

$$\left.\begin{array}{l} r_{sa} = V_{GC} \\ r_{st} = V_{GC} + V_{EC} \\ r_{mzt} = V_{GC} + V_{EC} + V_{GS} \\ V_{p} = 1 - V_{GC} + V_{EC} + V_{GS} + V_{ES} \end{array}\right\} \quad \ldots \quad (3)$$

where s denotes sibs, mz monozygotic twins, t or a brought up together or apart; and V_p the total phenotypic variance. These three correlations could be readily derived from observations collected by educational psychologists during surveys of the school population in their area. Values for the four hypothetical variances can then be calculated by successive subtraction.

Table 1 gives the correlations obtained for intelligence and attainments during one of our earlier London surveys. I have inserted correlations for intelligence derived from reports by various other investigators, taking in each case the median value (see Burt, 1966, table 3). By way of comparison I have added similar figures for stature. Table 2 gives estimates for the factor variances derived from these coefficients by the method described.

It will be seen in the case of height that genetic factors contribute nearly 90 per cent of the variance, about 80 per cent in the case of intelligence, and little over 60 per cent at most in the case of attainments. This last percentage is probably excessive, since here

Table 1: Observed correlations

Group	No. pairs	Height	Intelligence		Attainments
			(Burt)	(Other investigators)	
Monozygotic twins reared together	84	0·939	0·896	0·874	0·898
Sibs reared together	231	0·483	0·543	0·551	0·685
Sibs reared apart	156	0·431	0·468	0·472	0·401

Note. The 'No. pairs' refers to the groups on which the three investigations carried out by myself were based, not to those of 'Other investigators'.

the value has almost certainly been inflated by a significant correlation between the children's attainments and the cultural level of their homes. Of late several keen environmentalists have been echoing the statement that 'a test of intelligence is simply yet another test of attainment'. Figures like the foregoing plainly rule any such contention out of court. The proportionate influence of nature and nurture is here nearly the same for intelligence as it is for height, and widely different from what it is for attainments.

Table 2: Variances for genetic and environmental factors

Factor	Percentage of total			
	Height	Intelligence		Attainments
		(Burt)	(Other investigators)	
V_{GC}	43·1	46·8	47·2	40·1
V_{GS}	45·6	35·3	32·3	21·3
V_G	88·7	82·1	79·5	61·4
V_{EC}	5·2	7·5	7·9	28·4
V_{ES}	6·1	10·4	12·6	10·2
V_E	11·3	17·9	20·5	38·6
V_T	100·0	100·0	100·0	100·0

Instructive as they may seem, these results when published raised more questions than they solved. If intelligence is inherited in the same fashion as height, how is it that with both sets of data the influence of the 'common genetic factor' is apparently greater in the case of intelligence than in that of height, which after all can be far more accurately measured? One possible explanation is that correlations for sibs brought up apart are liable to be affected by selective placement; and in the case of intelligence this may have unduly magnified the value for r_{sa}. It may be practicable to devise methods which will check, eliminate, or allow for this and other irrelevant influences. But so far no such method has been actually tried in practice or seems likely to win general acceptance. In any case, it is plainly unwise to rely solely on values deduced from a minimum number of observed correlations.

In the case of intelligence there is undoubtedly a further influence at work, namely, that of preferential mating. Both men and women tend to choose their spouses from the same social class and from persons who have much the same intelligence and intellectual background. In respect of height this tendency is far less marked. It is therefore desirable to isolate and estimate the genetic effects of such preferences. When there is little or no preferential mating, we should expect the values for the common and specific genetic variances to be approximately equal. In the case of height the specific genetic variance is generally the larger. In a single set of samples, each containing at most little over 200 pairs, the difference is not significant; but it reappears in many other inquiries, and therefore demands an explanation. The most likely would seem to be the effects of dominance, another subsidiary factor too often ignored in psychological studies.

In spite of its limitations I still believe that the foregoing procedure may be usefully adopted by educational psychologists who (as correspondence shows) are exhibiting a renewed interest in the problems of nature and nurture, and are in a position to collect correlations of the types I have described. Nevertheless, it has long been clear that a more elaborate mode of investigation is essential if we are to attain a deeper understanding of mental inheritance. 'What seems to be needed', as I argued in an earlier report, 'is not just an empirical proof *that* mental characteristics are inherited, but a more systematic attempt to ascertain *how* they are inherited.'

In deriving the requisite equations we usually followed the

deductions set forth by Fisher (1918) in his classical study of the inheritance of bodily characteristics: a few incidental modifications appeared desirable, suggested partly by the later work of Mather and Sewall Wright, and partly by the peculiarities of psychological data. At the same time it seemed possible to simplify some of the proofs. The guiding principle was to start by deriving results for a single locus, and then to generalize the equations so reached to problems involving any number of loci. Instead of retaining the earlier and rather confusing symbols employed by these authorities I have mentioned, I shall here substitute the more familiar type of notation, now customary in quantitative genetics, for that adopted in earlier papers (cf. Falconer, 1967, *Glossary of Symbols*).

Formulae

The foregoing assumptions imply that the total 'phenotypic' or observable variance (V_P) is to be partitioned into at least four contributary components, i.e. that

$$V_P = V_A + V_{AM} + V_D + V_E \qquad \ldots \ (4)$$

We can, if we wish, split V_E as before into V_{EC} and V_{ES}. Here V_A denotes what is usually termed the 'additive variance' and specifies the amount of genetic variance that would be expected if neither dominance nor assortative mating were operative. Writers on animal genetics describe it as the 'variance of breeding values', since dominance has no effect on the resemblance between parents and their offspring. The ratio of the additive variance to the total observable variance, V_A/V_P, is therefore often designated the 'narrow heritability' (frequently the adjective is omitted).

V_{AM} denotes the variance due to assortative mating. This is a factor that is hardly ever mentioned in work on the genetics of plants and animals, no doubt because the experimentalist is nearly always able to ensure that mating is random. Since its effects are transmitted from the parents to their offspring, it will be convenient to expand the formula for heritability (in the sense of breeding value) so as to include this further component. Accordingly, let us write[1]

$$V_H = V_A + V_{AM} \qquad \ldots \ (5)$$

V_D denotes the variance due to dominance. When present, this is also a component in the total genetic variance. Thus we have now subdivided the entire genetic factor afresh into three distinct factors, and can write

$$V_G = V_A + V_{AM} + V_D \qquad \dots (6)$$

The additive and dominant components are necessarily independent, owing to the way they are defined and calculated; nor is there any evidence to suggest a correlation between assortative mating and the other two components. We can therefore assume that each of the factors is independent of the others.

The relation between this threefold method of partitioning genetic variance and the twofold method adopted in the earlier approach (eqn 3 above) is easily established. With the present method a simple but rather lengthy proof leads to the following expression for the correlation between ordinary sibs (Burt, 1971, table III, eqns 8 and 18; Burt and Howard, 1956, tables VI and VII and eqn 13b):

$$r_{st} = \frac{\frac{1}{2}V_A + V_{AM} + \frac{1}{4}V_D + V_{EC}}{V_A + V_{AM} + V_D + V_{EC} + V_{ES}} \qquad \dots (7)$$

(In deducing formulae for correlations between relatives the result obtained is intuitively plausible: the numerical coefficients of the several variances—here $\frac{1}{2}$, 1, and $\frac{1}{4}$, are simply the probabilities that a gene in one member of the pair will be identical with a gene in the other member.) Now by equation 2

$$r_{st} = \frac{V_{GC} + V_{EC}}{V_{GC} + V_{GS} + V_{EC} + V_{ES}}$$

Hence $\qquad V_{GC} = \frac{1}{2}V_A + \frac{1}{4}V_D + V_{AM} \qquad \dots (8)$

and $\qquad V_{GS} = \frac{1}{2}V_A + \frac{3}{4}V_D \qquad \dots (9)$

Taking equation 4 as our basic formula, we have four hypothetical quantities to determine. If, as before, we put $V_P = 1$, we shall need only three empirical observations. The most convenient to take are the following:

1. r_{mza}, the correlation for monozygotic twins reared apart. Fisher, who was concerned with adults not with children, made no use of correlations between identical twins or between sibs or twins reared apart, doubtless because no reliable figures were then available. Our choice of this correlation has been criticized on two grounds: the correlation actually observed, it is said, might well

have been augmented either by selective placement or by the similarity of the prenatal environment. However, in the case of twins the attempt at selective placement proves almost impossible in practice, because the need for boarding out one or both of them cannot be foreseen early enough to be sure of finding a foster-mother similar in social status to that of the children's own mother: that this was so in the case of our own data is confirmed by the figures we have given for the social and economic conditions of the homes. The embryological evidence indicates that the intra-uterine conditions of twins are more likely to produce differences than similarities; and such conditions as cytoplasmic asymmetry may even have the effect of a slight quasi-genetic difference. That being so, we may validly take $r_{mza} = V_G/V_P$, at least to a close approximation. This at once gives us a value for V_G.

2. To determine the presence and influence of dominance we can make use of the fact that it affects only the correlations between collateral relatives (sibs, twins, etc.), not the correlation between parents and offspring, r_{po}. Since each child derives half its genes from the father and half from the mother, the correlation between children and one or other of their parents, so far as it is due to genetic influences only, will be $\frac{1}{2}V_H/V_P$, where V_H, it will be remembered, denotes the variance due to inheritable genes. When mating is random, this will be $\frac{1}{2}V_A/V_P$, as can be directly shown (Burt, 1971, table III; Burt and Howard, 1956, table V). When, owing to assortative mating, some of the father's genes are identical with those of the mother, the value of V_H will be in-creased by a certain amount which we have termed V_{AM} (eqn 5). Let r_{pp} denote the observed correlation between fathers and mothers. Now, if the assessment for a particular parent, a father say, deviates from the mean for the population by a unit amount, then the other parent (the mother) will on an average deviate by a fraction equal to r_{pp}. The mean deviation of the parents will thus be $\frac{1}{2}(1 + r_{pp})$, and the expected deviation of the offspring will consist of the inheritable part of this, i.e. by V_G/V_P times the mean deviation of the parents. Thus the correlation between one parent and the offspring will be

$$r_{po} = \frac{1}{2}\frac{V_H}{V_P}(1 + r_{pp}) \qquad \ldots \quad (10)$$

(A formal algebraic proof can be obtained by making certain obvious modifications in the tables just cited.) Unlike inbreeding, which involves matings between similar *genotypes*, assortative mating increases the relative frequencies of the extreme homozygotes only, not of all homozygotes, and causes a much larger increase in the total variance. It follows that

$$\frac{V_H}{V_P} = \frac{2r_{po}}{1 + r_{pp}} \qquad \ldots \quad (11)$$

and, given observed values for these two correlations, we can at once calculate

$$V_D = V_G - V_H \qquad \ldots \quad (12)$$

3. However, the influence of assortative mating is of importance in and for itself. The obvious evidence for any such contribution is the presence of a positive and significant correlation between husbands and wives for the characteristic investigated (r_{pp}). But the value actually observed will be the correlation between the phenotypic assessments for the two parents; i.e. it will depend partly on acquired characteristics. What we need to know is the proportion of the full breeding value (V_H) contributed by the additional variance resulting from assortative mating, i.e. V_{AM}/V_H; this will evidently be $(V_H/V_P)r_{pp}$. Hence

$$\frac{V_{AM}}{V_P} = \frac{V_H}{V_P} \cdot \frac{V_{AM}}{V_H} = \frac{(V_H)^2}{V_P} r_{pp} \qquad \ldots \quad (13)$$

Wright's deduction leads to $V_{AM} = [r_{pp}/(1 - r_{pp})]V_p$, which yields slightly different numerical values; but his assumptions seem oversimplified (cf. Crow and Kimura, 1970, pp. 148–52, 156–9).

4. If, as before, we wish to split the variance for environmental factors into common and specific factors, we can take the difference between the correlations for identical twins reared together and reared apart, though, as we shall see later, it is a little precarious to rely on just one set of differences.

Main results

Let us now consider the results obtained when we insert in the formulae thus derived, values actually observed for the three kinds of correlations we have proposed. The figures set out in table 3 are taken from Burt (1966). The correlations for monozygotic twins therefore are slightly different from those available for our earlier investigations (table 1), and are based on a larger sample.

Table 3: Observed correlations

Group	No. pairs	Height	Intelligence		Attain-ments
			(Burt)	(Other investi-gators)	
Monozygotic twins reared together	95	0·962	0·925	0·874	0·983
Monozygotic twins reared apart	53	0·943	0·874	0·752	0·623
Parents and children	374	0·507	0·492	0·498	0·514
Fathers and mothers	95	0·280	0·379	0·403	0·678

Note. The 'No. pairs' refers to the groups on which the three investigations carried out by myself were based, not to those of 'Other investigators'.

Using the above coefficients, we can now calculate provisional estimates for the four component variances.

If we accept these estimates at their face value, the following conclusions may be drawn. Apparent intelligence, assessed in the way described, is influenced by much the same genetic factors and to almost the same extent as bodily characteristics. There is clear evidence for the effects of both dominance and assortative mating. Hence the common practice of calculating expected correlations on the basis of additive variance only (0·50 for both sibs and parents and children, 0·25 for grandparents and grandchildren, and so on) is scarcely justifiable. As we might have guessed from the differences between the observed correlations (table 3, line 3), and indeed from everyday observation, the influence of assortative mating is appreciably larger for intellectual than for bodily characteristics; the effects of environmental conditions are likewise far more marked. In the case of educational attainments, however, the large value for the environmental factor almost certainly includes the effects of the covariance between environmental conditions and innate intellectual ability.

A single set of figures derived from a single research and based on the minimum number of observed coefficients is admittedly inconclusive. But, as before, we can check the results by applying the same procedure to data collected from other investigators (table 4, col. 3). The main results are much the same. The variance

Table 4: Analysis of variance

Source	Height	Intelligence		Attainments
		(Burt)	(Other investigators)	
Additive genetic (V_A/V_P)	61·6	52·1	50·7	35·8
Assortative mating (V_{AM}/V_P)	17·5	19·3	20·3	25·4
Dominance (V_D/V_P)	15·2	16·0	4·2	1·1
Genetic total (V_G/V_P)	94·3	87·4	75·2	62·3
Common environmental (V_{EC}/V_P)	1·9	5·1	12·2	36·0
Specific environmental (V_{ES}/V_P)	3·8	7·5	12·6	1·7
Environmental total (V_E/V_P)	5·7	12·6	24·8	37·7
Total	100·0	100·0	100·0	100·0

for dominance, however, is reduced, while that for environmental factors is considerably increased; this, no doubt, is because most other investigators have relied on unchecked scores, usually obtained with tests that were largely verbal: the figures taken from our own studies are the 'final assessments', obtained after the raw test scores queried by teachers had been checked and corrected by a re-examination involving 'performance tests' and other supplementary data.

The three types of correlations selected as our initial data are by no means the only ones we could have used. When, for example, no trustworthy figure is available for the correlation between parents and children, we could, as before (eqn 3), use the correlation for sibs reared together. However, in that case one of the three equations that would need to be solved simultaneously would be a quadratic; and the calculations would consequently be far more complicated and less satisfactory. Instead let us inquire how the inferences derived from this second mode of analysis compare with those obtained from the first. Using equations 8 and 9 we can calculate fresh estimates for the variances of the common and specific genetic factors (V_{GC} and V_{GS}). For intelligence they are as follows: (*a*) estimated from our own data (table 4, col. ii) 49·3 and 38·1 per cent, total 87·4 per cent; (*b*) estimated from the data of other investigators (table 4, col. iii) 46·7 and 28·5 per cent, total 75·2 per cent. These results, it will be seen, are in close agreement with those we previously reached with an entirely different set of correlations, and entirely different method of analysis (table 2). The fact that, in the case of intellectual abilities though not of stature, V_{GC} exceeds V_{GS} is now seen to result from the effects of V_{AM}, i.e. of assortative mating.

It will have been remarked that in our various equations we have used the same value for the effects of a common environment, whether the relatives are sibs, identical twins, or (in other studies) fraternal twins. Now, as several writers have justly stressed, the similarity in environmental conditions of identical twins is almost certainly greater than for fraternal twins, and for fraternal twins than for ordinary sibs. This might conceivably account for the fact that in table 2 the value for V_E is larger than the value reached in table 4. Nevertheless, the real question is not whether these differences exist, but whether they are likely to affect the particular characteristic or type of assessment with which we are concerned. It is desirable that a survey should always include data for dizygotic and monozygotic twins as well as for sibs, and, if possible, for pairs reared apart as well as together (cf. Burt, 1966); estimates for the common environmental variances can then be computed for the different pairs, and, when necessary, a suitable correction made. Here I need only say that, with the small samples usually available, the slight modifications thus suggested, even if justified, are not statistically significant.

Testing the model

The conclusions we have reached have been derived from a hypothetical set of assumptions about the mode of mental inheritance. The crucial issue is: how far are the inferences so deduced confirmed by applying them to assess or predict other observable data? Let us therefore use the variances tabulated above to calculate expected values for correlations between relatives of varying degrees of kinship other than those on which these variances were actually based.

Let us begin with the correlations for ordinary sibs brought up together, obtainable from samples bigger and more numerous than those for any other pairs. For these I shall take the figures given in our latest survey (Burt, 1966), since they were derived from larger numbers and with better tests than the correlations used for our preliminary analysis (table 1). The appropriate formula for the expected values was given in equation 7. Inserting the estimates for the component variances from table 4, we obtain the figures shown in table 5 (line 1); the correlations actually observed are given in the line beneath. The agreement is reasonably close; it will be noted that the correlations between parent and child, are, as usual, somewhat greater. As our formulae suggest, this can now be explained as another consequence of assortative mating. In the case of intelligence, there are differences both in the theoretical and the observed correlations between my values and those for other investigators. These are doubtless due to the different methods of assessing intelligence—raw test results with most other investigators, carefully checked figures in our own inquiries.

Table 5: Correlations between sibs

Values	Height	Intelligence		Attainments
		(Burt)	(Other investigators)	
Expected	0·540	0·545	0·589	0·796
Observed	0·501	0·531	0·554	0·803

The comparison between expected and observed correlations can be extended to relatives of other degrees of kinship. In the course of our surveys we have collected correlations for a wide variety of relationships—ranging from monozygotic twins, full sibs, half sibs, etc., to unrelated children brought up together or apart. Fifteen of the most reliable coefficients are set out in the article just quoted (table 4) and compared with the values to be expected on the foregoing assumptions. It will be seen that, when due allowance is made for assortative mating, common environmental influences, and (when relevant) for dominance, the agreement is decidedly better than when (as is more usually done) these complicating factors are disregarded.

The values for the component variances tabulated above are by no means the best that could be attained. Here, in order to allow for an empirical confirmation of the method, the data used have consisted of the minimum number of observed correlations. Plainly, still better estimates might be secured if we included all the available correlations and applied either the method of least squares or (what in principle would seem preferable) that of maximum likelihood. Yet, once again the improvements that result prove as a rule to be much too slight to be statistically significant; and, until larger samples are obtained, it is doubtful whether the gain is worth the labour.

To decide such questions as these we evidently need some acceptable means of testing statistical significance. In comparing correlations Fisher's z-transformation has been used. In comparing variances a standard error for the difference between variances might in principle be used; but, since we are dealing with hypothetical estimates, not with values actually observed, the requisite calculations entail an almost prohibitive amount of labour. It seems better to start with the sampling errors of the quantities that have been directly observed, i.e. of the empirical correlations or covariances. In table 4 our figures for the total genetic variance are simply values of the correlations for monozygotic twins reared apart (r_{mza}), computed in the case of intelligence from 53 pairs (0·874): if we adopt a 'confidence coefficient' of 0·95, then, on applying Fisher's z-transformation, the confidence limits for such a correlation would be 0·785 and 0·925. In table 2 the values for the common factor variance were based on r_{sa}, e.g. for intelligence on a correlation of 0·468 obtained from 156 pairs; in this case the confidence interval extends from 0·405 to 0·529—a range almost as wide as before in spite of the increased numbers. The values of V_{AM} were based on two observed correlations: in such a case we can take the lower and higher of the confidence limits for one correlation and combine each of them with the opposite type of limit for the other correlation; from these figures we can then deduce limits for V_{AM}. And similarly for the remaining variances, and so finally for the expected correlations calculated for sibs or other relatives. The range of variation proves to be fairly wide, but not so wide as the variation in the fluctuations exhibited by the corresponding correlations that have been reported in the literature (cf. Erlenmeyer-Kimling and Jarvik, 1963).

Conclusions and practical implications

The prime requisite for a working model is that it should be as simple as possible, provided it yields an adequate fit to all the relevant data, i.e. provided the discrepancies that emerge are devoid of statistical significance. Judged by the investigations here described the model proposed appears eminently satisfactory. It is elaborate enough to furnish estimates that stand up to verification, and simple enough to demand only the most elementary types of calculation.

The two main conclusions we have reached seem clear and beyond all question. The hypothesis of a general factor entering into every type of cognitive process, tentatively suggested by speculations derived from neurology and biology, is fully borne out by the statistical evidence; and the contention that differences in this general factor depend largely on the individual's genetic constitution appears incontestable. The concept of an innate, general, cognitive ability, which follows from these two assumptions, though admittedly a sheer abstraction, is thus wholly consistent with the empirical facts.

The practical implications are obvious, though the problems involved are much more complex than is commonly supposed. First of all, we can safely assert that, provided we adopt the methods of assessment described above instead of merely relying on the raw test scores, our estimates of a child's innate general ability can claim a reasonable degree of accuracy, measured by $h^2 = V_G/V_P$; secondly, follow-up studies demonstrate that these estimates are closely correlated with the children's actual attainments both at school and in later life.

From this it is tempting to infer that each individual's innate capacity sets a fixed upper limit to what in actual practice he is likely to achieve under existing conditions. A favourite way of putting this is to interpret 'capacity' in terms of cubic content: 'it is impossible for a pint pot to hold more than a pint of milk'—a picturesque but misleading analogy. Twenty per cent of the children with I.Q.s of 90, for example, have educational quotients of over 100; and much the same is true at other levels (Burt, 1962, table XIX). Nor can these anomalies be explained away as errors of estimation. A given genetic endowment is compatible with a whole range of developmental reactions and consequently of acquired attainments. All that a knowledge of a child's genetic endowment permits us to infer are the limits of that range, where 'limit' is defined in terms of probability. The choice of a minimum probability will doubtless be decided in the main by financial considerations. Were more lavish funds available for the compensatory education of the dull and for the special education of the gifted, both would attain a higher level of achievement. What such levels are likely to be can be roughly predicted by a knowledge of genetics: a more precise determination can only be secured by pilot experiments.

Suggestions for further research

At the moment the most glaring need is for much larger samples. These can best be secured by accumulating results from a number of surveys carried out in different educational areas. In England something of this sort was practicable before the so-called '11-plus examinations' went out of fashion. Unfortunately the few that have been published were undertaken by relatively inexperienced postgraduate students. In my view such inquiries should be planned and supervised by educational psychologists who are members of the local staff and thus acquainted with the schools, the teachers and the social conditions, and they should be carried out by teachers with a psychological training, not by academic research students who enter the classrooms as strangers. The co-operation of a geneticist, proficient in quantitative techniques, would be invaluable.

Research in the human sciences is subject to obvious handicaps. Human beings are not amenable to full experimental control. We cannot mate men and women according to some methodological scheme, or backcross the hybrid offspring with one of the parents. It would therefore be useful if the validity of our basic assumptions and our working formulae were checked by applying them to creatures which impose no such restrictions and are available in far larger samples. We might, for example, test them on appropriate stocks of *Drosophila melanogaster* (the familiar banana-fly) by measuring various graded characteristics both physical (e.g. body weight) and behavioural (e.g. phototaxis). Assortative mating could be imitated by introducing a known amount of inbreeding, and the environmental conditions varied to ascertain the effect of correlations with genetic differences.

With human beings, when the problem is primarily psychological, statistical studies of populations should always be supplemented by case studies of individuals: early histories will often shed further light on the origin and development of this or that peculiarity. Tests should be supplemented by what Binet called the *méthode clinique*, and interpreted by introspective observations, designed to verify the tacit assumption that they really do test what they are intended to assess. After all each child is a complex and conscious organism, not a mere unit in a statistical sample.

In this chapter I have concentrated on the study of 'intelligence' defined as general cognitive ability. The next step should be to undertake similar inquiries with other mental characteristics, particularly with special abilities and temperamental qualities ('personality'). A few tentative researches in this direction, based on much the same methods, have already been published (cf. Burt, 1938, 1949, 1950 and refs). Here too we found it essential to begin with a preliminary factorial analysis; as a glance at the current textbooks suffices to show, psychologists, unlike their colleagues in other branches of science, are surprisingly inconsistent and arbitrary in the way they distinguish and classify what they suppose to be the basic processes of the human 'mind' (or of human 'behaviour' if that phrase be preferred). However, in studying mental qualities that are not cognitive, or cognitive qualities that are not general, the problems of inheritability have proved to be much more complicated and elusive.

Nevertheless, the results already obtained for temperamental qualities (cf. Burt, 1938) are promising enough to show that these further applications of the methods we have outlined are well worth following up; and many of our tentative inferences have since been confirmed by others who began their work at University College London (e.g. Cattell, 1946; Eysenck, 1953; despite minor divergencies in terminology and other details). Thus, notwithstanding the provisional nature of the results here recorded, one claim can, I think, safely be advanced. The recent cry that 'the old issue of nature versus nurture is now out of date' is itself outdated. Modern genetics, besides its many profitable applications to agriculture and stockbreeding, has already made valuable contributions to human physiology, pathology and medicine; it will assuredly prove yet more informative and fruitful in the field of psychology.

Notes and references

1 For variances derived from an analysis of variance I retain the upper-case subscripts used in my earlier papers. This should prevent V_G and V_H being confused with the symbols V_g ($=$ my v_A) and V_h as used by Crow and Kimura (1970, Glossary, p. 580).

Burt, C. (1938) 'The analysis of temperament', *Br. J. med. Psychol.*, *17*, 158–88.

Burt, C. (1949) 'The structure of the mind', *Br. J. educ. Psychol.*, *19*, 100–11, 170–99.

Burt, C. (1950) 'Factorial study of the emotions'. In Reymert, M. L. (ed.), *Feelings and Emotions*. New York: McGraw-Hill.

Burt, C. (1962) *Mental and Scholastic Tests*. London: Staples Press.

Burt, C. (1966) 'The genetic determination of differences in intelligence', *Br. J. Psychol.*, *57*, 137–53.

Burt, C. (1971) 'Quantitative genetics in psychology', *Br. J. math. statist. Psychol.*, *24*, 1–71.

Burt, C. (1972) 'The inheritance of general intelligence', *Am. Psychol.*, *22*, 3, 175–90.

Burt, C. and Howard, M. (1956) 'The multifactorial theory of inheritance and its application to intelligence', *Br. J. statist. Psychol.*, *9*, 95–131.

Cattell, R. B. (1946) *The Description and Measurement of Personality*. Yonkers: World Book Co.

Crow, J. E. and Kimura, M. (1970) *An Introduction to Population Genetics Theory*. New York: Harper and Row.

Erlenmeyer-Kimling and Jarvik, L. F. (1963) 'Genetics and intelligence', *Science*, *142*, 1477–9.

Eysenck, H. J. (1953) *The Structure of Human Personality*. London: Methuen.

Fisher, R. A. (1918) 'The correlation between relatives on the supposition of Mendelian inheritance', *Trans. Roy. Soc. Edin.*, *52*, 399–433.

Acknowledgment

This chapter is based on Burt's article on 'The inheritance of general intelligence', first printed in the March 1972 issue of the *American Psychologist*: copyright 1972 by the American Psychological Association and reprinted here in revised form by permission.

Appendix

Table 6: Correlations between relations

	(Burt)		(Other investigators)		Theoretical value
	Number of pairs	Correlations	Number of investigations	Median correlation	
Direct line					
with parents as adults	963	0·495	13	0·50	0·49
with parents as children	106	0·562	—	—	0·49
with grandparents	321	0·335	2	0·24	0·31
Collaterals					
between monozygotic twins					
reared together	95	0·925	13	0·87	1·00
reared apart	53	0·874	3	0·75	1·00
between dizygotic twins					
same sex	71	0·553	8	0·56	0·54
different sex	56	0·524	6	0·49	0·50
between full sibs					
reared together	987	0·507	36	0·55	0·52
reared apart	151	0·438	3	0·47	0·52
between half sibs					
paternal			97	0·21	0·25
maternal			138	0·28	0·25
between uncle (or aunt) and nephew or niece	375	0·354	—	—	0·31
between first cousins	552	0·215	2	0·26	0·18
between second cousins	127	0·164	—	—	0·14
Unrelated persons					
foster parent and child	88	0·193	3	0·20	0·00
children reared together	136	0·267	4	0·23	0·00
children reared apart	200	−0·042	2	−0·01	0·00

Table 7: Correlations for intelligence and attainments

	Number of pairs	Intelligence	Reading	Spelling	Arithmetic	General Attainments
Monozygotic twins						
Reared together	95	0·925	0·954	0·947	0·862	0·983
Reared apart	53	0·874	0·602	0·592	0·725	0·623
Dizygotic twins						
Reared together	127	0·534	0·915	0·923	0·748	0·831
Full sibs						
Reared together	264	0·531	0·836	0·848	0·754	0·803
Reared apart	151	0·438	0·497	0·483	0·563	0·526

CHAPTER TEN

The identification of the gifted

Definition

To define the gifted child a wide variety of formulae have been suggested. Some are based primarily on administrative considerations, others on the pet theories of the writers. In the main, as Dr Anastasi points out, 'British writers have put the prime emphasis on *g* (the general factor), while American psychologists nowadays focus upon "group factors", and regard *g* as minor and secondary', or indeed as non-existent.[1]

Both Hollingworth and Terman in their pioneer investigations accepted Galton's assumption that the primary factor determining the potential achievement of each individual was his innate allowance of 'general ability', and therefore based their definitions of the gifted child on the I.Q. as assessed by tests of intelligence.[2] Terman's borderline was 140 I.Q. Most British psychologists have adopted essentially the same principle with a somewhat lower borderline, usually determined by the requirements of the secondary (grammar) schools.

Later American writers have tended to adopt the standpoint taken by Thurstone in his early work on *Primary Mental Abilities* and to prefer a far broader and more generous type of definition. DeHaan and Havighurst (1957), in *Educating Gifted Children*, begin by describing 'intellectual ability' as 'composed of several parts, sometimes called "primary mental abilities" '. These constitute the basis of certain 'areas of talent'—'verbal skill, spatial imagination, science, mechanics, art, music, social leadership', etc.; and a gifted child is accordingly defined as one who is 'in the top 10 per cent of his age-group in one or more of the areas listed'. Differences in these potential abilities are assumed to be innate. But, since their development is so often uneven, it is considered quite unsuitable to base the 'screening' on tests of 'general intelligence'. The aim should be to discover 'as wide a variety of talent as possible', and therefore the most useful method will be to employ 'different aptitude tests' and construct 'individual profile cards'. Since eight or more areas are enumerated, it would follow that, if each was completely independent of the others, the number of gifted children in the population would amount to at least 80 per cent. Actually the number expected is about 20 per cent, or 'possibly as much as 25 per cent'. Hence there must be, as indeed the writers elsewhere recognize, a good deal of overlapping; and the figures cited seem far more consonant with a theory that recognizes a factor of 'general ability'.

Many writers hold that both the foregoing views contain elements of truth, and therefore recognize two groups—those who are 'gifted all round' and those who are 'specially gifted'. As representing this eclectic principle we may take A. O. Heck. The term 'gifted child' (without further qualification) 'refers to a child of high intelligence quotient'. Regardless of how talented a child may be along a particular line, if he does not have a high intelligence quotient he is not considered 'gifted' (where the word is used without any qualifying adverb). As a convenient border-line Heck suggests an I.Q. of 125 (which would cut off the top 5 per cent or thereabouts). In addition, however, he recognizes a further group whom he calls the '*specially* gifted'; and to these he devotes a separate chapter. They will be 'only average from the point of view of academic ability' (and so can easily be overlooked by the teacher), but may be exceptionally endowed with poetic, musical, artistic or mechanical talent.

Recently a number of American authors have sought to make 'creativity' the defining characteristic. 'No child should be designated "gifted" [so we are told] merely because he is proficent in those rather mechanical intellectual qualities which are measured by intelligence tests. His work must be original and creative.' The arguments for this view are based on the discovery that the tests of creativity devised by these writers show no correlation with the tests of intelligence which they employed. But, as I have tried to show elsewhere (*Br. J. educ. Psychol., 32*, 1962, 292–8), this result is rather a reflection on the efficiency of the tests used than a 'new discovery'. There is no genuine creativity without an equally high degree of general intelligence. But this is a problem we shall return to later on.

Scholarship examinations

If their supernormal achievements are largely dependent on supernormal abilities which are innate, it is plainly desirable, in the interest both of the community and of the children themselves, that those who are thus highly endowed should be discovered at the earliest possible age and accorded the educational and social opportunities which their abilities deserve. In Britain there has been for centuries a system of scholarships, provided either by educational foundations or by private bodies, which enabled 'scholars of promise' to attend places of higher education, such as grammar schools, public schools and the colleges of the older universities. After the passing of the Education Act of 1902, regulations were issued which obliged the new 'secondary schools' to allow 25 per cent of the annual admissions to be available without fee; and, in order to ensure that the entrants were capable of profiting by the education offered, applicants for these 'free places' were required to pass an entrance test, usually a written examination in English and arithmetic.[3]

Accordingly, in 1905 the Education Authority for London introduced a 'junior county scholarship scheme'. By 1913 nearly 2 per cent of the pupils in each age-group, as they arrived at the appropriate age, were awarded scholarships to 'secondary' schools of the 'grammar' type. However, a geographical survey revealed that the numbers varied widely from one electoral division to another: in the poorest the proportions were about 0·3 per cent; in the comparatively well-to-do between 6 and 7 per cent. And further investigations plainly demonstrated that a number of the brightest children were being missed because, owing to the low economic and cultural conditions prevailing in their homes, their scholastic attainments fell greatly below their real abilities.[4]

The introduction of psychological tests

Experiments were therefore made in introducing (i) a group test of intelligence into the written scholarship examination taken by all candidates, and (ii) a supplementary individual examination consisting of an interview and various additional tests for borderline cases and for those pupils who had been nominated by teachers but had failed in the written examination. However, most grammar schools were naturally reluctant to accept pupils, no matter how bright, who had not already acquired a good foundation in the basic subjects. And it quickly became obvious that the time for identifying children of high ability was not at the age of eleven, when the scholarship examination was taken, but at a much earlier stage—in fact, as soon as the child came up from the infants' department. Teachers were therefore urged to start a school record card for each child as soon as he entered the junior department and to examine their pupils at regular intervals with standardized tests both of ability and attainment, partly to ascertain which of them appeared to be definitely subnormal or supernormal, and partly to see that the child's school progress was keeping pace with his mental development.

Method of assessment

As we have seen, in the earliest researches on intelligence testing carried out in Britain the tests were mainly non-verbal, applied individually, and repeated at least once. In the more theoretical researches the essential principle was to test all the main types of cognitive processes—sensory, motor, associative, relational, reproductive and productive—and the assessments of a child's intelligence consisted in a weighted sum of his scores in each test, the weights being based on the partial regressions on the general factor common to all tests. For practical purposes it was deemed sufficient to administer a battery of tests for the most complex processes of which the particular children were capable: the resulting assessments were then submitted to the teachers for criticism, and, where discrepancies appeared, the child was examined afresh. Tests for scholastic aptitudes were kept separate from the tests of intelligence, and 'psychographs' were constructed to show in diagrammatic form the general pattern of the child's development, and in particular his special abilities or disabilities.

This would still seem to be the most appropriate procedure for the educational psychologist to follow, whether the child to be examined is subnormal or supernormal. For the teacher in the classroom much simpler methods are wanted; and there is still an urgent need for suitable tests designed expressly for English children.[5] For testing older children on a fairly extensive scale, as in the 11-plus examination, considerations of economy called for the use of written group tests, which of necessity tended to be largely verbal. In such cases, however, a good deal of misunderstanding would be avoided if the usual type of so-called 'intelligence' tests were rechristened 'general classification tests'.

Criticisms of intelligence testing

Recently, as we have seen, the selection of gifted children primarily on the basis of intelligence tests has encountered growing criticism. Such tests, it is argued, tend to pick out children typical of a particular type of culture and of a particular socio-economic class. Perhaps the fairest statement of this view is that of Dr Anastasi.[6] 'The original aim of intelligence tests', she writes, 'was to sample different abilities in order to arrive at an estimate of general level'; but, since 'the individual's standing in specific functions differs, such a general estimate is unsatisfactory. . . . Intelligence can only be defined in reference to a particular milieu.' Moreover, those who first studied the problem very naturally gave predominant weight to educational accomplishments. 'Literature and science were rated higher than (say) skating or cooking.' Hence the tests chosen to assess intelligence were 'overloaded with certain aptitudes', particularly verbal ability and 'the ability to succeed in our schools'. Geniuses selected by means of such tests would consequently be 'defined in terms of specific social criteria and a cultural frame of reference'.

These arguments, like those of so many contemporary critics, take it for granted that in psychology the word 'intelligence' has the same elastic meaning that it has in popular parlance. As already explained, however, the term was originally adopted as a convenient shorthand name for a well-defined concept, namely, inborn, general, cognitive capacity. The tests proposed were not selected because they were believed to measure those specific abilities that are most highly prized by Western communities, but because, as the statistical evidence showed, out of the whole range of cognitive abilities they furnished *the highest correlations with the general cognitive factor.* It is true that many of the problems are expressed in words; but, if the test is properly constructed and correctly selected, all the children to whom it is applied should be able to understand the words used, regardless of variations in their actual intelligence. That being so, the mere fact that the test is in verbal form does not convert it into a test of verbal ability.[7] But in any case the data furnished by tests should always be supplemented by information gained by systematic observation; and the teachers should be trained for this purpose.

Reliability and validity

The reliability of the best current tests of intelligence is between 0·90 to 0·95.[8] And their validity, it would appear, does not fall far short of these figures. An important study of the subject is contained in an authoritative report on the selection examination at 11-plus for entrance to grammar schools.[9] After a detailed check obtained by following up two age-groups and applying supplementary tests two or three years later, the investigators estimate that, of the various collections of tests and assessments they have examined, 'a fair number are able to provide validity coefficients of 0·90 or more'. This, however, would mean that 'even the best methods at present in use are likely to involve "wrong" allocations for about 10 per cent of the candidates'. Nevertheless, these 'wrong' allocations will not be *seriously* wrong. Those who were accepted and subsequently failed are not, as a rule, bad failures; and the rejected candidates who succeed in the later tests will not be remarkably successful. In short, nearly all the 'wrong' allocations are borderline cases anyway.

When the correlations are based on retests carried out after a longer interval of time, the values obtained vary far more widely. In a review of various investigations Thorndike reports that, in the course of five years, the average values dropped from about 0·90 to 0·70, i.e. roughly at a rate of about 0·04 per annum. The lowest values are usually obtained with (a) group testing, and (b) tests at an early age (6 to 8). 'If the first test is given as late as ten years of age, prediction may be much better.' Byrns and Henmon located 250 college students who had been examined eight or ten years previously with the Natural Intelligence Test, and found that the results correlated to the extent of 0·81 with the results of a test administered at college. Honzik found that Terman–Merrill scores obtained at the age of eight correlated with those obtained at the age of fourteen or fifteen to the extent of 0·83.[10]

Most of the foregoing results are derived from tests applied, not for purposes of research, but for the more practical purpose of academic selection. They consequently suffer from three disadvantages: (i) they are in almost every case based on incomplete samples. Candidates for the 11-plus examination, for instance, included neither pupils who are educationally subnormal nor the brightest children from the professional classes who would seldom attend the ordinary elementary school. (ii) The predictions are commonly derived from the results of a single examination, taken as they stand. (iii) The follow-up is usually confined to groups still more highly selected and is rarely continued to the adult stage. A longitudinal study begun in London over fifty years ago to some extent avoids these shortcomings. Between 1915 and 1920, at the outset of my work for the London County Council, my co-workers and I tested what we believed to be a completely representative sample of school children at the age of ten in one of the more typical London boroughs. The results obtained were carefully checked by the teachers, and doubtful cases retested. The pupils were then followed up and re-examined at intervals until they were grown up. Approximately ten years later, all those who could be traced (782 out of an original batch of about a thousand) were examined afresh; and the correlation between the initial and terminal assessments amounted to 0·84. The average change in I.Q. was 6·7. Of those originally assessed as 'highly intelligent' (122·5 I.Q. or over), two-thirds were similarly assessed on the later occasion, and one-third as only 'moderately intelligent' (107·5 to 122·5 I.Q.).[11] Leta Hollingworth followed up fifty-six highly intelligent children who at 8½ had Stanford–Binet I.Q.s averaging 156. At 15 they were still in the top 1 per cent. At 18½ years, forty-six were still in the top 1 per cent, and all but one in the top 3 per cent.[12]

Psychiatric theories

In London and elsewhere these novel proposals were at first strongly opposed by many of the school doctors. To introduce a formal examination at this early age, particularly one on which the child's whole future might depend, would be to subject the candidates to an intolerable strain. There would, it was predicted, be many a nervous breakdown as a result. In any case, so they argued, the whole underlying theory rested on a gross misunderstanding of mental development.

Before Galton succeeded in placing individual psychology on a sound scientific basis, almost the only attempts to study mental differences by the methods of the older sciences were those undertaken by practising physicians.[13] As Stern points out, doctors in those days, 'commonly classified mankind into qualitative types; the normal or average individual was considered to be sharply separated from the aberrant or exceptional types, whether the aberration took the form of underdevelopment or over-development'. Genius was widely assumed to be as much a sign of pathological disorder as imbecility. The culmination of this theory is to be found in a celebrated work by Lombroso (Professor of Legal Medicine at Turin) entitled *The Man of Genius*. After a lively description of selected cases, illustrated by numerous anecdotes, he concludes that 'genius is a degenerative psychosis of the epileptoid group'.

Even today the theory is by no means defunct. It has been defended by Kretschmer, Lange-Eichbaum, and several psycho-analytic writers,[14] and is still widely accepted by numerous parents, school doctors, and popular writers on child psychology. Every-one is familiar with the stereotyped picture of the infant prodigy painted for us in such romances as Marie Corelli's *Mighty Atom*— a pale, sickly, nervous little bookworm, with bulging forehead and big round spectacles, hopeless at games, haunted by night-mares, pining away and dying prematurely, or else ending the tragedy of precocious childhood by a pathetic suicide. How far is this familiar portrait borne out by the actual facts?

The method adopted by most of the medical writers just quoted was to select an impressive series of cases exemplifying their conclusions, with no attempt to compare the frequency of the various symptoms reported among the geniuses (pallor, spinal curvature, premature baldness, tics, alcoholism, sexual abnormali-ties, visionary experiences, fanatical beliefs, and the like) with their incidence among the general population of the same place and period. Clearly, the only satisfactory procedure is to carry out an *ad hoc* survey either of the general population itself or of an un-selected and representative sample, and thus obtain comparable data, not only for the gifted individuals but also for a control group of ordinary or average individuals, all tested and assessed by the same objective procedures. This was, in fact, the scheme advocated by Galton.

London surveys

In 1915, as Psychologist to the London Education Authority, I was able, with the aid of teachers and others, to organize a series of surveys in London schools, beginning with a study of the entire school population in one of the largest of the boroughs (St Pancras). At the upper end of the intellectual scale we selected the ablest pupils in each age-group and compiled a brief but systematic case-history for each one. The borderline adopted was one which would pick out the brightest 3 per cent.[15] So far as possible, each of these was followed up for the remainder of his school career, whether or not he obtained a scholarship to a 'secondary' school. Particular attention was paid to those who either failed in the scholarship examination or, after winning a scholarship, failed to fulfil their early promise.

The Californian investigation

But by far the most thorough inquiry of this kind is that begun in the schools of California by Professor Terman and his collaborators in 1921, and followed up at intervals until quite recent years.[16] Since it is beyond question much more comprehensive than any other investigation, and since the results obtained seem for the most part to agree with those obtained elsewhere, I shall make it the basis of my review.

For purposes of the research a gifted child was defined as one with an I.Q. of 140 or more. A small number were also included with I.Q.s slightly below this borderline. In London, as the survey was carried out from within the Education Department, it was possible to screen every school in the area chosen; in the Californian survey this was impracticable, and the search was mainly confined to the five largest cities. The teachers were asked to nominate (a) the brightest three or four in each class, and (b) the youngest. Their nominees were then progressively sifted in turn with (i) a group test, (ii) an abridged version of the Stanford–Binet scale, and finally (iii) the complete Stanford–Binet. This yielded 661 cases (354 boys and 307 girls) aged, with few exceptions, between seven and seventeen. These formed the main experimental group. Expressed as percentages, the number discovered varied from 1·00 per cent in Berkeley to 0·35 per cent in San Francisco, and 0·30 per cent in Los Angeles. An additional batch, less elaborately selected, brought the total up to well over 1,000. Control groups drawn from the ordinary population were also studied for particular aspects of the inquiry.

Socio-economic level

1. *Californian survey*. The occupational status of the fathers of the gifted groups is indicated in the second column of table 1. That of the adult male inhabitants of California is shown for comparison in the first column.

Table 1: Classification of occupations (Californian children)

Occupational category	1. All males in California	2. Fathers of gifted children	3. Gifted children when adults
Professional	5·7	33·3	45·4
Semi-professional and higher business	8·1	32·4	21·9
Skilled, including clerical	36·7	25·8	6·2
Semi-skilled	31·6	7·6	0·7
Day labourers	17·8	0·9	—

The proportion of fathers belonging to the professional or semi-professional classes is more than four times that in the general population; comparatively few are drawn from the ranks of semi-skilled or unskilled labour.[17] The condition of the majority is described as 'fairly comfortable, rarely wealthy'; a few were 'living in what might truly be called poverty'. The number of Jewish children was about twice what would be expected from their proportion in the general population. The number who were of Scottish origin was also unexpectedly high.

2. *London survey*. Corresponding figures obtained from the London surveys are shown in table 2. The classification adopted is virtually that drawn up for an inquiry on vocational guidance carried out jointly by the National Institute of Industrial Psychology and the Psychological Committee of the Medical Council.[18] It is somewhat similar to the fivefold classification introduced by the Census in 1911, but based on the average intelligence of persons following the occupations included in each class. The first column shows the number of adult males (expressed as percentages of the total population) following the types of occupation

Table 2: Classification by occupations (London children)

Occupational class	1. Percentage of all occupied adult males	2. Children of scholarship ability in each class	3. Children to whom scholarships were awarded in each class	4. Proportion of each class possessing university ability	5. Proportion of those with university ability in each class
1. Highest professional work (lawyers, doctors, higher administrative posts in state or business, university and secondary school teachers)	0·3	0·2	0·2	23·8	4·6
2. Lower professional and technical work (including elementary teachers and executive posts)	3·0	16·6	27·8	10·2	19·2
3. Clerical and highly skilled (clerks of lower grade and highly skilled labour)	12·0	24·4	30·1	3·1	23·7
4. Skilled labour and minor commercial posts (small-tradespeople, shop assistants)	26·0	39·7	32·5	1·6	26·5
5. Semi-skilled labour and poorest commercial positions	32·5	13·6	7·1	0·9	18·7
6. Unskilled labour and coarse manual work	19·0	5·2	2·3	0·5	6·4
7. Casual labour	7·0	0·3	—	0·2	0·9
8. Defectives and other institutional cases	0·2	—	—	—	—
TOTAL or AVERAGE	100·0	100·0	100·0	1·5	100·0

Note. The figures in columns 4 and 5 are to be read as follows. In col. 4: out of all the children belonging to class 1 (highest professional) 23·8 per cent possess ability fitting them for entrance to a university; out of class 2 only 10·2 per cent; and so on. In col. 5: out of all these children who possess the ability requisite for a university, only 4·6 per cent come from class 1; 19·2 per cent from class 2; and so on. (For the way this column is calculated see text.)

specified; the second and third the occupations of the fathers of (*a*) pupils whose general ability (as assessed in the survey) should have enabled them to win junior county scholarships, and (*b*) pupils who actually succeeded in winning such scholarships. At the time of the survey, hardly any parents belonging to the higher professional or administrative classes sent their children to ordinary elementary schools. The low figures for the first occupational category, therefore, are scarcely comparable with those obtained in the United States or New Zealand, where there were no such class distinctions.

The most important conclusion emerging from the figures is that in this country able pupils from the so-called working classes—i.e. children of skilled, semi-skilled, and in particular unskilled workmen—failed to obtain scholarships so long as the examination was based on purely scholastic tests. The introduction of intelligence tests into the examination itself, and still more their increasing use by teachers in classifying and promoting children at the early stages, to some extent corrected this defect. But even at the present day much of the old discrepancy still persists, though there is as yet little evidence as to its precise incidence or amount. For the post-war period the most informative evidence comes from two surveys carried out by Mrs J. E. Floud and her collaborators—one in the industrial town of Middlesbrough and the other in the rural area of south-west Hertfordshire. This shows that, in spite of the abolition of fees, 'the sons of manual workers do not represent more than 45 to 50 per cent of the annual entries to the grammar schools'.[19]

The figures in column 4 of table 2 were obtained at a somewhat later period (1939–40), and relate not to the elementary school population, but, like those in column 1, to the population as a whole. The object of the inquiry was to estimate what proportion of the children in the several social classes are endowed with sufficient ability to undertake academic courses of university standard. At that date the number of new full-time entrants to the universities of England and Wales amounted to just over 1·5 per cent of those in the appropriate age. This implies a borderline of 2·17 S.D., or about 132·5 I.Q. on a scale with an S.D. of 15. Taking the average I.Q. and standard deviation of the children in each social class, it is possible to calculate the approximate percentage in each class having an intelligence of 132·5 I.Q. or over. These figures are entered in column 4. Then, weighting these proportions by the approximate number belonging to each class in the total population (col. 1), we can estimate what percentage of the university entrants should, with a perfect scheme of selection, be drawn from each class. This yields the percentages shown in column 5.

The proportions among actual university entrants were very different. About 65 per cent, at the time of the survey, were drawn from what were then fee-paying classes (i.e. roughly the first two classes in table 2), and about 35 per cent from the elementary schools; whereas, owing to their vast numbers, classes 3 to 7 must contain three times as many children of university ability as in the two small professional classes (see col. 5). This would imply a wastage of nearly half the available talent latent in the non-professional classes.[20] How far the position has been altered by the radical changes that have taken place since the end of the war it is impossible to say. Fresh surveys are urgently needed.

It would be instructive to know how far the differences shown in column 4 are attributable to genetic differences between the different social classes. Several sociological investigators—Mrs Floud and Mr Halsey, for instance—have maintained that the proportion of able individuals in the different classes are in fact approximately the same and that the apparent differences are due to environmental conditions. On the other hand, most British geneticists—Sir Ronald Fisher and Professor Darlington, for example—believe that, as a result of the constant interchange between the classes that has obtained over many centuries—the more highly endowed individuals tending to rise in social class, and those of low ability tending to drop to a lower grade—the genetic composition of the various social groups has become markedly differentiated.[21]

3. *New Zealand survey*. Parkyn's surveys of New Zealand children[22] yield very similar conclusions. Table 3 gives the figures for 11,421 Dunedin children tested with the Otis Intermediate group tests. The occupational classification (drawn up by McQueen and generally used for educational research in New Zealand) is slightly different from ours. The lines of division are based, not on ascertained I.Q.s, but partly on salary or wages and partly on social prestige.

The table indicates, that, of the entire school population in the area selected, 3 per cent had fathers in the 'professional' class, and

Table 3: Classification by occupations (New Zealand children)

Occupational category	General male population	Percentage of total gifted contributed by each group (High I.Q.)	(V. high I.Q.)	Percentage of each group contributed to total gifted (High I.Q.)	(V. high I.Q.)
1. Professional	3	9	20	11.1	6.0
2. Semi-professional and executive	5	12	12	9.0	2.1
3. Clerical and highly skilled	11	19	13	6.7	1.1
4. Skilled	21	21	26	4.1	1.2
5. Semi-skilled	20	15	14	2.9	0.7
6. Unskilled	13	6	3	1.8	0.2
7. Farmer	21	13	9	1.8	0.4
8. Father deceased	6	5	3	3.1	0.1
	100	100	100	3.9	3.9

that this small group contributed 9 per cent of the gifted children with 'high I.Q.s' (125–134) and 20 per cent of those with 'very high I.Q.s' (135 or over); moreover, of those belonging to this group as many as 11·1 per cent had 'high I.Q.s' and 6 per cent 'very high I.Q.s'; similarly for the other rows; Parkyn concludes that 'more than anything else the correspondence between the occupations of the fathers and the I.Q.s of their children would appear to be due to the inheritance of intelligence and the importance of intelligence and schooling in the different occupations'.

It follows that, in contemplating the characteristics that seem at first sight to be distinctive of gifted children, we must consider how far each is due to giftedness as such, how far it is due to the social conditions in which the child has been brought up, and how far to an interaction between the two, differing perhaps in the case of those from the middle and the working classes respectively.

Notes and references

1 A. Anastasi, *Differential Psychology* (1958), p. 328.

2 'By gifted children we mean those who test much above average on standardized scales for measuring intelligence' (L. S. Hollingworth, in Nat. Soc. Stud. Educ., *Twenty-third Yearbook*, 1924: cf. *id.*, *The Gifted Child*, 1926, p. 42; L. M. Terman *et al.*, *Mental and Physical Traits of a Thousand Gifted Children*, 1925).

R. F. DeHaan and R. J. Havighurst, *Educating Gifted Children* (1957). Since eight or more areas are enumerated, it would follow that, if each was *completely* independent of the others, the number of gifted children in the population would amount to at least 80 per cent. Actually the number expected is about 20 per cent, or 'possibly as much as 25 per cent'. Hence there must be, as indeed the writers elsewhere recognize, a good deal of overlapping; and the figures cited seem far more consonant with a theory that recognizes a factor of 'general ability'.

3 Board of Education, *Regulations for Secondary Schools in England* (1907) (Cd. 3952).

4 C. Burt, *Report of the Council's Psychologist to the Education Officer* (1914–15).

5 The tests recommended for London teachers were collected in a *Handbook of Tests for Use in Schools*. But by now they need revision. The method of constructing 'psychographs' (or 'mental profiles' as they are sometimes termed) is described in the LCC *Report on the Distribution of Educational Abilities* (1917), with diagrams (facing p. 65) giving illustrative instances. It should be noted that the common practice of using American tests—such as the Terman–Merrill or the Wechsler—without restandardizing the norms

for British children is apt to yield very misleading results. The reader may usefully refer to P. E. Vernon, *Intelligence and Attainment Tests* (1960).

6 A. Anastasi, *Differential Psychology* (1958), esp. pp. 368 ff. It is only right to observe that the theory of intelligence testing, which she rightly criticizes, is held by many educationists and teachers; my objection merely is that it does not represent the views of those psychologists who first advocated the use of 'intelligence tests' in this country. For still more vigorous criticisms from English writers, see D. Stott, *Unsettled Children and their Families*, and F. Campbell, *Intelligence Tests and All That*.

7 The statement that children rated as highly intelligent are chiefly children showing a predominantly verbal aptitude (cf. Anastasi, *loc. cit.*, p. 369) is not borne out by the actual results. For example, when such children, at the age of 12 or less, succeed in the Terman–Merrill tests for a 'Superior Adult III', the tests which they pass are the tests of reasoning, orientation, memory, and paper-cutting: their success in the specifically verbal test (Vocabulary) may be only a year or two above their actual age. The 'Opposite Analogies' test ('A rabbit is timid, a lion is . . . ?') is verbal in form; but plainly, a young child who succeeds in this does so not because of any unusual familiarity with the words employed, but because of his unusual capacity for educing and applying relations.

8 These, for example, are approximately the values calculated for different I.Q. levels with the recent revision of the Stanford–Binet tests (Q. McNemar, *The Revision of the Stanford–Binet Scale*, 1942). They are also the figures commonly reported by British investigators for the better type of group test.

9 A. Yates and D. A. Pidgeon, *Admission to Grammar Schools* (National Foundation for Educational Research in England and Wales, 1957).

10 R. L. Thorndike, 'The effect of the interval between test and re-test', *J. educ. Psychol.*, 24, 1933, 543–9; *id.*, 'The constancy of the I.Q.', *Psychol. Bull.*, 37, 167–86; R. Byrns and V. A. C. Henmon, 'Long-range prediction of college achievement', *School and Soc.*, 41, 1935, 877–80; M. P. Honzik *et al.*, 'The stability of mental test performances between two and eighteen years', *J. exp. Educ.*, 17, 1948, 309–32.

11 cf. *Mental and Scholastic Tests* (1921) and Institute of Education (Univ. London), *Studies in Education*, no. vi (1954). During the follow-up the tests or assessments had to be carried out by a number of different co-workers, and this must have somewhat reduced the accuracy of the later assessments. The high correlation is doubtless due to the wide range of our sample (roughly 50 to 150 I.Q.). With very rare exceptions, those who made the later assessments were quite unaware of the earlier figures.

A further attempt was also made to determine how far the assessment of intelligence in childhood would predict social efficiency still later. At the age of 30 or thereabouts, every person who could be traced received a rating based on the occupation he had followed (virtually on the average I.Q. for that occupation), and this was modified according to his type of work and degree of efficiency within that occupation. On weighting the numbers in the final group to allow for those who could not be traced or rated, the correlation between the ratings and the original assessments proved to be 0·61.

12 I. S. Lorge and L. S. Hollingworth, 'Adult status of highly intelligent children', *J. genet. Psychol.*, 49, 1936, 215–26.

13 e.g. P. Lélut, *Le Démon de Socrate* (1836); *id.*, *Amulette de Pascal* (1846); Moreau de Tours, *Psychologie Morbide* (1859); J. A. Schilling, *Psychiatrische Briefe* (1863). The occasional studies of gifted individuals carried out by Gall, Spurzheim, Combe, and their phrenological followers deserve a passing mention, but are of little scientific value. For a popular modern discussion, see Sir Russell Brain, *Some Reflections on Genius* (1960).

14 E. Kretschmer, *The Psychology of Men of Genius* (1931); W. Lange-Eichbaum, *Das Genie-Problem* (1951); S. Freud, 'The relation of the poet to day dreaming', *Collected Papers*, IV (1925); E. Hitchmann, *Great Men: Psychoanalytic Studies* (1956). Sir Russell Brain (*Some Reflections on Genius*, 1960, pp. 10ff.) describes genius as a 'nervous abnormality'. 'Most geniuses', he concludes, 'are perfectly sane'; but, particularly among the more creative specimens, there is a 'close correlation between genius and mental instability'. The theory of a close alliance between great wits and madness goes back to the days of the Greek schools of medicine. 'Men illustrious in poetry, politics, and the arts', says an oft-quoted writer, 'have often been melancholic or mad, like Ajax, Empedocles, Socrates, and many others' (Pseudo-Aristoteles, *Problemata*, 37, cited in many medieval books on medicine).

15 The reason for choosing this figure was that in those days approximately 2·8 per cent of each age-group were selected by the junior county scholarship examination for free places in the 'secondary' schools. With an I.Q. scale having an S.D. of 15, this proportion (3 per cent) would imply a borderline of about 128 I.Q. For details as to the surveys, see the LCC Reports on *The Distribution and Relations of Educational Abilities* (1917) and on *Mental and Scholastic Tests* (1921), and the various *Annual Reports* of the Psychologist to the Council.

16 L. M. Terman *et al.*, *Mental and Physical Traits of a Thousand Gifted Children* (1925); *The Gifted Child Grows Up* (1947); *Genetic Studies of Genius* (1958); *The Gifted Group at Mid-life* (1959). The Californian investigation was financed by the Commonwealth Fund of New York, the National Research Council, and various bodies and private benefactors, and with subsequent follow-up studies, appears to have cost about $150,000.

17 Unlike the figures for 'all males' in col. 1, those obtained in Terman's survey (cols 2 and 3) included comparatively few representatives of the rural population. The studies of leading American men of science and men of letters, carried out by J. McK. Cattell and E. L. Clarke, showed that an appreciable proportion were drawn from the 'agricultural classes'; and similarly, Galton's and Havelock Ellis's studies of British men of genius showed that many of their parents belonged to the 'yeoman and farming class'.

18 *Medical Research Council's Reports*, no. 33 (1926). The classification and the figures shown in the first column of table 2 are reproduced in *A Survey of Social Structure in England and Wales*, 1937, pp. 55 ff., table XXXI.

19 J. E. Floud *et al.*, *Social Class and Educational Opportunity* (1956).

20 In all classes, of course, the biggest source of wastage is to be found among the gifted members of the female sex. For the inquiries on which the statements in the text are based, see *Br. J. educ. Psychol.*, *13*, 1943, 83–98. Very similar figures are reported from the USA. Thus, President Henry of the University of Illinois states that of those who have the rating of at least an average college graduate, 'little more than half enter college and fewer than half finish'; for more detailed information, see National Manpower Council, *Student Department and National Manpower Policy* (New York, 1952), and Educational Policies Commission, *Manpower and Education* (Washington, 1956). Further data will be found in the reports cited later and in the list of references.

21 R. A. Fisher, *The Genetical Theory of Natural Selection* (1930); C. D. Darlington, 'The control of evolution in man', *Eugen. Rev.*, *50*, 1958, 113–23. For a detailed discussion of both sides of the problem, see the symposium on 'Class differences in intelligence', *Br. J. statist. Psychol.*, *12*, 1959, 1–34.

22 G. W. Parkyn, *Children of High Intelligence* (1948), pp. 117 ff.

Acknowledgment

Much of the material which appears in this and the two following chapters is reprinted, in slightly revised form, from Burt's Introduction in *The World Yearbook of Education*, 1962, by kind permission of the publishers, Evans Brothers (Books) Ltd, London.

CHAPTER ELEVEN

The characteristics of the gifted

Physical condition

The anthropometric measurements obtained for the Californian children showed that 'the gifted children as a group are above the best standards for American-born children both for height and weight'. The majority apparently were of an athletic rather than an asthenic or leptosomic physique; they had 'broad shoulders, well-developed lungs, and strong muscles'. The proportion of weakly children was only two-thirds of that found in the general population, and the number of ill-nourished children only one-third. As regards more specific disabilities, 'the incidence of physical defects [including defects of sight and hearing] and of abnormal conditions of every kind was well below that reported by school doctors in medical surveys of the general population'. The frequency of nervous disorders—tics, chorea, stuttering, etc. —was also lower—13 per cent as compared with 16 per cent among the control group; timidity and worrying was slightly commoner, but the difference was statistically insignificant. At birth the mean weight of the gifted children was ¾ lb above the mean for the general population, 4·4 per cent were born earlier than the usual term. On an average they learnt to walk one month earlier, and to talk 3½ months earlier than the ordinary youngster. Dentition and pubescence began somewhat sooner; change of voice occurred earlier in the boys, and 48 per cent of the girls had reached puberty before thirteen as compared with 25 per cent in the general population. In physical development they were thus well ahead of the average child at almost every stage.

The data obtained for London school children are fully consistent with the conclusions drawn by Terman, but, taken by themselves, could hardly be accepted as evidence for those conclusions, since they could in large measure be accounted for by differences in the material conditions of the different social classes in this country at the time of the inquiry.[1]

Educational attainments

In Terman's survey the average age of the gifted children on entering school was $6\frac{1}{4}$ years. By then nearly one-half had already learnt to read, usually with little or no formal instruction. One boy of only 2 years 3 months was already able to read as well as the average child at the end of the first grade. Early indications of precocious intelligence—quick understanding, retentive memory, large vocabulary, persistent curiosity, and an exceptional interest in such things as numbers and their relations, encyclopedias, atlases, and the like—were frequently reported. Few of the parents had given any systematic training, and many thought it wiser to hold the child back.

On entering school, 20 per cent of the children had skipped the lower first grade almost at once; and, at the time of the initial survey, as many as 85 per cent had already skipped one or more half grades. There was, however, comparatively little correspondence between each child's actual merits and the amount or rate of promotion in school; indeed, the teachers' assessments proved to be amazingly unreliable. Examined with standardized tests of attainments, the children's average achievement quotient proved to be 144, i.e. at the age of ten their attainments would be those of an average child of nearly fourteen and a half. This was well above their 'grade progress quotient', which was only 114. 'More than half the children had mastered the curriculum to a point at least two full grades beyond the one in which they were enrolled'; and even so their accomplishments were still below their actual capabilities, since their mean intelligence quotient was 150 or rather more. Thus, on an average, they were educationally retarded by at least a year.

Almost identical results were reported by Paul Witty with a group of fifty highly intelligent children. Their average intelligence quotient was 153, but their average 'school progress quotient' only 112.[2] In the more recent study carried out in Dunedin, Mr Parkyn found that pupils having I.Q.s ranging from 125 to 134 had 'progress quotients' of only 111, while pupils having

I.Q.s of 135 or upwards had 'progress quotients' of 118, dropping to 114 a year or two later.

Similar discrepancies were found in the London surveys. The 'supernormal' children were divided into two groups: (i) those with I.Q.s between 115 and 130, and (ii) those with I.Q.s over 130 (corresponding at the time of the inquiry with the borderlines for entrance to a central school and for a junior county scholarship in a secondary or grammar school). Their average intelligence quotients, educational quotients, and progress quotients were (i) 123, 111, 109, and (ii) 135, 121, and 118 respectively.[3] In the London schools, it will be seen, the divergence between the child's actual ability on the one hand and his school attainments on the other, though often striking, was by no means so wide or so general as it was in the American schools, or still seems to be in the New Zealand schools. Mr Parkyn himself hints at one of the most likely causes. After pointing out the difference between the system of selective schools in Britain and of non-selective schools in New Zealand, he remarks on 'the difficulties caused for those concerned with the education of the able minority' by a policy, such as that adopted in New Zealand, which 'attempts to provide for the needs of children of widely varying abilities within the framework of non-selective schools by simply modifying or supplementing a central core of studies'. His own results, he believes, 'justify the conclusion that adequate differentiation is not being made in the curriculum for the benefit of the brighter children, and that there is a tendency to undervalue the claims of scholarship'; nevertheless, he adds, 'the social philosophy of most New Zealanders is such that they regard the values to be achieved by maintaining the essential unity of all post-primary schools as more than compensating for the difficulties of organization thus involved'.[4] This, however, raises issues which fall outside our present scope.

The specialization of abilities

As we have seen, it is widely believed that gifted individuals, whether children or adults, are usually gifted in some particular ability or talent, so that their mental growth is apt to become one-sided and their development in one direction to be achieved at the cost of a more general advance. In Terman's investigation, evidence bearing on this point was sought by examining results not only from standardized tests of the ordinary school subjects but also from supplementary tests of general information in subjects such as music, art, science, literature, and the like. He gives a table of intercorrelation for the more important subjects. The coefficients, which are all positive, range from 0·20 to 0·88. The values are slightly lower than would be obtained from the complete population: but that is only to be expected with a group already selected for general ability,[5] and detailed calculation shows that the proportion of the individual variance which is attributable to specialized ability is no greater than in the ordinary population.

The varying achievements of a few of the more interesting cases are illustrated by 'psychographs' similar to those published for London children. One interesting instance is that of H. M. J., aged 6¾ by the calendar, with a mental age of 13·0 (I.Q. 192), working in the upper third grade at school. Her highest score is in arithmetical reasoning, namely +5·0 S.D. (12½ in mental years). Her score for reading is only 3½ S.D. (11 in mental years and two years below her intelligence level). Her spelling, composition ('language usage'), and, as might be expected, her general knowledge, are lower still. As the child is so young and has been such a short time at school, Terman rightly argues that her outstanding achievement in arithmetic is indicative of an innate aptitude. Several other children show markedly irregular 'profiles'; but then, so do many average pupils. The fact is that, whether his ability is approximately average or definitely supernormal, the development of *every* child is unique. As Terman observes, with gifted children the special aptitudes of each particular individual are reinforced by his high general ability, and are thus more likely to attract attention. Yet even in their poorest subjects they are still superior to the average child of the same age. There can therefore be no truth in the popular notion that high development in one direction is a 'compensation for inferiority in others'.[6]

According to Terman, the two subjects in which special ability or disability appear most frequently are spelling and arithmetic. Unfortunately no tests of technical or mechanical abilities seem to have been included. With Londoners the commonest types of special ability were as follows (the list is given in terms of the so-called 'group factors' established by the means of factor analysis): (i) verbal ability (reasoning, composition and spelling), especially frequent among girls; (ii) numerical ability (arithmetic and allied subjects) and (iii) technical ability, both more frequent among boys; (iv) artistic ability (drawing and painting) and (v) musical ability, both more frequent among girls[7]; and finally (vi) creative ability. Of these supplementary 'factors' the last deserves a slightly fuller discussion in view of the controversies which it has aroused in the past.

Originality

Those who have insisted that the difference between the genius and the ordinary man is a qualitative rather than quantitative difference have commonly chosen for the distinguishing characteristic a quality which they variously term 'originality', 'inventiveness', or 'creativity'. 'Genius', says an eighteenth-century writer, 'is commonly confounded by the vulgar, and sometimes even by the more judicious, with mere capacity. The two are totally distinct. Genius is properly the faculty of invention—the ability by means of which a man produces original works of art or makes original discoveries in science.' Ravaisson echoed the same doctrine: 'Le génie consiste surtout à créer, à inventer.' And Kant sums it up in the dictum: 'Genie ist eine musterhafte Originalität.' This was the theory preached by James Ward in his famous attack on Galton's *Hereditary Genius*. Psychology, he maintains, will do justice to genius only if it abandons its attempts at 'lifeless psychographs constructed with the help of statistical and correlational methods', and substitutes 'a living interpretation from within'. 'Genius is something that pertains to the Subject or Person, not to his psychoplasm; and, if that is so, the evidence for heredity, which is ample in the case of mere talent, will be lacking in the case of genius; and that is what we find.'[8]

Now, as Ward himself insists, the 'originality' of the genius does not consist in mere novelty as such. The novel product is 'the result of a subjective selection of what is relevant to an intention or meaning—a result synthesizing and fitting together into an "intellectual system" the *disjecta membra* which themselves have first to be found'. But the mental process of fitting together or 'synthesizing', as we have seen, is the hallmark of 'intelligence' as we have defined it; and, in point of fact, most of the illustrious names enumerated by Ward to support his theory appear in Catherine Cox's *Genetic Studies of Genius*, and are there credited with an intelligence quotient well above the average. Nevertheless, the most recent evidence does not support Spearman's notion that the originality of genius is '*no more* than a striking manifestation of *g*', and that 'no *special* "creative ability" exists'. The latest applications of those 'statistical and correlational methods', which Ward himself so sternly deprecated, furnish unquestionable evidence for something very like a 'special factor' of creativity, and indicate roughly in what it consists. It consists (so it would seem) partly in an active 'productive' imagination rather than an imagination or memory which is merely 're-productive' and partly in a tendency to rely on what is sometimes termed 'relative suggestion' rather than on so-called 'reproductive suggestion', or, in less antiquated jargon, on 'relational associations' rather than 'mechanical associations'[9]; and it seems most effective during moods of high excitement or intense absorption. But whatever may be its precise psychological nature, its proportionate contribution, if we may trust the figures obtained in the various factorial studies, is only about one-third that of 'general intelligence'. Creativity *without* general intelligence produces nothing of interest or value.

This conclusion, if it can be accepted, carried with it important practical corollaries. As a glance at their contents indicates, the commoner types of test used to pick out children of high ability tend to select what may be termed the 'analytic' or 'abstract' types and to overlook the 'synthetic' or 'concrete' types, and often to favour those with good reproductive capacities rather than those with special productive abilities. It may be added that DeHaan and Havighurst go farther still, and argue that 'creativity is something that can be taught'.[10] Most psychologists who are familiar with the day-to-day work of the ordinary classroom, particularly that conducted with one eye on impending examinations, will readily agree with them that 'creativity in children is all too frequently stifled', and that much more might be done to feed and foster it.

Early development

Our own case-histories indicate that in many instances the accelerated development of the most intelligent children is foreshadowed very early in their school career and often even before they enter school. They learn to walk five weeks earlier than the average, and talk eleven weeks earlier. They talk precociously in complete and complex sentences; and, on entering school, their vocabulary is nearly twice as large as that of the ordinary child of the same age. Their parents constantly comment on their inquisitive habits: they want to know the reason why, and are exceptionally quick to discover relations of cause and effect. The boys display a special interest in numerical relations—counting, telling the time, and grasping the details of the calendar; the girls invent and relate elaborate little tales and stories. Alike at home and at school both sexes show an unusual capacity for quick and sustained attention. They are not only quick at learning; they also seek to learn. Hence, no doubt, the frequent statements in our reports—that they are 'highly observant' and 'have well-stocked memories'.[11]

Leisure interests

Terman's inquiries into the interests and out-of-school activities of his gifted group furnish further information in keeping with the foregoing conclusions. Most of the gifted children were inveterate readers. Whereas hardly any in the control group had read a single book before the age of eight, the average child in the gifted group had read ten books before he was seven; and by that age he would be spending about six hours a week on home-reading, and by the age of twelve more than double that amount. As compared with the control group, the majority showed far greater interest in abstract subjects, and the range of their interests was much wider; the sex differences in interests, however, seemed much the same in both groups.

In the London inquiry the general results were, with minor exceptions, very similar. Here, too, the outstanding difference between the supernormal children and the rest consisted in the amount of time devoted to reading. The younger would read almost anything that came their way; the older tended to specialize and follow up their individual interests; and in doing so they displayed a keenness and tenacity quite unlike anything found in the average youngster of the same age. The boys showed marked preferences for science, engineering, aeronautics, the latest inventions, and, as lighter reading, travel, detective stories, and tales of the sea. The girls preferred poetry, biography, history, and natural history. Both made regular use of libraries and of encyclopedias and similar works of reference.

With the Londoners, particularly the boys, the time spent on hobbies distinguished the gifted children from the average almost as much as the time spent on reading. This seems to be a point in which the London children differed from the American.[12] Scientific hobbies were especially frequent—building ingenious working models with Meccano sets, constructing wireless receivers, toy theatres and toy aeroplanes, performing electrical and chemical experiments, observing stars and making effective telescopes, collecting stamps, fossils, and the like. With the girls, painting, drawing, photography, and writing stories and composing poems were the most popular pastimes.

The third main difference between the gifted children and the ordinary London youngster related to the time spent at the cinema. The ordinary boy spent more than twice as much time 'at the pictures' as the gifted child.[13]

In games, as in most other things, the gifted children appear more mature in their preferences. According to Terman's account they are far less attracted by games of a competitive type— baseball or football, for example—than the average lad, and tend to favour quieter pastimes, particularly those requiring thought and skill rather than strength or speed, such as chess, checkers, and card games. They are by no means solitary or unsociable. On an average they spend $2\frac{1}{2}$ hours daily with other youngsters out of school hours; and, so far as the teachers' impressions went, 90 per cent of the boys and 97 per cent of the girls seemed quite normal in their choice of amusements. Only in comparatively rare cases was it reported that the child 'prefers reading to play' or 'shows no interest in ordinary games'.[14]

Personality and character

To determine the emotional and moral characteristics of his gifted groups, Terman not only collected detailed reports from parents and teachers, but also applied 'character tests'. The main result was that 'although these tests do not make possible a very reliable comparison, they warrant the conclusion that the gifted group is decidedly superior to the control group, and the superiority greater for girls than for boys'. In tests for honesty, however, the boys made a better showing than the girls. The characteristics most conspicuous among the gifted were originality, self-confidence, desire to excel, forethought, perseverance, leadership, sense of humour, and cheerfulness. In emotional stability and social adaptability they were well ahead of the average child of similar age.[15]

In Britain the conditions affecting the development of social and moral behaviour are more complex. There is a sharper differentiation of social classes and a wider variation in their codes and traditions. At the time of our initial surveys these differences were even more marked than they are today. Children of high intelligence, drawn from the wealthier or upper professional classes, were for the most part educated at the 'public schools', which claimed to lay special stress on the training of character through games and sport and social pursuits. With children of this class the superiority in social and moral qualities was still more striking than in Terman's group. On the other hand, with gifted children who came from the 'middle' or 'lower' classes the situation was very different. Cases of maladjustment were frequently noted.

In the poorer classes the bright child was often more intelligent than his parents. He might, with the teacher's encouragement, develop intellectual ambitions at variance with the aims and habits of his family. As a result, conflicts at home, open or suppressed, were by no means unusual. Awarded a 'free place' at a secondary school where most of the pupils paid fees, his accent, manners and dress at once betrayed him; and he became a misfit at school as well as out of it. Even the bright child from the middle classes experienced a similar strain, especially since he was, as a rule, only too well aware of the sacrifices made by his impecunious parents to secure him the best possible education.

In the primary school there are other difficulties to be overcome. There the commonest cause of maladjustment springs from the combination of intellectual superiority with a physical, emotional and social development that is relatively immature. If, in view of his high ability, the bright child is promoted to a class that is in keeping with his intellectual development, he has to mix with older children who are bigger, stronger and more worldly wise than he. If, however, the teacher thinks it better to keep him with pupils of his own age and size, and possibly even fails to recognize how exceptional his abilities are, then his mind will privately run far ahead of his companions'. In grasping new ideas, learning new facts, and solving new problems he may be nearly twice as quick. He is compelled to mark time while the rest catch up; and as a result soon becomes bored, restless or lazy. The others in their turn will resent his superiority, and perhaps twit him for being the teacher's pet. Thus, in whatever class he is placed, he is unable to join with his fellows on equal terms and is thrown back upon himself.

It is no doubt for reasons such as these that so many physicians and psychologists in this country, who have had occasion to study children of exceptional ability, have gained the impression that an appreciable proportion are of an 'asthenic' or introverted type—shy, solitary, highly strung, distinctly lacking in social qualities and strength of character; in short, as one of them puts it, 'sheer bookish misfits'. In point of fact, however, definite neurosis was found to be comparatively rare.[16] Now and then some of the maladjusted are tempted to react in the opposite fashion, exploiting their unexercised abilities in ways that are definitely anti-social and frequently persistent, owing largely to the fact that such children are skilful enough to evade or circumvent discovery. Nevertheless, delinquent cases are far rarer than popular opinion imagines. The intellectual criminals of history—Villon, poet and thief, Vidocq, burglar and detective, Eugene Aram, philologist and murderer, Wainewright, the art-critic and art-collector who poisoned his insured relatives to pay for his gems, Professor Webster, who used his own laboratory for cremating his wealthy victims—these and other gifted scoundrels have captured a disproportionate interest by the very ingenuity of their offences. The resourceful organizer of crime, the brilliant leader of the lawless gang, is fortunately as scarce in fact as he is ubiquitous in fiction.

The net result of our inquiries may be summed up as follows. Among our gifted groups those who were of a definitely 'asthenic' or introverted type amounted in all to 7·3 per cent, as compared with 5·1 per cent in the control group; those who were of a definitely 'sthenic' or extraverted type amounted to 12·8 per cent as compared with 5·4 per cent in the control group.[17] But barely 1 per cent were so markedly maladjusted as to become definitely neurotic or delinquent. The actual figures were: neurotic 0·8 per cent, delinquent 0·2 per cent, as compared with 2·6 and 1·2 per cent among the controls.[18] In general, where parents and teachers are able to meet the requirements of the gifted child, defects of personality, whether in the direction of neurosis or of delinquency, prove to be decidedly uncommon. As a rule, children of high intelligence have a somewhat higher rating for 'general emotion-ality' than children of average intelligence, but at the same time they are able to exercise a more intelligent control over it. In our inquiries the gifted boys and girls were almost invariably de-scribed as more amenable to discipline, and, with few exceptions, as both ready and able to take an effective lead in social activities. Compared with others of their age, a larger proportion belonged to clubs and similar organizations; many were Boy Scouts, and a fair number were members of juvenile debating societies. With-in such organizations they frequently held office as secretaries, treasurers, presidents, chairmen, or the like. In addition they were reported as far more regular in their attendance at church, chapel, Sunday school, or Bible classes.

In the New Zealand inquiries Parkyn used a method of trait-rating similar to Terman's, and obtained similar results. He notes, however, certain minor differences. With his children, as his table of ratings shows, moral and especially social qualities stand out far more strongly; and the children themselves appear to have been more definitely extraverted and free from nervous disorders of every kind. 'As for the type of emotionality', he writes, 'whether "sthenic" or "asthenic"—to use Burt's terminology—there appears to be a tendency for the intelligent children to be "sthenic" rather than "asthenic" in the nature of their dominant emotions.' But, as he rightly observes, these minor differences between the gifted children studied in different countries relate to 'the traits which are most liable to be influenced by environmental conditions'.[19]

The highly gifted

Often the child's intelligence is so exceptional that it is almost impossible for either home or school to satisfy his needs, unless they too are equally exceptional. Accordingly, we have found it helpful to distinguish two main types—the 'moderately gifted' with I.Q.s below 150 (or thereabouts), grades D and E in Galton's classification—and the 'highly gifted' with I.Q.s above that level—grades F and G ('geniuses' in Galton's sense). A child of this latter type may be as much ahead of the majority of the gifted children as these are ahead of the average child. And though their numbers are too few for generalization, it would seem that within this group maladjustment may tend to increase in severity and frequency with the increase in the intellectual disparity.

Children of this high level are so few and far between that their existence as well as their special problems passes almost unrecognized by teachers and by parents.[20] However, one eminent member of the group has himself published an autobiographical account of his own early childhood, namely, Professor Norbert Wiener of the Massachusetts Institute of Technology—'the inventor of cybernetics and the trainer of many of America's most eminent physicists and electronic engineers'. At the high school, which he entered at the age of ten, his fellow students, who were seven years older, already seemed to him 'full-grown adults', and 'the seats were much too big'. For some of the lessons the teacher even took him on her lap. He entered Harvard at the age of twelve, and felt still more like a shrimp out of water. 'A deep strangeness fell upon me', he writes, 'which has made me feel all my life a sojourner on this planet rather than a native. . . . I had therefore to create for myself a fantastic personality and become an actor in real life: only then could I adapt myself to the various parts I was called on to fulfil.'[21] Bernard Shaw has similarly described the secret embarrassment he felt during adolescence; and his solution was much the same—to invent a mask and a role for himself and live up to it.

Summary

The results recorded in these three independent surveys, carried out in widely distant parts of the world, thus lead to conclusions which appear both clear and fairly consistent. In general, gifted children, whether boys or girls, differ from the average child in (1) intellectual, (2) volitional, (3) physical, (4) emotional, (5) moral and (6) social characteristics, and roughly in that order, i.e. the differences are greatest in intellectual and least in moral and social characteristics. The order varies somewhat in the different researches. But, as a rule, the groups from the three different communities resemble each other most, and differ most from their fellows, in those characteristics which may plausibly be assumed to have a genetic and therefore an organic basis. They differ from each other chiefly in those qualities that are most strongly affected by environmental and social conditions.

Contrary to the traditional picture of the precocious youngster, the gifted child is, as a rule, taller, stronger and healthier than the average. He is on the whole freer from abnormality of whatever kind, physical, intellectual, emotional and nervous. Until they begin to specialize, most gifted children are gifted all round. Their abilities in every direction are highly developed, and at least in earlier years are developed fairly evenly. They show a much greater fund of common sense, originality and intellectual curiosity than others of their own age. They are in nearly every respect more mature; they work harder; they are more scrupulous, conscientious and truthful; they readily take the lead; and, unless disheartened by repeated frustration, display greater self-confidence and finer social qualities. The defects that a few occasionally exhibit are usually traceable to the specific conditions under which they have developed, and especially to the fact that their exceptional abilities have been overlooked or their needs inadequately met.[22]

Notes and references

1 cf. J. Kerr, *Fundamentals of School Health* (1926), pp. 22 ff. and refs. Possibly, too, as more recent evidence suggests, they may also be due in part to differences in the genetic constitution of the different social classes; but this point will be taken up later.

2 P. Witty, 'A genetic study of fifty gifted children', *Nat. Soc. Stud. Educ. Thirty-ninth Yearbook* (1940). See also *The Gifted Child*, edited by P. Witty (1951).

3 C. Burt, *Mental and Scholastic Tests* (1921), pp. 174–80.

4 *loc. cit.*, pp. 216 ff. My former colleague Dr F. H. Spencer, Chief Inspector of London Schools, also observes, after a visit to New Zealand schools, that 'the rate of progress . . . was considerably slower than in the selective central or technical schools of Britain'.

5 Terman, *op. cit.*, table 119, p. 319. On factorizing the table in the usual way, I find the general factor contributes just over 35 per cent to the total variance (rather less than with an unselected group) and the special factors 14 per cent (much the same as for the general population of the same age).

6 cf. 'The structure of the mind', *Br. J. educ. Psychol.*, 19, 100–11, 176–99.

7 However, the only instances of *outstanding* musical ability were found among the boys. This is in keeping with the fact that in the past (with the exception, perhaps, of Ethel Smythe) hardly any women have achieved fame as first-class composers or conductors.

8 Gerard, *An Essay on Genius* (1774), p. 7; Ravaisson, *Philosophie en France*, p. 245; Kant, *Kritik der Urtheilskraft*, sect. 49 (Ward misquotes Kant's phrase as '*meisterhafte* Originalität'); J. Ward, *Psychological Principles*,

pp. 450 ff. Ward's theory does not imply (as Spearman supposes in *Abilities of Man*, p. 33) that 'this creative faculty, unlike intelligence, is wholly emancipated from the laws of heredity' as the biologist would understand that phrase. According to Ward, 'genius is innate but not inherited', where (from the examples he cites—Shakespeare, Newton, Beethoven, etc.) it is evident he interprets heredity in the old-fashioned way as connoting resemblance between parents and children. Ward's theory is thus perfectly compatible with the *Mendelian* 'laws of heredity'.

9 The terminology here used is largely that of Stout's *Analytic Psychology* (which Ward himself quotes with approval): see especially his discussion of 'noetic synthesis', 'unconscious inference', 'inspiration', and 'mental productiveness' generally (*op. cit.*, s.v.). The factorial evidence is summarized, and the above interpretation more fully explained, in 'The structure of the mind', *loc. cit. sup.*, pp. 180 ff. Here it is perhaps relevant to note that one of the commonest criticisms of current intelligence tests, advanced by the more enlightened teachers, is (to quote one of their number) that they 'depend too much on the faculty of memory and too little on the faculty of imagination'.

10 See their instructive chapter on 'Developing creativity' (*Educating the Gifted Child*, pp. 162 ff.). Of the available tests, those which we have found most helpful for this purpose are (*a*) tests for so-called 'fluency'; (*b*) an 'analogies' test so arranged that the child himself has to supply correlates instead of just selecting one of those given; (*c*) tests of inductive reasoning, like those described by Wheeler (*Br. J. statist. Psychol.*, 11, 137 ff.) and by Piaget, Inhelder, and their colleagues; (*d*) tests of imaginative design carried out with coloured blocks; and (*e*) simplest of all, tests of creative writing (see *Br. J. educ. Psychol.*, *19*, esp. 180 ff.). For purposes of research, particularly with older individuals, the tests described by Guilford and his fellow-workers seem most promising (cf. J. P. Guilford *et al.*, 'A factor-analytic study of creative thinking', *Psychometrika*, *19*, 1954, 297–311). This, however, is to my mind one of the many fields where systematic observation is likely to be more effective than mere testing.

11 It may be remarked that systematic notes or leaflets drawing the attention of teachers and parents to these diagnostic points have proved a valuable aid in identifying gifted children at an early age and in encouraging an appreciative interest among the adults concerned.

12 Among New Zealanders Mr Parkyn noted a similar prevalence of scientific and technical hobbies among the gifted groups. 'Their versatility', he remarks, 'was amazing, and the competence in planning and the precision in execution wholly admirable.' Terman's groups seem to have shown little interest in practical and technical subjects. In the teachers' lists of favourable traits, 'mechanical ingenuity is the only one on which the control group rated higher than the gifted group'. However, as Terman remarks, the teachers probably had rather limited opportunities for observing activities of this type.

13 In recent inquiries into television nearly every investigator has noted analogous differences between gifted and average children, both as regards time spent and the type of programme preferred.

14 See also M. Stewart, 'The leisure activities of grammar school children', *Br. J. educ. Psychol.*, *20*, 1950, 11-34.

15 Similarly, H. Hartshorne and M. A. May (*Studies in Deceit*, 1927) found in their experimental studies that, on the average, the most intelligent children were not only more stable emotionally, but far superior to the control group in their resistance to temptation.

16 See also P. Witty and H. C. Lehman, 'Nervous instability and genius', *J. abn. soc. Psychol.*, *24*, 1930, 486 ff.

17 This is in keeping with Sir Russell Brain's observation that the characteristic temperament most closely associated with genius is cyclothymia (moods of elation and hyperactivity with short periods of depression). This seems true of the geniuses best known to the general public (Dickens, Johnson, Shakespeare, Goethe). But many of the ablest philosophers (e.g. Kant) and scientists (e.g. Cavendish) have been introverts. The former group, however, seems to have been the most original and creative.

18 The somewhat arbitrary definitions adopted for the purposes of statistical comparison were the same as those adopted in the reports on educational subnormality and delinquency (e.g. *The Young Delinquent*, 1925, p. 515). In my study of juvenile delinquency only $2\frac{1}{2}$ per cent of the delinquents had I.Q.s over 115; those with I.Q.s over 130 were rarer still. Healy's experience was much the same (W. Healy and A. F. Bronner, *Criminals and Delinquents*, 1928). See also C. L. C. Burns's investigation of cases of maladjustment from grammar schools ('Maladjusted children of high intelligence', *Br. J. educ. Psychol.*, *19*, 1949, 137-41).

19 Parkyn, *loc. cit.*, pp. 54 ff.

20 Among my own cases one type of difficulty appeared again and again as a cause of emotional disturbance—a difficulty rarely suspected by the parents and commonly concealed by the child himself, namely, the problems of human life as such, particularly the enigmas of birth and death. It is popularly supposed that children only take an active interest in sex and religion when they reach adolescence. Freud has taught us that tiny children may puzzle over sex and reproduction; but even psychologists and psychiatrists fail to realize how early the highly intelligent youngster may begin to worry over metaphysical and philosophical questions. And the moral or religious conflicts that ensue may sometimes precipitate a temporary nervous breakdown.

21 N. Wiener, *Ex-Prodigy: my childhood and youth* (1953). Terman made a special study of individuals who were highly supernormal, taking as his borderline an I.Q. of 170. He reports, however, that the average ratings for mental adjustment and nervous stability were 'almost identical for the high group as for the total gifted group'. On the other hand, Leta Hollingworth found several instances of maladjustment among her group of highly

supernormal children, and devotes an illuminating chapter to the subject (*Children above 180 I.Q.*, 1942, esp. ch. 20).

22 For further reviews of the main findings, see more particularly Paul Witty (ed.), *The Gifted Child* (1951), and the *Fifty-seventh Yearbook of the National Society for the Study of Education* (1958).

CHAPTER TWELVE

The gifted child in later life

The value of after-histories

One of the most widespread beliefs about the youthful prodigy is that, as he grows older, he will in all likelihood revert to the general average. And the parent is frequently warned that any attempt to spur on such a child to advance at a speed greater than the normal will merely hasten the eventual collapse. 'Early ripe, early rot', says the proverb. The story of Henrick Heineken is held up as an awful warning. Before he was twelve months old, little Henrick had memorized the best-known stories from the Pentateuch. Before he was three he could add, subtract, multiply and divide. Before he was four he could read German, French and Latin, and his fame was spreading through Europe. He was summoned to appear before the King of Denmark. But before he was five he had died, 'a wonder for all time', as his tutor records.[1]

Obviously, the generalization which such stories illustrate is not one that can be established simply by examining biographies or tables of mortality. What are needed are 'longitudinal studies'—comparable after-histories of intelligent children and of average children to determine how often the members change over from one category to the other. A number of investigations have been completed in which the after-histories have been carried to the end of the school period; but in only a few has the follow-up been continued into adult years. Of the latter, by far the most detailed is that published by Terman and his colleagues, in which the group of gifted boys and girls already described was kept under observation for thirty-five years. Reviews were made at intervals of about twelve years down to 1955, when the group had reached an average age of about forty-five.[2]

HEALTH

Throughout the period covered by the case records the general health of the gifted groups remained well above that of the average population, and the occurrence of specific ailments or defects seemed comparatively rare. When fully grown, the males were three inches taller than the general average, and two inches taller than the average college student. For the female groups the differences were similar but smaller. The over-all mortality was only 84 per cent of that reported for the ordinary population of California.

INTELLECTUAL STATUS

A brief test of adult intelligence was applied in 1940. At the outset, when tested with the Terman–Binet tests, the average I.Q. of the gifted group was 152, i.e. 3·2 S.D. above the mean for the general population. Eighteen years later, tested with new tests appropriate to their age, they were still 2·1 S.D. above the general mean, which, in terms of the Terman–Binet scale, would be equivalent to an I.Q. of about 134. The drop in I.Q. does not imply any *actual* decline of intelligence. The results of single tests are of necessity somewhat inaccurate; and the second test, which was newer, shorter, less thoroughly standardized, and applied under far less rigorous conditions, must have been even more unreliable than the first. Terman therefore contends that the apparent diminution in the scores could be fully accounted for by statistical regression due to unreliability. In any case, it can safely be said that the group as a whole unquestionably remained well above the average for persons of the same age, and might still be as much above the average as when they were first tested.

EDUCATIONAL HISTORY

Ninety per cent of the gifted men and 86 per cent of the gifted women entered college. The majority graduated, usually a year or so earlier than the average college student; 20 per cent won undergraduate scholarships or fellowships. But still more could have earned and profited by a monetary grant had it been available; and one of the practical conclusions drawn is that 'greater financial assistance for gifted students is a pressing need'.

OCCUPATIONS AND ACHIEVEMENTS

In later life the majority rose to positions of responsibility or leadership: 46 per cent were working in some professional occupation (i.e. were lawyers or judges, members of college faculties, physicians, scientists or engineers, and school administrators or teachers—roughly in that order of frequency), and another 41 per cent in some semi-professional capacity (i.e. were business officials, managers, executives, or the like). At the latest survey the income of the men ranged from $4,000 to $400,000, with a median of just under $10,000. As many as 111 have found their way into *Who's Who in America, American Men of Science*, or the *Directory of American Scholars*. Three have been elected to the National Academy of Science—an honour comparable to a Fellowship of the Royal Society in Britain; and at least a dozen have achieved an international reputation. The publications of the group comprise over ninety books and monographs (including textbooks translated into several languages), 2,000 scientific or technical articles, and more than 700 plays, essays, short stories, or the like—not counting mere journalistic contributions. And all this at an age when many illustrious men have still been unknown.[3]

LEISURE INTERESTS AND HOME LIFE

The group showed a remarkable versatility in their non-vocational pursuits. In a long list of leisure activities, sport held the first place for both sexes. With the men photography came next, and music with the women. Fiction—particularly classical fiction, detective stories and historical novels—proved to be the most popular type of reading; poetry ranked high with the women. As regards political preferences, 39 per cent of the men and 38 per cent of the women described themselves as 'Republican', and 23 per cent of the men and 27 per cent of the women as 'Democrats': the remainder were non-committal.

The incidence of marriage and the age at marriage was much the same for the gifted as for the general population. In this they differed from ordinary college graduates with whom marriage was somewhat less frequent or was contracted somewhat later in life: the discrepancy, we are told, 'was particularly striking in the case of gifted women'. Gifted persons, it was found, tend to marry those who are themselves above average in general intelligence. The divorce rate was only 11 per cent for the men, 13 per cent for the women, and still lower for those who had passed through college. The average I.Q. of their children was 133. This figure, it is stated, 'conforms fairly well to what would be expected in virtue of Galton's law of filial regression'. No information seems to have been obtained regarding interest or active participation in social or philanthropic work or in local politics.

Causes of failure

Every investigator who has followed up a group of children, selected for their high abilities at or before the middle of their school careers, has recorded that a certain proportion failed to fulfil their early promise. It is therefore important to inquire what are the commoner causes of such failure. Most of the available information relates to failure at the secondary school stage; some to failure among university students; comparatively little to the failure of gifted individuals during adult life. Let us therefore begin by reviewing the apparent causes of scholastic failure. For this I shall rely principally on data obtained from after-histories of pupils transferred to grammar or technical schools in Britain at the age of eleven or thereabouts. Later we may consider how far the same conclusions hold good of failure in adult life; and for that we must depend chiefly on the Californian investigations.

1. *Faulty assessments.* The explanation most commonly put forward, particularly by critics of the whole idea of selection, is that verdicts reached at the early age of 11-plus, at any rate with existing procedures, are bound to be very frequently misleading. Before the introduction of intelligence testing, the after-histories of those who had passed or failed in the scholarship examination already indicated the inadequacy of relying solely on a single written examination—and that of a strictly scholastic type—for assessing the abilities of children at these tender years; and the fact that such examinations cannot do justice to the bright child from an uncultured home is now a platitude. But it does not seem so widely realized that a child of only mediocre intelligence, who is reasonably industrious and comes from a fairly good home, can answer most of the questions in the ordinary type of question paper in English and arithmetic, provided he has a retentive memory to compensate for his lack of outstanding ability.[4] With what are commonly called 'tests of intelligence' a dull pupil is far

less likely to succeed; but it is still quite possible for a bright pupil to come to grief owing to some physical or emotional upset on the day of the examination. Cheating is nowadays largely forestalled by the methods of invigilation. Coaching is a more troublesome problem; but its effects can also be eliminated if proper care is taken in the construction and marking of tests. But, when all is said, causes of this kind are far less frequent than is generally supposed. They accounted for no more than 7 per cent of the cases in our later surveys.

2. *Ill-health.* A far more important cause of failure consisted in serious illness or prolonged ill-health during the secondary school period. (*a*) Acute illness (noted in 3 per cent of the cases)—resulting in most instances from a definite infection (scarlet fever, influenza, pneumonia, or the like)—was often followed by a serious decline in the child's school progress. (*b*) Still more frequent, and much more frequently ignored, were the mild but chronic forms of weakness prevalent among children coming from the poorer type of home—anaemia, malnutrition, recurrent catarrh, and what the school doctor usually labels 'general debility'. Where such conditions were detected and dealt with at an early stage (e.g. by provision of school meals, country holidays, regular exercise in the fresh air), the consequences could often be averted. They were noted in over 6 per cent of our cases. Today they would probably be less frequent; but they have by no means been wholly removed. (*c*) Physical disturbances associated with puberty sometimes formed a contributory factor. Often the observable symptoms were nervous or emotional. Such causes were noted in 4 per cent of our cases (chiefly girls). (*d*) Specific physical disabilities, such as are frequently responsible for educational backwardness among children of average or slightly subnormal intelligence—defects of vision and hearing, stammering, left-handedness, and the like—were much rarer among the gifted, and particularly among those who had already succeeded in securing entrance to schools of the 'grammar' type (2 per cent). Altogether physical causes accounted for 15 per cent of the failures.

3. *Fluctuations in development.* The curve of a child's development is not like the curve of a planetary orbit: you cannot, by noting his position and growth-rate at one point of his course, foretell with perfect accuracy what position he will reach at some later point. Although the *average* curve of growth is fairly smooth and

regular, the curves for individuals often exhibit well-marked variations. A few seem precocious in the narrow sense: they mature rapidly and come to an early arrest; yet well-attested cases of this type appear to be almost as exceptional as the so-called late bloomers. Far commoner is the type of child whose mental development is swift and steady up to the stage of puberty, and then undergoes a series of minor setbacks (traceable quite as often to external as to internal causes) from which he may or may not eventually recover. Nearly 12 per cent of the failures encountered in our inquiries appeared to be due to unforeseen developmental changes of this kind.

4. *Special abilities.* During the later stages of the child's school career his abilities tend more and more to specialize. This presumably is due largely to the delayed maturation of what are called 'special aptitudes', and partly perhaps to the emergence of new and special interests. As a result, some of the gifted children apparently belong to a definitely 'intellectual' (or academic) type, others to a 'practical' (or technical) type. The former, usually at a somewhat later stage, subdivide into a verbal or literary type and a scientific or mathematical type. Clear-cut examples of the three main types are rare; the distinction is a matter of degree rather than of kind. And, although a few children may reveal a definite bias at quite an early age, it would be quite impracticable to effect a general classification on this threefold basis at 11-plus, as was at one time proposed. Consequently, when at eleven or thereabouts nearly all the brighter pupils are creamed off by a scholarship examination or other type of selective test and transferred forthwith to a school of the 'grammar' type, a large proportion will later on turn out to be children whose latent aptitudes would have fitted them far better for an education of a more practical, technical or scientific type. The number of failures due to this cause varies according to the provision made for technical education and the methods and age of selection. In London, during the periods of our surveys, the proportion attributable to this cause amounted to 8 per cent.[5]

One further cause of failure belonging to this general group calls for passing mention at this point. As we have seen, many highly intelligent children display an ability that is creative rather than assimilative. They may have poor mechanical memories; more often, perhaps, they are simply bored by the drudgery of routine and rote work that the current examination system demands. As a result, during the grammar school stage, particularly when judged by examination standards, they are apt to be set down as 'disappointing pupils, who have failed to fulfil their early promise'. In after life, as artists, poets, or inventors, or perhaps as enterprising captains of industry, they may achieve astonishing success; and once again we note the obvious danger that, in dealing with its most gifted pupils, the secondary school of today is liable to stifle rather than stimulate originality and inventiveness, and to favour the reproductive at the expense of the productive type of mind.

5. *Motivational conditions.* By far the most important factors (noted in 32 per cent of our cases) arose from those emotional elements of personality which underlie motivation, and in particular from the child's attitude towards school. In teachers' reports the commonest complaint is that the child is lacking in the 'will to work' or 'devoid of interest in school subjects'. In many cases the school itself is largely to blame: the deep and lasting influence exercised by an enthusiastic and scholarly teacher is constantly mentioned in the autobiographical or retrospective comments of pupils who have effectively developed their potential gifts, and the lack of a sympathetic teacher by those who have felt frustrated. Still more frequently, as we shall see in a moment, the favourable or unfavourable attitude of the child is determined by the attitude prevailing in the home. In yet other instances, as the family histories themselves suggest, the weakness appears constitutional. This, I fancy, is one of the commonest reasons why scholarship winners from the lower occupational classes so often fail to fulfil their early promise; again and again in cases such as these we find that the parents and other relatives seemed to have suffered from a similar lack of ambition or industry, with the result that the family as a whole has drifted or sunk to their present low level.

Gifted children, like children of average or subnormal intelligence, have all varieties of temperament from the highly excitable to the completely apathetic, and from the abnormally introvert to abnormally extravert. Any exceptional deviation of this kind is apt to hinder steady concentration on the daily tasks of the classroom.[6] To achieve success in the intellectual sphere the learner needs not only high intellectual ability, but certain qualities of character as well—a stable temperament, a driving curiosity about intellectual problems, a capacity for sustained hard work, and a determination to do well, together with ideals and aims that look forward to the remoter future and to scholastic success instead of hankering after immediate pleasures or mere monetary rewards. By the time the child has reached the age of early adolescence he has acquired a repertory of implicit values and a fairly definite notion of the type of person he wants to be and the sort of life he hopes to enjoy. Many a sharp teenager fails in the grammar school because he has come to look on the world as a kind of fun-fair. The inducements of an easily earned wage and of irresponsible freedom, untrammelled by the restrictions of home and school, may all too readily overcome any initial resolve to stick at sedentary tasks day after day and year after year. Every school-master can quote disappointing instances of this sort—bright, responsive, talented youngsters, marred by some lack of stamina, allured by the profuse attractions of this modern age—the Micawbers, the Jingles, the Uncle Ponderevos, who, when he meets them in after years, bring to his mind Brutus' reflection on Casca:

'What a blunt fellow this is grown to be!
Yet he was quick mettle when he went to school.'[7]

6. *Home conditions.* An almost equally important factor, often overlapping with one or more of the others, consisted in the unfavourable conditions obtaining at home. The attitude of the child is determined by the attitude of his family. Many of the parents appeared to be entirely indifferent to the child's success either in school or even in later life; and thus did nothing to help or encourage him in what of necessity formed an arduous undertaking for all but the most gifted. 'Homework' in such cases was a frequent difficulty, since there was no quiet place where the child could concentrate on his evening tasks. An even larger number of parents seemed actively hostile to the idea of further education. They wanted their youngster to contribute as soon as possible to the family income, and looked on academic pursuits as a pedantic affectation unworthy of a working-class lad and liable to make him feel superior to his own family. 'Book larning', said a burly bus-conductor to me once, 'is not for kids that'll have to earn their own bread'; adding, with the ambiguous pronunciation of the Cockney, 'It's for them as like to give theirselves the hairs of the

eyebrow.' Conditions of this kind were noted in as many as 28 per cent of the cases.

Failure and success in adult life

Terman's follow-up inquiries continued, as we have seen, well into adult life, and furnished unique opportunities for studying the various factors making for success or failure in later years. Three colleagues were invited to make independent assessments of the 730 men who had reached or passed the age of twenty-five. Taking as a criterion, 'the extent to which the subject had made use of his superior ability', the three judges were asked to select the 150 most successful and the 150 least successful. The previous histories of the two groups were then systematically compared. It appeared that many of the 'prognostic differences' had been already discernible almost at the very start of the whole research.

There were, to begin with, marked differences between the two groups in regard to parents and home backgrounds. In the successful group those who had parents from the professional classes were twice as numerous as in the unsuccessful group; and generally the educational tradition was far stronger in the families of the former. Men of Jewish extraction were three times as numerous. At school the more successful had been promoted much more rapidly: 90 per cent had graduated, as compared with 37 per cent among the least successful. Among the latter many declared that they had just drifted into the jobs they occupied, and a good many would have preferred a different type of employment. Nevertheless, quite a large proportion had deliberately selected a comparatively humble career, free from responsibility, and many preferred to exercise their talents on hobbies and other pursuits which brought 'content rather than hard-earned fame'.

Ill-health, an unhappy home, and the various types of misfortune that are liable to overtake men through no fault of their own were occasionally to blame. But, on the whole, the medical history of the two groups showed comparatively little difference. The most striking contrasts were found in the assessments for temperament and personality. Even during childhood the least successful received far lower ratings for emotional stability, perseverance, self-confidence and social adjustment. Later on, quite in keeping with these early ratings, they appeared to change their jobs far more frequently and found it harder to settle down. The marriage rate was lower; the divorce rate twice as high; and among the married the wives were far less intelligent or ambitious than those of the more successful members. Perhaps the most significant difference between the two, as revealed by ratings and actual test results, was a difference in the 'level of aspiration' and as the investigators term it, 'the drive to achieve'.

From a practical standpoint, however, the conclusion of greatest importance is one on which Terman himself lays special stress: 'Eighteen years prior to the classification made by the judges on the basis of adult achievements, the teachers and parents had already discerned those differences of personality which later on would distinguish the most successful individuals from the comparative failures.'

Where the loss of talent occurs

The foregoing inquiries into the causes of failure may be supplemented by a still more recent investigation undertaken for the National Science Foundation in the USA. The inquiry involved a review of all relevant national statistics and a series of intensive studies made in individual States and among selected samples. The results obtained indicate (as the Dean of Harvard puts it) 'the measure of our failure as educators at the present day'. Of the brightest 10 per cent of American children, it was found 'about 90 per cent of both boys and girls graduate from high school; about 80 per cent of the boys and 60 per cent of the girls get to college; and some 55 per cent of the boys and 40 per cent of the girls finally graduate from college'. From this highly superior group the total number who thus drop out at one stage or another amounts, we are told, to over 125,000 a year. A similar inquiry was made with a lower borderline, cutting off the top 30 per cent —a figure suggested by the high proportion of the general population who enter college in the USA; the percentages indicating the wastage at each stage were much the same as before. In both cases what perhaps is particularly striking is the fact that the greatest loss occurs not in the transition from school to college but after college entrance.

Further inquiry revealed a multiplicity of reasons why these young people fail to enter college in spite of their high intelligence; the commonest appear to be financial need, lack of interest, the attractions of full-time jobs, and, with the girls, early marriage. The reasons for dropping out after entry are rather different; lack of effective habits of work, lack of appropriate motivation, loss of interest in the subjects of the course, and dissatisfaction with the quality of teaching or the type of counselling provided; at this stage apparently financial considerations are far less important. The places of those who should reach college but do not are filled by others of lower potential talent. For the country as a whole, it appears 'over half the college entrants are drawn from school graduates *below* the top 30 per cent level of ability. . . . Have we', the writer asks, 'unduly stimulated a demand for college education among men who will not gain from it the advantages they are seeking?'[8]

Potential ability and realized ability

Most of the knowledge and skill acquired by a member of a civilized society depends on the environmental facilities which he has enjoyed from infancy upwards, particularly on those provided in his home and school. And there can be little doubt that the intellectual and practical efficiency of each and every individual could be increased by improving those facilities. Supply the average schoolboy or the average undergraduate with a personal tutor or coach, and he will very likely pass an examination in which he would otherwise have failed. But while it is right to insist on the value of a favourable environment, there is no need to belittle the influence of genetic factors. The fact that certain conditions are highly advantageous does not justify us in concluding that they are also sufficient.

Educational and social writers frequently assure us that the conditions provided by the ideal home or school can and should 'stimulate mental growth'. But the phrase contains a fallacious metaphor. It implies the old-fashioned notion that the effects of exercise and training tend to become generalized or transferred. Transfer, however, is effective only in very restricted and specialized ways. No doubt, in the absence of propitious conditions in the environment, the child's potentialities will not be realized to the full. But it is equally possible that his genetic potentialities may themselves be severely limited.

One of the experiments most frequently cited is the Demonstration Guidance Project carried out in the poorer quarters of

New York. The brightest pupils were selected for a specially intensive education. In the course of six years their scholastic attainments had greatly improved. Yet their average I.Q. had only risen from 94 to 97·6—a change which probably demonstrated not so much an improvement in the children's real intelligence but rather the liability of nearly all such tests to be affected by environmental circumstances. To secure a maximum supply of fully developed or *realized* ability we certainly need a maximum of encouragement and opportunity in the environment—at least for all who are potentially capable of such high development. But the maximum amount of *potential* ability depends on, and is strictly limited by, the individual's inborn constitution. Potential ability can be changed (if at all) only by changes in the factors affecting that constitution.[9]

The effects of changes in the birth-rate

The remarkable success that has followed the application of genetic principles in agriculture, horticulture and stockbreeding naturally prompts the inquiry whether similar methods might not be exploited to improve the genetic make-up of the human race. The answer is that human genetics, and particularly what is sometimes called psychogenetics, are specialized branches of a novel science about which far too little is at present known. Quite apart from the ethical and political issues involved, we are still much too ignorant even to sketch in outline a sound scheme of eugenics such as could be put into actual practice. Analogies from other fields and the results of fairly simple calculations would certainly seem to indicate that the relatively low fertility, which commonly distinguishes highly intelligent families, must in the long run tend to diminish the proportion of highly intelligent offspring born in each successive generation; but it is too soon to seek any clear or convincing confirmation from the data so far available from successive population surveys. It may, however, be safely said that, despite the pessimistic prognostications put forward a quarter of a century ago, there has been, during the last fifty years or so, no *great* deterioration in the average level of intelligence in this country. On the other hand, it certainly seems conceivable that there may have been a *small* decline, amounting perhaps to about 1 to 2 I.Q. points per generation; and a drop of 1 point only in the general average would imply a loss of over 15 per cent in the number of gifted children at the upper end of the scale (130 I.Q. or upwards).[10]

The effects of changes in matrimonial customs

The characteristics of the individual depend not only on the simple transmission of genes, but still more on the recombination of genes brought about through sexual reproduction; and, as genetic researches on plants and animals have abundantly shown, the quality of each new generation may be profoundly affected by modifications in the mating system. From history we know full well how changes in the balance between inbreeding and out-breeding can influence the destinies of human populations, re-moulding them sometimes for good, sometimes for ill. Most of the highly civilized nations seem to have started their career from the mingling, friendly or forcible, of a number of different races, and to have been distinguished by the formation of inter-fertile classes, which work together without, as a rule, breeding together —a system which is found in no other form of animal life.[11] Our own society has been marked by fairly stringent limits to inter-marriage between distinct social classes, together with an in-creasingly free mobility of the exceptionally able or exceptionally incompetent upwards or downwards from one class to another. But during the past fifty years vast changes have taken place in the whole structure of modern society. New methods of transport, new means of production, new modes of government, a lowering of barriers between different races and different social classes, and in our own country a marked improvement in the educational ladder—all these transformations have visibly altered the balance and stability of the various nations and of the constituent bodies within the same nation. Groups that have been inbred for cen-turies are now shifting over to outbreeding. What effect all this will have on the genetic composition of each community it is impossible to foretell. But, as the genealogist would be the first to agree, the possible changes undoubtedly present an urgent subject for research and for reflection.[12]

The discovery of the gifted

Meanwhile, much can be done by introducing more efficient methods for identifying the gifted, and more appropriate modes of training them according to their varying needs. A good deal of the recent criticism of the 11-plus examination is no doubt both misconceived and misinformed; yet it is to a large extent based on a genuine sense of the inadequacies of present methods of selection.

To begin with, the procedures employed tend chiefly to pick out those who are most likely to succeed in a grammar school education of the traditional type. As we have already noted, they favour the verbal mind rather than the technical, the analytic rather than the intuitive or synthetic, the assimilative rather than the creative. However, fresh tests are already available which have been tentatively used for studying these neglected aspects of intellectual activity; and some of them might be tried out systematically to discover practicable ways in which current selection tests could be modified or developed. But intelligence is by no means the sole criterion to be adopted in deciding who are the gifted individuals. Special abilities and disabilities, and above all the relevant traits of temperament and character, must also be taken into account. In short, the focus should be on *the person as a whole*, not on mere intellectual capacity. All this implies that the process of selection must be based on the information secured, not only by formal standardized tests but also by the continued observations of the experienced teacher during his daily contacts with each pupil both in the classroom and outside it.

It is equally important to start identifying those who are potentially gifted at the earliest possible age, and (so far as is practicable) to ensure that their curriculum at school and their training and occupations at home shall be suited to their unusual capacities well before they are eventually transferred to special types of secondary school. Furthermore, since the course of mental development is often liable to marked fluctuations, and since so many special aptitudes are comparatively late in maturing, the allocations made at 11-plus should be regarded not as fixed for the rest of the child's school life, but as subject to repeated review.

The need for selection

Although, as a rule, it is the method of selection which forms the ostensible object of criticism, the chief reason for popular opposition has to a large extent been the principle of selection in itself. The fact that many are called and few chosen naturally comes as an unwelcome shock to those who are rejected. Apart from all personal feelings, the very notion of segregating children according to their inborn gifts seems to many a misguided attempt to substitute an ill-conceived meritocracy for the hard-won principles of democracy.[13] It magnifies the minor differences between one individual and another at the expense of the universal human nature which binds us all together.

This, it has been said, should be the golden age of the common man. It is our duty first and foremost to do the best for the vast mass of the population who, after all, consist of just ordinary mortals of just average ability. Our next obligation is to provide extra help and extra care for the subnormal and the handicapped. Nevertheless, in the interest not only of national survival but of the progress of the race as a whole, there is no escaping the obvious conclusion that in the long run it is the highly intelligent few who can confer the greatest benefits on the less intelligent many— including, it may be, in a time of crisis the gift of life itself.

In our laudable anxiety to improve the lot of our own generation we are apt to close our eyes to the effects of present policy on the generations to come. The society which pays most attention to its genetical future will be the society that is most likely to have a future. The influence of great men on the course of history is a well-worn platitude. But too often both historian and biographer have allowed us to forget the many occasions on which disaster has befallen nations and empires just because the great man was not forthcoming at the crucial moment. What catastrophes might have been averted had Athens found another Miltiades in 413 B.C., Jerusalem another Judas Maccabaeus in A.D. 70, Rome another Julius Caesar in the fifth century. Or—to pick but a single instance from science—suppose that Ptolemy, the author of *The Great Syntaxis* (or 'Almagest'), had possessed the brain of a Newton or an Archimedes, what a world of difference that one exchange of genes might have made to the development of astronomy, technology and religion during the next fourteen hundred years.

In spite of popular prejudice there is, or there should be, no insuperable conflict between equality as a principle of justice and inequality as a fact of genetics. In education equal opportunity means equal opportunity to make the most of differences that are innate. The ideal is a free and fair chance for each individual, not to rise to the same rank in life as everyone else, but to develop the peculiar gifts and virtues with which he is endowed—high ability if he possesses it; if not, whatever qualities of body, mind and character are latent within him. In this way, and this way alone, can we be sure of realizing to the full our untapped resources of talent, and warding off the decline and fall that has in the end overtaken each of the great civilizations of the past.

Notes and references

1 H. Lehndorff and L. Falkenstein, 'Christian Henrick Heineken: the miracle boy from Lübeck, 1720–4', *Arch. Pediatr.*, 72, 1955, 360–77.

2 L. M. Terman *et al.*, *The Promise of Youth: follow-up studies of a thousand gifted children* (1930); *The Gifted Child Grows Up* (1947); *The Gifted Group at Mid-Life* (1959).

3 *The Gifted Group at Mid-Life*, chaps 7 and 11. Although Terman's list mentions scientists and industrialists of international influence and reputation, it includes no poet, musician or artist of the same high rank. It is tempting to suggest that here again we have some evidence that the psychologist's methods of selection tend to pick out the analytical and logical types rather than the synthetic, intuitive or creative.

4 It should be noted that in later years the types of question set by the LCC examiners were drastically changed so that, although they were couched in the form of questions in English and Arithmetic, the answers turned more on the child's capacity for problem-solving than on the retentiveness of his memory. I may add that similar misjudgments may occur at a much higher level. I have known several students with I.Q.s between 105 and 115 who had succeeded in obtaining second-class honours in their final examinations mainly by dint of a good memory and a little luck in the questions set.

5 The evidence for these conclusions is set out in a number of articles dealing with the reorganization of education contemplated under the Butler Act: e.g. cf. 'The education of the adolescent: implications of the Norwood Report', *Br. J. educ. Psychol.*, 13, 126–40; and the *Symposium on the Selection of Pupils for Different Types of Secondary Schools*, ibid., esp. 17, pp. 62 ff.

6 The ways in which such conditions affect school work is discussed in detail in *The Backward Child* (1946), ch. 15. Their operation is much the same in the supernormal as in the subnormal.

7 Among historical celebrities who exemplify what I have called 'realized genius', a high degree of emotionality is extremely common, especially in the more creative personalities. With those who become practical organizers —leading politicians, captains of industry, social reformers, or the like— it is concentrated and controlled, supplying an incessant drive; with artists and men of letters, particularly the poets, *genus irritabile vatum*, the control is often lacking. See also P. Witty and H. C. Lehman, 'Drive: a neglected trait in the study of the gifted', *Psychol. Rev.*, 34, 1927, 364 ff.

8 Donald S. Bridgman, 'Where the loss of talent occurs and why', ap. *College Admissions 7: the search for talent* (College Entrance Examination Board, New York, 1960), pp. 30–5. The evidence as to reasons for dropping out during

the college is taken from R. E. Iffert, *Retention and Withdrawal of College Students* (U.S. Government Printing Office, 1957). Bridgman's figures for wastage are somewhat smaller than the estimates given in the earlier study by Dael Wolfle (*America's Resources of Specialized Talent*, 1954); but Wolfle's study suffered from the after-effects of the war and other somewhat exceptional factors operating at the time. Let me add that it is high time a similar set of inquiries were undertaken in Britain.

9 See D. N. McIntosh, *Educational Guidance and the Pool of Ability* (University of London Press, 1959).

10 For a summary of the various arguments, with detailed references, may I refer to my memorandum on *Intelligence and Fertility* (1952), originally prepared at the request of the Royal Commission on Population. As I there pointed out, 'to predict an alteration in traits from a knowledge simply of the selective factors at work may be altogether rash in the absence of adequate knowledge about the way those traits are genetically determined': e.g. if the heterozygotes (or hybrids) were superior to the homozygotes, repeated selection of the superior types would be ineffective. In their final *Report*, the Commission conclude that, although the calculations submitted by their witnesses differed appreciably in detail, 'all of them point to a rather serious drop in average intelligence with a more than corresponding increase in mental deficiency and decrease of high intelligence' (p. 154). The view tentatively suggested above would appear to represent that of the majority of British geneticists. Thus P. B. Medawar, in his chapter on 'Intelligence and fertility', concludes that 'if innately unintelligent people have larger families, we can infer that the average level will decline, but . . . the decline will be slow—much slower than the negative correlation between intelligence and family size might tempt us to suppose' (*The Future of Man*, 1960, p. 86); and J. B. S. Haldane's estimate of the decline is practically the same as my own, '1 or 2 points per generation' (*Heredity and Politics*, p. 117).

11 cf. R. A. Fisher, *The Genetical Theory of Natural Selection* (1950), pp. 170 ff.; C. D. Darlington and K. Mather, *Genes, Plants and People* (1950); C. D. Darlington, 'The control of evolution in man', *Eugen. Rev.*, 50, 1958, 169–78.

12 cf. J. Conway and C. Burt, 'Class differences in general intelligence', *Br. J. statist. Psychol.*, 12, 1959, 5–34 for a discussion of the genetic aspects; also S. M. Lipset and R. Bendix, *Social Mobility and Industrial Society*, 1959, esp. ch. 9.

13 Here, I fancy, the mistake lies not in the selection of the gifted individuals, but in the way they are trained and treated after selection. As I have argued elsewhere, simply to give such children an academic education at a grammar school and university, and thus in effect to transfer them from the humbler class in which they were born and which so urgently needs leaders of high ability, to an aristocracy consisting of an intellectual élite may in the end prove both wasteful and harmful. Take but a single illustration: suppose

Ernest Bevin, having gained scholarships at Rugby and Oxford, had then passed the examination for the Civil Service (like so many of the ablest graduates of his day), what a loss that would have meant both for the trade union movement and for the nation as a whole.

CHAPTER THIRTEEN

The education of the gifted

The foregoing conclusions, I suggest, provide the best available clues to the basic principles which should guide the education of the gifted child. Let us consider in turn their practical implications.

As we have seen, the intelligence quotient, by its origin and form, expresses a rate. It measures the average speed of mental development during the immature years of growth: a child of six with a mental age of nine has developed, and probably will continue to develop, at a rate which is 50 per cent faster than the average. From this it is sometimes inferred that the school progress of such a child, and therefore his rate of promotion, should be half as fast again as that of the ordinary pupil. To draw practical inferences direct from theoretical generalizations is always rash and often misleading. In point of fact, as my own case records demonstrate, if such a child happens to have been placed in a special type of school where practically all the pupils are of the same high calibre, and if the school curriculum is adapted to the actual capacities of the pupils, then their rate of progress in the more elementary subjects proves to be on average nearly twice that of the average child. The same holds good, so far as my experience goes, of those children who have been taught wholly at home by highly intelligent parents or by competent tutors.

This at first sight may seem paradoxical. But it is fully confirmed by the results of other investigators. Dr Hollingworth, for example, writes: 'We know from measurements we have made over a three-year period that a child of 140 I.Q. can master all the mental work provided in the elementary school, as ordinarily established, in half the time allowed; and a child of 170 I.Q. can do all the studies required, with top marks, in about one-fourth of the time' (op. cit., p. 287). The reason no doubt is that such a child, in addition to superior intelligence, is also characterized by a quicker insight, a more retentive memory, and greater keenness and industry. Unless adequate provision is made to meet their needs and capabilities, such children are liable to waste half their time, and as a result to feel frustrated and dissatisfied. Unrecognized and consequently held fast in the lock-step of the ordinary class, the potential genius drags and drifts along, gradually acquiring a habit of idleness, daydreaming, or inventing mischief. School for him becomes a place in which day by day he experiences intolerable boredom, and which not unnaturally he soon begins to detest.

The autobiographies of men of high ability are full of retrospective complaints. Darwin, writing of Shrewsbury—the school which is now so proud of him—declares, 'Nothing could have been worse for the development of my mind than Dr Butler's school: to me as a means of education it was simply a blank.' Not infrequently he played truant, and spent his time studying the plants, the animals and the birds which he observed in the country lanes. During these solitary strolls, he tells us, he became so addicted to following his own inner train of thought that, during one of his rambles along the fortifications, he actually stepped over the edge, and fell seven or eight feet. Galton, looking back on his life at his first boarding school, says the place 'was hateful to me in many ways, and lovable in none'. At King Edward's School, Birmingham, where he went a few years later, he says, 'I learnt nothing, and chafed at the limitations.' In a letter to his father he writes: 'How much better to remove me before it is too late.' Nor in this respect have schools greatly changed. I could quote equally emphatic criticism of the curricula of today. Here is an extract from a diary kept by a child of ten. 'All the sums were so easy I wrote down the answers at sight. The others took nearly an hour. Squeers [his Dickensian nickname for the master] said I had guessed, and I was to write the working out in full . . . It isn't only that the others are all so slow. The teachers are equally stupid. Twice this week I got the answer right, and Squeers got it wrong. He owned up after a bit of argy-bargy, but rather sarcastically'.

One of my research students has made a special study of the ablest pupils in a selected batch of comprehensive schools, and, after testing their intelligence, interviewed all who had an I.Q. over 140. Three types of criticism occurred again and again. (*a*) In regard to subjects, more than half the pupils complained that the curriculum made no provision for the particular topics in which they were specially interested and for which they possessed a special aptitude (e.g. with boys higher mathematics, nuclear physics and molecular biology; with girls various aesthetic subjects, such as poetry, painting, instrumental music, ballet-dancing, and the like). (*b*) As regards teaching methods, a large number protested about 'the waste of time in playing down to the dunces —learning things by games and childish examples, when they are obvious at a glance', in short, about what are supposed to be 'progressive methods'. A few, however, approved of the heuristic methods in science, 'especially when you are left to go ahead on your own'. (*c*) As regards the teachers themselves, 'the commonest complaint [we are told] was that the pupil so often realized that he himself was quicker at seeing the point and in solving problems, and had a better knowledge of his special subjects, than those who were trying to teach him. The remarks of the teachers [it is added] not infrequently bore out this conclusion. In the words of one of them, "the presence of a couple of pupils who are excessively bright can be more of a nuisance in the day-to-day work of the classroom than half a dozen who are excessively backward".' According to the Foundation's Report, 'nearly 850 teachers out of approximately 11,000 state that they are called upon to teach, often at a highly specialized level, subjects for which they are imperfectly prepared'. The moral would seem to be that, instead of pursuing a policy which demands a greater uniformity in the nation's schools, we should aim at a greater diversity.

The child who suffers most is the bright child from the humbler ranks. Those whose parents are themselves professional people often enjoy the requisite facilities and encouragement at home. Boys whose parents are themselves of mediocre ability, with no intellectual interests, are doubly handicapped. Nowhere, either at home or at school, are they given the opportunities or the materials to develop their own intellectual interests. In the commoner type of 'intelligence test' (so-called)—usually a verbal group test—they fail to do themselves justice. The outlook of their friends and relatives leads them to aim rather at immediate financial gain than at educational advancement. They quickly discover that their own intelligence is superior to that of both parents and teachers. They become restless and resentful; and their main object is to break loose from school and home and secure an independence of their own. Plainly, therefore, these quick learners confront the educationist with practical problems that are even more urgent than those of the 'slow learners' of whom we have lately heard so much.

So long as we think solely of the child's rate of progress, the natural solution may seem obvious: promote such pupils twice as fast as the others. This was the principle explicitly adopted in the two oldest of the recorded attempts at catering for 'superior scholars'—St Louis (1868) and the 'Cambridge plan' (1891); in these early American schemes the promotions were made twice a year, so that eight grades could be covered in four years. This by itself, however, is far from satisfactory. For one thing it means placing tiny youngsters in classes intended primarily for those who are very much older and very much bigger. The seats and desks are too high; the rest of the class are far more mature and worldly wise, and what is the child to do when he gets to the top class in the school? By the time he is ten or eleven the mental gap between him and the average pupil is so large that a separate type of school seems needed. This argument appeared to be the only valid psychological ground for introducing selection and separation at the early age of eleven (see the memoranda which I drew up at the request of the Consultative Committee of the Board of Education and printed in their *Reports*). It should be remembered that what educational officials were originally concerned with were the brightest 3 or 4 per cent (roughly corresponding to the former 'scholarship winners')—pupils who might reasonably hope to become honours candidates at a university. To gain a scholarship at a university, it was said, such a boy should start his special subjects—Latin, Greek, Advanced Mathematics, Chemistry or the like—not later than eleven. If, however, we are thinking rather of the top 25 per cent, then at that early age the gap between the borderline pupil and the average child is much narrower and discrimination consequently more difficult. The solution preferred by many teachers was an internal organization of schools into a series of 'streams'; the curriculum for pupils in the 'A' stream kept to the courses laid down in official 'recommendations', but covered them at a more rapid pace; but then the difficulty is to find enough specialist teachers for the brightest 3 or 4 per cent.

Accelerated programmes of these various types may meet part of the problem; but they are far from adequate. After all we do not want the brighter pupils to be just rushing on to topics that they will be able to cope with much more effectively when they have had a longer experience of worldly life. And, while concentrating on the knotty question of transfer to a 'secondary school of grammar type' at the age of eleven, we have tended to ignore the equally urgent needs of such children during the 'primary' stage.

Accordingly, as several writers, particularly in the United States, have recently pointed out, what is really needed is not merely a faster programme, but a richer programme. One of the problems which has of late been worrying teachers and educationists is the tendency towards premature and one-sided specialization in the higher forms of the grammar school. This is very largely the result of the requirements prescribed for entrance to a university. It is too often forgotten that these requirements are relics of the days when tutors at the older universities and headmasters in the older grammar schools thought first and foremost of those exceptionally bright youngsters who were likely to obtain a First in Literae Humaniores or to become wranglers in the Mathematical Tripos at Cambridge. The problem might, I think, be partly met if we could frankly recognize the distinction between the exceptionally gifted pupils who deserve a fair chance to achieve these or similar successes at the university, and the moderately gifted who deserve a university training but can hardly be expected to aim so high as first-class honours. The exceptionally gifted pupil can start his special subjects quite early without entirely sacrificing his interest in other fields of human knowledge.

As we have seen, one of the outstanding characteristics of the gifted child is the wide range of his potential interests. A boy of ten was referred to me as 'an incorrigible truant and a constant nuisance in the classroom'. With the Northumberland Tests (mainly verbal, the forerunner of the present-day Moray House Group Tests) his I.Q. was 132; with an individual test (British adaptation of Terman–Binet) it was 168; and his quotient rating on a test of general information was 187. In reading, arithmetic and handwork his test score was superior to the average for children of fifteen; in spelling and composition it was barely eleven. I found that the days on which he was absent from school were commonly spent at the Science Museum at South Kensington or at one or other of the nearest borough libraries, or occasionally with one or two fellow-truants at various railway stations. He was surprisingly well informed about the history of locomotives and the working of railway and aeroplane engines and he had picked up a wide knowledge of elementary physics, mechanics and geology, and of the lives of famous inventors. A year later it was possible to transfer him to a junior technical institute, and subsequently to a school of engineering. He is now a well-known designer of aircraft.

Another youngster, encountered during my surveys, the son of a schoolmaster with the run of his father's library, had by the age of seven read all Scott's poems, and most of his novels. This led him to read Green's *History of England*, and learn the genealogies of the kings. When he was nine he started Hogben's *Science for the Citizens* and this was followed by *Mathematics for the Million*. Meanwhile he had unearthed a copy of the Hebrew scriptures and a Hebrew grammar; and he was able to translate for me the whole of the story of Joseph, not from his memory of the English Bible (which, of course, he had used), but literally, word by word, with very few mistakes.

A talent for dancing, for music, and for mathematics may show itself quite early—even at the infant school. But these are exceptional. So far as my own case-histories go, few of the brighter children exhibit signs of highly specialized abilities until they approach adolescence, though special interests, sometimes transitory, not infrequently predominate at an early age. Given the chance, nearly all evince at the earlier stages an intelligent appreciation both of general literature and of general science. Of late there has been a growing preference for scientific subjects, notably astronomy, fostered largely by programmes seen on television. During the primary school period any adequately trained teacher should be able to meet their youthful needs. Up to the age of eleven or twelve what such children need is not specialized instruction, but facilities for self-instruction—a variety of suitable books and magazines, a little apparatus, and a word or two of well-timed advice on choice of reading or the conduct of home-made experiments. At a later stage assistance can often be obtained from expert outsiders who are not members of the teaching staff. Local specialists from industry or the professions—a doctor, lawyer, artist or musician, an engineer or the borough librarian—can usually be discovered who will give talks or lectures, and often help with individual pupils who show a precocious interest in their own particular subjects.

Teachers themselves, I find, in the suggestions they offer to pupils of this type, are apt to adopt an attitude that is far too

academic. The approach they favour is commonly one that would
in the end enable such pupils to pass a written examination in the
subjects proposed. The real need, however, is for a plan of study
which will give the children a clearer understanding of what is
going on around them in ordinary life and at the same time help
them to become familiar (in Matthew Arnold's famous words)
'with the best that has been thought and said in the world'. During
their earlier years their minds are largely occupied with the
exploration—physical as well as intellectual—of the world into
which they have so recently been born. The evolution of common things, the story of the town or county in which they live,
the design of household furniture and crockery, electricity in the
home, the chemistry of cookery, of clothing, of plastics and
detergents, of drugs and disinfectants—these are the kinds of
topic in which their interest can readily be aroused. Even at the
primary stage the brightest might well be encouraged to learn a
foreign language—in general I would suggest French (Dumas by
way of introduction); for those with a scientific bias German. The
bright child always picks up a strange language best if he starts
when very young; for one thing, pronunciation and accent are
more readily mastered before the child's articulatory habits are
rigidly fixed. Later those intending to specialize in the Arts can
nevertheless profit by a general course on the history and philosophy of science; and both the future Arts student and the future
Science student can be introduced to the topics of local government, elementary economics and current affairs. Biography and
travel are popular at every age.

Those who are highly gifted tend at an unexpectedly early age
to take a spontaneous interest in—and, not infrequently, to become gravely worried by—problems of birth and death, of
religion and metaphysics. In my own experimental teaching I
have found it quite practicable to discuss with such youngsters in
homely language the traditional problems of philosophy and
ethics; and elementary instruction along these lines should, I
think, form a regular part of their training for future leadership.

When available, so-called 'teaching machines' are well suited to
the requirements of the older children. But the mechanical gadget
is not itself of paramount importance. What is wanted is a well-
devised programme for self-instruction—printed or roneod
schemes giving the bare essentials, definitions of technical concepts, skilfully worded statements of important generalizations and

results, and an outline of the method of investigation or proof, whether experimental or logical, adapted to the special needs of the pupils in question. Successful programmes of this type have still to be compiled; and their compilation is not a mere exercise in book production, but calls for careful trial and research. For foreign languages the elementary broadcasts on sound or television, and above all a suitably selected set of gramophone records, are invaluable.

The intelligent child is usually also a creative and inventive child. As we have seen, the high correlation that obtains between creativity and intelligence is often attenuated and obscured by the type of so-called intelligence test at present in vogue: it favours the acquisitive mind rather than the constructive mind, the assimilative rather than the inventive. Yet it needs no knowledge of history to realize that all national, intellectual and scientific progress has resulted primarily from the enterprise and innovations, the discoveries and the inventions, of a small handful of imaginative pioneers. Unfortunately in the ordinary classroom initiative and originality tend to upset the steady methodical routine of the day-to-day tasks. The youngster who is perpetually bursting with bright ideas or overflowing with awkward questions is consequently looked upon as a nuisance, a disturber both of the peace and of pace. His new-fangled notions meet with ridicule; and he is taught to hold his tongue. Initiative is suppressed, and atrophies for lack of exercise.

Better outlets for creativity are therefore essential. As our case-histories show, many children of this type pass their time in writing stories, composing poems, designing plans for model theatres or mechanical toys which they rarely have the chance to construct. Efforts in these directions should be deliberately encouraged in the classroom. Handicraft might play a much larger part. The popular superstition that the intelligent child is 'poor with his hands' dies hard. In point of fact, given materials suited to the tiny fingers of the very young or the more ambitious projects of the older child, the bright youngster often shows great mechanical ingenuity. In the ordinary work of the class they do much better with what used to be called the 'heuristic method', whereby the pupil discovers things for himself instead of being expected to take his facts and concepts at second hand from the teacher and just commit them to memory.

One marked characteristic of the highly intelligent child, perhaps his most distinctive characteristic, is his capacity for perceiving and applying logical relations. Where the average child links his sentences à *l'écriture sainte* with 'and . . . and' or an occasional 'when', his compositions are dotted with 'ifs' and 'thens', or 'because' and 'therefore'. This facility means that he can readily be taught to reason systematically. His favourite type of fiction is the detective story—particularly of the old-fashioned Sherlock Holmes and Austin Freeman kind, where the chief fun is to be got by trying to deduce the solution from the various clues which the author supplies. I suggest therefore that a more important and valuable part of such a child's education should consist in lessons or exercises in the techniques of reasoning—especially in the skill required to lay bare and criticize lurking fallacies. The elementary algebra of probability is a topic rarely taught in schools; yet for the scientific reasoner more especially it is a topic of supreme importance. It comes easily to the intelligent child at a comparatively early age. Both types of training—logical and statistical—can be made enjoyable if the teacher has at hand an assorted collection of puzzles and brain-teasers gleaned from the pages of weekly papers and magazines.

But the most conspicuous of the many problems presented by the child who is highly gifted is the wide disparity between his mature intelligence and his immature emotions. Until adolescence is complete his emotional level, as we have seen, corresponds far more closely with his chronological age than with his mental age. The child is painfully aware that he is exceptional; he feels isolated from his fellows, and in the ordinary school has the greatest difficulty in finding congenial friends. He gradually comes to realize that, because he is exceptional, he is understood neither at home nor at school. In our study of maladjusted children, it will be remembered, feelings of this kind were noted in more than 6 per cent of our cases. A large proportion were cases of 'highly gifted children', i.e. pupils with I.Q.s well over 150, those who, because of their rarity, form some of the community's most valuable assets. In Terman's 'thousand gifted cases', I fancy, the method of selection (based initially on teachers' nominations) probably led him to underestimate the frequency of neurotic disturbances; but even he noted that they were especially frequent among the brightest of all.

With children whose I.Q.s, though well over the average, are nevertheless below 150, instability and maladjustment are relatively rare. The mere fact that the child is intelligent imparts a certain measure of steadiness and self-control. In such cases the child's ambitions, industry and energy tend to be more or less in keeping with his abilities: and he is able to fend for himself and solve his own problems. Children who, though bright, are temperamentally lazy are apt to be a source of disappointment to the parents or teachers who recognize their abilities and a serious nuisance to those who do not. The most troublesome cases of all are those in which the child comes from a poor and semi-illiterate home and attends a school that recruits its pupils chiefly from the lower and duller levels of the so-called 'working classes'. Both at home and at school he develops all too often an aggressive attitude to all forms of authority; and his very shrewdness makes him doubly difficult to handle. The following case is perhaps worth reporting in some detail, not only because it illustrates the kind of difficulties that arise, but also because when fully grown the individual in question was able to recall and relate pretty frankly the experiences that he had been through.

Billy Brown, as I shall call him, was a youngster of eight and a half, referred to me because his mother complained that he suffered from constant nightmares and 'hated the school they made him attend'. His teacher described him as 'always gay and lively; a bit too fond of playing the buffoon and showing off; rather childish in his jokes, but quite popular with the others'. Billy was well nourished and well grown, but had a quaint owl-like face and curious tripping gait. He peered at you through big round lenses, with a solemn expression that somehow seemed scarcely natural. With the Terman–Binet scale his mental age was 14·6, and his I.Q. therefore 172. In scholastic tests his scores (in 'mental years') were: Reading 15·0, Spelling 12·4, Arithmetic 14·0, Composition 13·5, Writing 9·5, Drawing 11·5. He was an only child. His father, a self-educated journalist, had died when Billy was only four. The mother, not herself highly intelligent or highly educated, said the boy had 'always been precocious'. He was exceptionally early in walking, talking, and learning to read and write. Before he was six he had half filled an exercise book with unfinished stories and a number of poems. Two of them I transcribe. The first, which was headed 'Shoping baskit', and had a picture of Mrs Brown with her 'baskit' beneath the title, ran as follows:

'If you were Sinder Ella and I was Grandma Brown
Ide hold my magic wand out and you should ride to Town

if wishes were just horses then you would have to ride
but I would give you a big motor car and then youd sit inside.'

(To avoid identification I have changed the surname to 'Brown',
and to preserve a rhyme I have substituted for the name of the city
the simple word 'town'.) As a tailpiece he has appended a sketch of
the 'big motor car' with Mrs Brown seen through the window.
The second poem is in a different metre.

'Sylvie and Bruno used to play
for Sylvie was Bruno's sister
now Sylvie's gone far far away
and oh how Bruno missed her.'

The names are, of course, taken from Lewis Carroll's story.
Sylvie was the boy's pet name for his favourite playmate, a girl of
seven, named Sybil, who had lived next door, but later left with
her parents for Canada. Bruno (sometimes Browno) was the
nickname for himself. After their parting, so his mother explained,
he 'began to mope' and ceased to play with other children.
Actually, so I found, he had invented an imaginery 'Wild West',
full of Red Indians from whom he used regularly to rescue
Sylvie, and then in fancy continue their games as before.

Much of his time he spent poring over his father's books. As a
result he was widely read in English literature and history. He had
taught himself algebra as far as quadratic equations, and studied
Euclid to the end of Book I. He discovered how to use a plani-
sphere, and could name most of the larger constellations. Both his
abilities and his knowledge were well over the head of his own
teacher. He explained to me, for example, how the teacher had
told the class that the 'Venus pencils' which they used for drawing
were 'named after the bright star you could see in the southern
sky'. 'I told him', he said, 'that it wasn't a star but a planet, and it
couldn't be Venus, because Venus is always near the sun, not in
the South. It isn't Jupiter or Saturn because they're near Spica, and
you can only see Spica in the summer' (that is, of course, if you're
an evening observer) 'so it must be Mars'—a remarkable specimen
of correct reasoning, quite apart from the knowledge shown.

He disliked children of his own age; but at school made friends
with one or two of the older boys. Inwardly he was painfully
aware of his inferior strength and size, and his queer appearance
provoked a certain amount of teasing and chaffing. In the class-

room he found it difficult to hide his superior knowledge and ability; and he quickly gained the title of 'Professor'. Possibly he suggested it; certainly he played up to it; his model (as he afterwards explained) was 'the Professor in Lewis Carroll's story'. He used to strut about the playground, like Lewis Carroll's Professor, 'with a big book under each arm', wearing a little raincoat—the nearest he could get to 'the Professor's flowered dressing gown'. Many of his would-be smart retorts were modelled on 'the Professor's'. Under this mask he managed to give himself a certain measure of confidence, and by his comical repartees successfully turned aside the kicks and cuffs that are so often the lot of the youngster who is cleverer than his schoolmates. Even when grown up, his customary pose was that of the slightly cynical wag. The nightmares and the childish outbursts at home were the natural reactions to the repressed emotional strain that he not infrequently experienced at school.

On my recommendation he was moved to a higher class, and as a 'Wolf Cub' placed under the eye of an intelligent Scoutmaster, who himself was a Cambridge graduate. He gained first a junior county scholarship, and then a university scholarship in mathematics. By then he had become perfectly well adapted. To quote his own words, 'Everything became quite easy as soon as I found myself just as tall and as big as the fellows I was with.' He is now a professor no longer in fancy but in fact; his publications include, not only scientific researches, but also under a *nom de plume* a short book of verse.

Finally, as we have observed, those who are exceptionally bright, like those who are exceptionally dull, differ far more widely among themselves than children of average or normal intelligence. Nowadays we draw our main borderlines for subnormal and supernormal at I.Q.s of 85 and 115 or thereabouts. This gives a range of 30 points for the normal. But the supernormal may have I.Q.s up to 200 or possibly more—a range nearly three times as wide. Moreover, because intellectually they mature more rapidly, they often develop at an early age well-marked special interests and sometimes well-marked special abilities. And in character and temperament as well they display a range of variation far wider than a group of average individuals.

If therefore these children are to receive an appropriate training, each should be systematically studied as an individual. His abilities should be observed, tested, and formally recorded at the earliest possible age; and a 'personal file' or 'school record card' should be compiled and regularly brought up to date. Tests of educational achievements as well as of general and special capacities should be applied annually; significant observations on personality and behaviour promptly entered; and specimens of work in and out of school preserved. The general plan for such records will be similar to those already in use for the educationally subnormal. The file should follow the child from class to class, and from school to school. Not only will it serve the practical purpose of enabling his successive teachers to meet his growing needs with greater understanding; such records will also prove invaluable for purposes of research.

Possibly the most satisfactory way of providing for the brighter cases would be to establish a special type of residential school for the highly gifted. Brought together in daily contact these youngsters learn as much from each other as they do from their teachers. Such a school should offer not merely an intellectual training based on a specially advanced and comprehensive curriculum, but also training in character and what is sometimes called 'a training for leadership'—by which is to be understood not education for a particular social class but an education for those who will almost certainly take a lead in science, art, commerce, industry and the various professions. One or two preparatory schools and public schools have in the past aimed vaguely at something of this type. How far such a measure is advisable or practicable I shall not attempt to discuss. I will merely suggest that a small venture of this sort, specifically for those from poorer or less cultured homes, might be well worth undertaking if only as a tentative experiment.

Conclusions

Until recently, increasing attention has been paid to the needs of pupils of moderately high ability—more particularly those of a grammar school type. By means of scholarship systems, selective transfer to various types of secondary school, and selective classification (or 'streaming') within the school, some degree of special educational provision has been effected, mainly from the age of eleven onwards. Little or no consideration, however, has been devoted to the special requirements of those who are *exceptionally* gifted, i.e. children whose abilities are as much above those of the average grammar school pupil as those of the average grammar school pupil are above those of the general population. Yet these children are among the nation's most valuable assets.

The neglect seems largely the result of a twofold misconception. First of all, teachers and others greatly underrate the abilities of the ablest children. They realize that they are intelligent; but they do not realize *how* intelligent they are. Secondly, the prevailing notions about the way differences in intelligence are distributed have led to a gross underestimation of the frequency with which such children occur in the general population. The evidence in the preceding pages indicates that the number of those with I.Q.s of over 140 is nearly four times as great as current estimates would suggest.

References

BEREDAY, G. Z. F. and LAUWERYS, J. A. (1962) *World Yearbook of Education: The Gifted Child*. London, Evans Brothers.

BOARD OF EDUCATION (1931) *Report of the Consultative Committee on the Primary School*. London, H.M. Stationery Office.

BURT, C. (1959) The examination at eleven plus. *Br. J. educ. Stud.*, 7, 99–117.

BURT, C. (1961) The gifted child. *Br. J. statist. Psychol.*, 14, 123–39.

BURT, C. (1962) The number of highly gifted children. *Br. J. statist. Psychol.*, 15, 145–51.

BURT, C. (1962) *Mental and Scholastic Tests* (4th edition). London, Staples Press.

CITY OF OTTAWA PUBLIC SCHOOL BOARD (1956) *A Study of Gifted Children*. Ottawa, Government Printing Office.

COX, C. M. (1926) *The Early Mental Traits of Three Hundred Geniuses*. Stanford, Stanford University Press.

DAVIDSON, C. L. (1929) Special classes for children of superior mental ability. *Third Yearbook of the Division of Education Research, Los Angeles*. Los Angeles, School Publications.

DEHAAN, R. F. and HAVIGHURST, R. G. (1957) *Educating Gifted Children*. Chicago, University of Chicago Press.

EDUCATION POLICIES COMMISSION (1950) *Education of the Gifted*. Washington, D.C., National Educational Association.

GALTON, F. (1869) *Hereditary Genius*. London, Macmillan. Fontana Library Ed. (1962). London, Collins.

HAVIGHURST, R. J., STIVERS, E., and DEHAAN, R. F. (1955) *A Survey of the Education of Gifted Children*. Chicago, University of Chicago Press.

HOLLINGWORTH, L. S. (1942) *Children Above 180 I.Q.* New York, World Book Co.

HOWARD, M. and BURT, C. (1952) The nature and causes of maladjustment among children of school age. *Br. J. Psychol. Statist. Sec.*, 5, 39–58.

LOOMIS, G. I. (1951) *Survey of Literature and Research concerning the Education of the Gifted Child.* Oregon, University of Oregon School of Education.

NATIONAL MERIT SCHOLARSHIP CORPORATION (1959) *Recognizing Exceptional Ability among America's Young People.* Illinois, National Merit Scholarship Corporation.

NATIONAL SOCIETY FOR THE STUDY OF EDUCATION (1924) Report on the Education of Gifted Children. *Twenty-third Yearbook.* Bloomington, Public School Publishing Co.

NATIONAL SOCIETY FOR THE STUDY OF EDUCATION (1958) *Education for the Gifted.* Chicago, University of Chicago Press.

SUMPTION, M. R. (1941) *Three Hundred Gifted Children.* New York, World Book Company.

TERMAN, L. M. (1925) *Mental and Physical Traits of a Thousand Gifted Children.* Stanford, Stanford University Press.

U.S. OFFICE OF EDUCATION (1946) *Bulletin No. 1: Curriculum adjustments for gifted children.* Washington, Government Printing Office.

WALL, W. D. (1961) Highly intelligent children. *Educational Research,* 2, 101–11, 207–17.

WIENER, N. (1953) *Ex-prodigy: My Childhood and Youth.* New York, Simon and Schuster.

WITTY, P. (1951) *The Gifted Child.* Boston, Heath.

Index